"*churchfails* cleverly illustrates two immutable facts: First, there has never been a shortage of bad ideas in the church, and second, were it not for Jesus the church would fail miserably. This book marches out the blunder-makers one by one with their boneheaded ideas in full view. With a dose of mercy, the contributors then offer advice on how to avoid joining this parade of fools. But beware: the saying 'He who laughs last didn't get the joke' surely applies. If you read this book without a sense of humor, it might just mean that you or someone you know is represented inside. So, read the book, take their advice, and laugh out loud."

Anthony Chute, professor of church history, California Baptist University, Riverside, California

"The subject sounds boring, and the chapter titles even more so—but the READING brings interest and entertainment that are refreshing."

Dave Gustafson, Eden Prairie, Minnesota

"People who think church history and theology are no laughing matter should read *churchfails*. The authors provide humor, alliteration, and wit to highlight colorful characters in church history."

Dr. Adam Harwood, Associate Professor of Theology, New Orleans Baptist Theological Seminary

"Who said history was boring? *churchfails* sets that rumor to rest immediately. We owe a great debt to those who made so much Christian history so accessible and interesting. Laughter and learning are great companions. You won't find a more delightful way to improve your knowledge of church history than *churchfails*."

Dr. Chuck Kelley, president, New Orleans Baptist Theological Seminary

"This is a delightful book. These brief vignettes of historical figures give us insight into how sincere Christians (or so-called Christians) have often erred, quite convinced that they were discerning 'the will of God.' You don't have to agree with every assessment of these 'heretics' in order to kick back, relax, and marvel that the church has actually survived despite its many very flawed leaders and often foolish preachers! And along the way, you will notice that history often repeats itself!"

Dr. Erwin W. Lutzer, senior pastor, The Moody Church, Chicago, Illinois

D1024477

churchfails

DAVID K. STABNOW, GENERAL EDITOR

churchfails

100
BLUNDERS
in Church
History
(& What We Can
Learn *from* Them)

SIMEON STYLITES

HOLMAN
BIBLE PUBLISHERS

NASHVILLE, TENNESSEE

Churchfails: 100 Blunders in Church History
(& What We Can Learn from Them)

© Copyright 2016 by B&H Publishing Group

Published by B&H Publishing Group
Nashville, Tennessee
All rights reserved.

ISBN 978-1-4336-0817-9

Dewey Decimal Classification: 270
Subject Heading: CHRISTIANS/LAITY/CHURCH HISTORY

Scripture quotations are from the *Holman Christian Standard Bible*® Copyright 1999, 2000, 2002, 2003, 2009 by Holman Bible Publishers. Used by permission.

Printed in the United States of America
1 2 3 4 5 6 7 8 9 10 • 21 20 19 18 17 16
VP

CONTENTS

Medieval churchfails 73

churchfails in the Reformation   105

churchfails in Modern Times   121

Momentary churchfails   177

Apocalyptic churchfails   209

Contributors

Rex Butler was a shoe salesman in his former life, then God called him to teach when he was 40 years old. He went from selling soles to schooling souls as Professor of Church History and Patristics at New Orleans Baptist Theological Seminary—following in the footsteps of William Carey and D. L. Moody!

Ken "Deep Dish" Cleaver grew up in the Windy City, a land flowing with cheese and sausage. Although he teaches church history, theology, and apologetics at Liberty University's School of Divinity, we actually invited him to be on our team of authors because he's an avid unicyclist, and we needed the balance.

Rodrick K. Durst was raised and trained in California, moving between campuses of Golden Gate Seminary to catch all the earthquakes. When not teaching theology or history, he serves as director of the seminary's Bay Area Campus, which really won't exist until fall 2016.

Lloyd A. Harsch is a parent, professor, pastor, political pundit, and punster. What better job can there be for a wannabe comic than teaching church history and Baptist studies at New Orleans Baptist Theological Seminary? He has a captive audience that is pressured to applaud his puns because he submits their grades!

James Lutzweiler is a part-time mushroom picker, concert pianist, and unpaid poet laureate trapped in the almost dead but still somewhat Herculean body of a widow-chasing archivist in search of the papers of their preacher- or professor-husbands.

Stephen O. Presley hails from the Lone Star State but ventured out to study theology among the brave-hearted kilt-wearers of the far northern territory. After enduring his fair share of freezing gales and bagpipe renditions of "Scotland the Brave," the prodigal son returned home to the blessed sun-kissed land of Texas, our Texas, where he teaches church history at Southwestern Seminary.

David K. Stabnow gave up a dead-end career digging graves in the frozen soil of Minnesota in favor of herding cats and shepherding words as Bible and Reference Book Editor at B&H. He lives in Nashville but doesn't listen to country music.

Introduction

Groucho Marx once said, "I refuse to join any club that would have me as a member." If Christianity is a club, it has featured innumerable inglorious members. As abashed affiliates of said club, what can we do? We can try to deny our past and present peccadilloes, but covering up a crime is like poking a polecat: it's worse in the end. So, we can rant and rave, or we can laugh and learn. This book settles on the second strategy.

Definition of "churchfail"

The dictionary definition of *fail* is simply "be unsuccessful." For this book, there's a much finer nuance—even though it's questionable whether these epic fails can be nuanced in any way.

Certainly there is a difference between a secular and a sacred fail. For the former, consider the title characters in *Dumb and Dumber* and their injudicious ilk. They neither seek nor attain redemptive qualities, though they may lay claim to some sort of likability in the end. A sacred fail, on the other hand, involves a person who has explicitly or inherently made certain claims, against which his actions are set in bold relief. Upon conversion, a Christian's mind is supposedly renewed (Rom 12:2) and given over wholly to loving God (Matt 22:37). We pious persons purport to fear the Lord, which (we are told) is the beginning of wisdom (Ps 111:10; Prov 9:10).

Perhaps *beginning* is the crucial word here. A little understanding of God's ways is a dangerous thing. It's like a beginner in swimming lessons or a white belt in karate—if such people sally forth to employ their newfound skills, they will quickly find themselves under water or knocked silly, respectively. This explains the failures of those who have merely dipped a big toe into the vast ocean of theology before succumbing to the Siren of apostasy. But there are others who don't have this excuse to fall back on.

"Stupid is as stupid does." Forrest Gump introduced this saying into the American milieu. By contrast, the juxtaposition of "brilliant is" and "stupid does" is a fascinating facet of philosophy. In *De Divinatione* Cicero observed, "There is nothing so absurd but some philosopher has said it." Augustine noted,

> All the perversities of all errors, all sects, preaching deviant morals and ungodliness, have had as their authors men of great brilliance. They weren't

the brain-children of any sort of men; they were started by men of the sharp-est intelligence.[1]

Thus a churchfail does not proceed from a person of low intelligence. These are brilliant people who have delved deeply into the exegesis of Scripture and the synthesis of theology, but somewhere along the way they came up a goose short of a gaggle, a few clowns short of a circus, all wax and no wick, one tree shy of a hammock, a sheep shy of a sweater. In some cases, it is amazing how clear the error is to those of us who observe their train wrecks with the advantage of hindsight. In one *Calvin and Hobbes* comic strip, Calvin is reprimanded for something he did and is told that he lacks com-mon sense. He replies, "I've got *plenty* of common sense! I just choose to ignore it."[2]

So it seems with churchfails. These are smart people; they just do dumb things.

To the churchfail fool—and sometimes to his pals and peers—it seemed at the time perfectly reasonable, rational, and right. I'm the same way; most everything I do seems perfectly sensible and sound. But if "I don't know much about history," as Sam Cooke says, I'll be condemned to repeat it, just like I repeated ninth-grade German. This book is our chance to learn from history.

---

[1] Augustine Sermon 374:5:2, in *Newly Discovered Sermons* (Hyde Park, NY: New City Press, 1997), 394.

[2] Bill Watterson, October 15, 1986.

Patristic

churchfails

It took a few centuries to iron out proper expressions of theology. In *Heretics*,[3] a book of essays by G. K. Chesterton, we find this observation: "Truths turn into dogmas the instant that they are disputed. Thus every man who utters a doubt defines a religion." These people did the church a great service by exploring every possible way theology could go wrong.

---

[3] "Concluding Remarks on the Importance of Orthodoxy," *Heretics* (New York: John Lane, 1905).

Simon Magus

"belief" without repentance?

pull of power orientation
was his answer to Peter unwillingness to repent?
this

Date: AD 35

Synopsis: Simon Magus rejected Christ and claimed to be the true Messiah, having come to redeem humanity through his knowledge.

Biography: Mr. Magus shouldn't be confused with Mr. Magoo. The latter was an *affluent* cartoon character. The former, also known as Simon the Magician, had more of an *effluent* character. He was a Samaritan and rather popular throughout the region (especially at birthday parties and midway arcades). He is mentioned in the account of Philip's preaching in Acts 8, where Simon rather infamously tried to buy the Spirit— whence the term _simony_ derives. Little is known about his personal life except for his relationship with his assistant, Helen, a Phoenician prostitute. He eventually made his way to Rome, where he died under Nero around the same time as Peter and Paul.

churchfail: Simon was a false messiah who, through his own pride and interest in mysticism, claimed to be the true God and redeemer. According to Acts 8:9-25, those who witnessed Simon's magic shows were so impressed that they exclaimed, "This man is called the Great Power of God" (v. 10). While such acclaim probably inflated his ego, he had a moment of humility when he heard the gospel, believed, and was baptized. However, he later revealed his true colors when he saw Peter lay his hands on believers and they received the Spirit. Thinking that was some powerful prestidigitation to complement his collection of conjurations, Simon Magus tried to buy from Simon Peter the capability to convey the Comforter. Rather than charging him for services rendered, Peter charged him to repent. *apparently he did not!*

Nothing more is said in Scripture about Simon. The early church, however, knew him as the oft-imitated but never duplicated father and founder of Christian heresy. The Fathers' writings are replete with references to the branches of heresies that sprouted from the tree of Simon, most of which are known by the general title "Gnosticism." This notorious arch-heretic constantly challenged the apostles' teaching, making him one of their chief opponents.

common cultural source

Simon's messianic delusions derived from his own deliberations, beginning with how he saw his mistress, Helen. Simon taught that the spirit inside Helen was actually very ancient (called the "Thought of his mind" and the "Mother of all things"). In fact, it was through the spirit of Helen in primeval times that Simon (who thought he was

6

also God the Father) originally created all spiritual beings. But these intractable angels turned on him and abused the female spirit with him by imprisoning her in a human body. This same spirit was passed down through great women of the ages (including another "Helen"—of Troy) but became impounded in the very Helen who accompanied him. Simon proclaimed himself the Savior who had come to rescue this woman, together with all humanity, through his knowledge. Simon also prophesied that the wicked angels and all those who rejected his message would be destroyed, while those who believed in him would be saved.

Simon's teaching spread as far as Rome and—while some of it may seem outrageous—he impressed people through sleight of hand and divination. People reported dramatic illusions, including levitation. He was so famous that his acolytes later erected

The Death of Simon Magus

statues of him and Helen in Rome. His followers would worship the images, offering sacrifices and incense. One tradition suggests he died when he was buried alive for three days in order to rise again like Christ, proving he was a superior messiah. Oops.

Application: It is unfortunate that Simon deceived so many. Jesus, however, warned His disciples that there would be false teachers and false prophets (Matt 24:5), and in the case of Simon, it didn't take long for them to show up. Simon's heresy reminds believers that the only way of salvation is through Jesus Christ, the true Son of God. Teachers of various faiths and traditions will, like Simon, claim that they have received a special revelation and have discovered another way to gain Paradise. They may even claim that many paths lead to a right relationship with God. The bold proclamation of Christ, however, is that He is the only way and the only means of salvation (John 14:6). Christians do not look for another messiah or another path to salvation; Christ has already opened up the path to heaven for all who believe in Him.

S.P.

Menander and Menandrians

Date: ca. 90

Synopsis: Menander created a special form of spiritual baptism and convinced his followers that those who were baptized would never die . . . that is, until they did.

Biography: Menander was a late-first-century Gnostic and the most influential student of the late Simon Magus (the magician mentioned in Acts 8:9-24; see previous article). After Simon's death around AD 75, Menander took charge of the Simonians and began a regular speaking tour to every conference center, stadium, football field, and cricket pitch of every major city throughout Syria.

A Samaritan, Menander grew up in the small village of Capparetaea. He was exceedingly fascinated with magical arts—the Harry Houdini of the ancient world—and reputedly achieved the highest level of magic powers and knowledge. Many people seemed to enjoy his shows, and he had quite the reputation for magical powers. He ended up mentoring Saturninus (this is a person, not a planet) and Basilides (p. 16), who became influential Gnostic thinkers in their own right. All of his little magicians-in-training were called the Menandrians (not to be confused with a tasty citrus fruit), and they continued to exist at least until the fourth century.

churchfail: Menander's tenets followed a meandering trail away from the truth. One of his major problems was that he made his theology personal, but in the wrong way. He didn't bother with giving credit to anyone else, but announced that he himself was the true redeemer sent by God to save people. He also taught that he did not have a normal origin, but rather sprang forth through the work of another deity named Wisdom (*sophia*). Thus Menander, not that insignificant Jesus guy, was the true expected Messiah who was coming to save mankind.

Most of the early church fathers accused Menander of being possessed by a demon, but it didn't seem to slow him down much. He actually convinced others that a great invisible power above sent him. His job was to teach everyone about this deity and impart the true knowledge of this previously unknown god. Like other Gnostics, he taught that wicked angels—who were really bad guys and caused all kinds of problems for people—created the world. Through the knowledge imparted to him, Menander outsmarted and conquered the wicked angels that created the world by discovering and teaching the true knowledge of the great invisible power above. He was like an

8

ancient magical warlord sage who could deceive angels with his special tricks and awe people with his wise sayings—he would have gone far in any RPG.

His particular ploy was a patented, proprietary peculiar baptism. He taught that everyone he baptized received a spiritual resurrection . . . at that very moment! Menander thought that any talk of a physical resurrection—as if Jesus actually rose from the dead—was foolishness. The only true resurrection was the spiritual resurrection in the mind through Knowledge. Menander taught that anyone baptized and received as one of his followers would never die, but would live eternally and spiritually without ever growing old. In fact, he persuaded his followers that *he* would never die. Even after his death, his followers kept assuring everyone that Menander was still alive. "Pay no attention to that decaying man behind the curtain!"

Application: While there are several lessons to be learned from the life and teaching of Menander, his use of the ordinance of baptism and his views on resurrection are particularly important. Gnostics like Menander often appropriated biblical imagery and language to give their teaching a sense of authority. The way Menander borrowed the Christian practice of baptism reminds the church of the importance of

Menander

teaching and understanding the true significance of believer's baptism. Menander blended magic with the ordinance to spiritualize the event and to teach his own version of a mystical Gnostic spiritual resurrection through knowledge. Baptism, as it is presented throughout Scripture, is best understood as an act of obedience that symbolizes the believer's confession of faith in the gospel (Matt 28:19; Acts 8:12). The practice of baptism does not communicate any kind of spiritual resurrection in the present life of the believer, but instead serves as a testimony of the future resurrection that is promised for all who believe in Christ (Rom 6:3-5).

S.P.

Nicolaus and the Nicolaitans

Date: ca. 90

Synopsis: The Nicolaitans were a Gnostic sect that indulged in a mixed bag of immoral behaviors and didn't give a hoot about holiness.

Biography: The heresy of Gnosticism was a rather formidable challenge from the earliest days of the church. The Apostle John mentions one lively group of heretics, called the Nicolaitans, making the rounds among the churches in Asia Minor (Rev 2:6, 15). Mystery shrouds the origins and beliefs of the Nicolaitans, but according to the early church fathers they stem from the early Christian leader, Nicolaus. Acts 6:5 mentions Nicolaus as one of the seven chosen to defuse a food fight in the fledgling flock. He must have been an influential leader in the early church—or at least like all good pastors, he knew how to organize a good luncheon. The passage also mentions that Nicolaus was a proselyte, a Gentile convert to Judaism, from Antioch. But it doesn't say, "Oh, by the way, he founded a Gnostic sect."

Some church fathers were convinced that Nicolaus was really a good guy and only branded as a fornicator by his ruthless, back-stabbing, no-good followers, the Nicolaitans. The church father Eusebius, for example, took up the defense of Nicolaus and argued that he was exceedingly virtuous. He reported how Nicolaus was so devoted to his own purity that he offered to give up his natural relations with his wife in order prove that he had mastery over his passions. That sounds like silly grandstanding.

Still, in letters to two of the churches in John's revelation, Jesus condemned the Nicolaitans for their

Peter Consecrates the
Seven Deacons

immorality. While the church at Ephesus wisely and rightly rejected their teachings, there were some at Pergamum that found the allure all too alluring.

Their influence was short lived—by the end of the second century the Nicolaitans per se were passé. However, some early Christians connected the Nicolaitans with Cerinthus and Valentinus (pp. 12, 30), so it may be that they just took the party elsewhere. A ruse by any other name still smells.

churchfail: Because the Nicolaitans only get less than one column inch in Scripture, the early church fathers help fill in the details. Apparently the Nicolaitans enjoyed their fair share of promiscuous adventures and regularly ate meat sacrificed to idols. They gave in to every craving and scratched every itch, allocating no resources to trivial things like propriety or holiness. Their starting point in Gnostic dualism, exacerbated by a hyper view of election, made heresy inevitable. In general, the Gnostics held that the material world was born out of sin and evil and, therefore, inherently corrupt. This fundamental fallacy sent Gnostics on one of two tragic trajectories: radical asceticism or lavish licentiousness. If the world and the body are a one-way path to destruction, it's best either to hunker down and avoid as much of the world as possible, or to simply enjoy the ride. The Nicolaitans went with the latter and became essentially indifferent to all villainies and vices. They did not believe the wicked material world—including their own corrupt carapaces—made any difference in spiritual salvation. Obviously, this didn't put them on a path of pious purity or a call to Christlikeness.

Application: While there's almost no connection between orthodontics and orthopedics, the heresy of the Nicolaitans serves as an important reminder about the interrelationship between orthodoxy (right belief) and orthopraxy (right practice). This Gnostic sect believed in a cosmic dualism that resulted in a rejection of any view of the goodness of creation, and thus they deduced that their spiritual lives were unaffected by participation in immoral behavior. However, the Scriptures teach that Christians are not merely called to *believe* in the gospel but also to *live out* the implications of the gospel faithfully. The Bible provides the basic guidelines for sanctification and how Christians should live in light of the gospel. This growth in godliness comprises a variety of aspects of the spiritual life including the way we Christians treat our families, other Christians, the poor and destitute, and so on. Christians should not participate in immorality or continue in the same desires we had before we came to believe the gospel. Instead, in response to the grace of God in Christ, we should live as obedient children and seek holiness in every aspect of our lives (1 Pet 1:14-16).

S.P.

Cerinthus

Date: ca. 100

Synopsis: Cerinthus rejected the God of the Old Testament, denied the divinity of Christ, and thus grieved the Holy Spirit, completing a heretical trifecta.

Biography: Cerinthus earns the dubious distinction of being the earliest heretic mentioned entirely outside of the Bible. A Gnostic teacher influenced by first-century Jewish thought, he became (in)famous throughout Asia Minor and likely had a significant following in Asia and Galatia. Privately, he had quite the reputation for indulging his impulses and was known to have savored a variety of vices.

churchfail: Cerinthus lived during the waning years of the first century and, along with Simon Magus (p. 6), was a real burr under the apostles' saddles. The church father Irenaeus mentioned one occasion when the apostle John was about to enter a bathhouse in Ephesus, but upon learning that Cerinthus was inside, exclaimed, "Let us flee, lest the bath fall in, as Cerinthus, the enemy of the truth, is within." Besides wanting to avoid becoming collateral damage when God struck Cerinthus down, apparently the thought of washing up around heretics made John feel unclean!

Cerinthus was one founder of the fad of dualism, which the Gnostics would all embrace. He distinguished sharply between the transcendent *Father God*—who dwelt far above in the heavenly *plērōma*—and the *Creator* of the world, who was universally depraved (so God in Genesis 1 was really the bad guy). This Creator employed several attending angels—it was creation by committee. This same Creator was also the one wreaking havoc on people throughout the Old Testament—the dark side of this dualism.

Cerinthus rejected the virgin birth of Jesus and taught that Christ was born to Joseph and Mary as a mere man and not God-in-flesh. He admired the *man Jesus* as more righteous, wise, and prudent than anyone else, but He was nevertheless a man and not the Savior. Cerinthus identified the true savior as the *spirit Christ* (so *Jesus* and *Christ* are two separate beings—another aspect of his dualism). He also argued that the spirit Christ—sent down from the transcendent Father above (not from the corrupt Creator)—descended upon Jesus at his baptism.

Now *adoption* is eminently commendable, but Cerinthus's view of Christology, known as *Adoptionism*, was a heretical bad penny that has resurfaced throughout church history. According to Adoptionism, the spirit Christ took possession of the man Jesus and became a distinct power working within Him—kind of like Professor X. Through the power of Christ, Jesus performed many miracles and revealed the secret knowledge of the true transcendent God who is greater than the foolish Creator in Genesis. Then immediately before Jesus was crucified, the spirit Christ abandoned the man Jesus, since the spirit Christ was "impassible"—he could not suffer.

Bathhouse in Ephesus

Cerinthus's fallacious philosophy was not fully fledged like that of the later Gnostics such as Basilides or Valentinus (pp. 16, 30), but he presents an early example of the dismissal of the divinity of Christ.

Application: The story of Cerinthus reminds believers today of the importance of clearly defining the doctrines of creation and Christ as well as the theological connections between the deeds of God in the Old Testament and His work in the New Testament. The God of the Old Testament is, in fact, not some spiteful deity plotting to pounce on His people every time they fail and fall. Instead, the loving God of the Old Testament has been working out a plan of redemption from the beginning of creation that culminates in the person and work of Jesus Christ.

Cerinthus's bifurcation of the man Jesus and the spirit Christ anticipates many christological heresies throughout Christian history. From the earliest days of the church, Christians and heretics alike struggled to make sense of the full deity and full humanity of Christ. It is easy to think of the man Jesus as having some kind of superhuman power and virtue that exceeds everyone else, but that is not what He claimed or the apostles taught. It is also hard to understand Jesus's full divinity as He suffered and died on the cross—that His human body was capable of death but His divine nature was impassible. It would take many more years of controversy and debate for the church to find the right words to express how Christ is fully God and fully man, but this clarification had to be made in order to explain how Christ Jesus redeemed and restored God's people so that we might have right standing before God.

S.P.

Sethianism

Date: ca. 125

Synopsis: Sethian Gnostics claimed to be descendants of Seth (Adam's third son) and superior to everyone else, including the prophets and apostles.

Biography: When most people think of the stories of Genesis 1–3, Adam and Eve's appletarian diet or Cain's liquidation of his brother usually come to mind. Not so for the Sethians. They really liked Seth, the third son of Adam and Eve . . . and I mean *really* liked him. Sethians believed Seth was the paragon of truth and the manifestation of the ultimate divine reality. Seth was even more important than Christ, since the Redeemer was simply another appearance of the Great Seth (yes, that's actually what they called him). I don't know why they choose such an obscure figure—Seth is only mentioned a few times in the Old Testament and exactly once in the New Testament (Luke 3:38). Nevertheless, they must have been quite the salesmen: they flourished throughout the Mediterranean region from the second to the fourth centuries.

While it is hard to identify their founder, several ancient writings communicate their ideas, including *The Holy Book of the Great Invisible Spirit* (aka the *Gospel to the Egyptians*), *Trimorphic Protennoia* (a real page-turner), and the *Three Steles of Seth*. The Sethians even claimed that *The Holy Book of the Great Invisible Spirit* was composed by the Great Seth in ancient times but hidden away on a high mountain (in a mayonnaise jar?) until after the prophets and apostles wrote the Bible. Only then was the true

Seth

story of the ancient world revealed to the followers of Seth through the teachings of the Great Seth.

churchfail: Like other Gnostics, Sethians did most of their underlining, crossing out, and marginal notes in Genesis. They loved the creation story but didn't buy the idea that the God who created the world was really a good guy. Instead, they believed that the good God, who was floating way up in the heavenly realm, consisted of a divine triad including the Father (the Great Invisible Spirit), the Mother (Barbelo), and the Son (Autogenes). We won't get into the interactions of these divinities right now, but suffice it to say that they had little to do with the material world below. The present world was instead ruled by the wicked world-craftsman Yaldabaoth (good luck saying that five times fast!).

According to the Sethians, Adam was a heavenly creature closely associated with the spiritual triad above. Seth was the true spiritual offspring of his father, and thus the ideal human. They also believed that they were the one pure race whose line went back directly to the truly spiritual one. So if the Sethians were around today their T-shirts would say "I ♥ ancestry.com" because they were constantly babbling on about genealogies and family lineage. They often announced to anyone who would listen, "We are the Seed of Seth!"

Those who were in the genuine genealogy of Seth also contained within their material bodies a small splinter of the spiritual sphere. The Great Seth came and secretly indwelt the man Jesus so that He might teach about the presence of this spiritual element to the few true followers in the line of Seth. Then, when they awakened to the knowledge of the spiritual element within, it could return back to the heavenly world after death. Of course this was bad news for anyone born into the wrong family, because only those in the line of Seth had any hope.

Application: The heresy of the Sethians reminds Christians of the importance of the authority and sufficiency of Scripture, and of the accessibility of the gospel to all who believe regardless of family line or citizenship.

While there are many theological problems with their beliefs—especially their elevation of Seth—their root error is rejecting the teaching of the Scriptures. They invented extra-biblical revelation and claimed that it superseded the writings of the prophets and apostles. For Christians, on the other hand, the writings of the Old and New Testaments are the final authority in all matters of faith and practice and are sufficient for communicating the truth of the gospel.

At the same time, the Sethians also erred by assuming that only those of a particular genealogical line have salvation. As Jesus commanded, Christians are to go to *all nations* and preach the gospel to *all people* (Matt 28:19-20). The gospel is not offered to only a few, but to anyone who will believe in the saving work of Christ.

S.P.

Basilides of Alexandria

Date: ca. 132

Synopsis: Mr. B rejected both the deity and the humanity of Christ and held to several forms of dualism.

Biography: Basilides taught for many years in Alexandria, Egypt, beginning around 132. Mere scraps of what he wrote made it to the twenty-first century, but his teaching spread and persisted well into the fourth century. Little is known about his personal life—apparently he avoided patristic paparazzi—except that he had a son named Isidore. He and his son taught in the same school, creating an influential father-son philosophizing tag team.

churchfail: Basilides, an early Gnostic, held to several distinct forms of dualism. He claimed to have received his philosophy from several significant somebodies, including Matthias (who replaced Judas in Acts 1:23-25) and some bloke named Glaucias (who in turn claimed to know the apostle Peter). Basilides may have provided the malign nascent seed of many Gnostic sects, and he even influenced the teacher Valentinus (p. 30; not to be confused with Valentine, the third-century patron saint of greedy florists). Basilides even arrogantly attempted to compose his own Gospel, not-so-humbly dubbed the *Gospel according to Basilides*.

Basilides's dualistic philosophy permeated his theology like the smell of burned popcorn in a dorm room, and especially affected his Christology. He snubbed his nose at monotheism and skipped right over the Trinity on his way to a primordial Ogdoad—a group of eight supreme deities. The highest of the octogods was the unoriginate and ineffable Father of all. From these spiritual beings emanated 365 lower angels who lived in various levels of the heavens and had unusual names like Caulacau and Abrasax. But all of them got involved creating the world and human beings: each angel got to take a turn forming a separate part of Adam's body. While they created, they were probably singing, "The shin bone's connected to the (clap!) knee bone," just to make sure they didn't get anything out of place.

This disjointed anthropology set the stage for Basilides's view of Christ and salvation. Like other Gnostics, Basilides denied the full deity and full humanity of Jesus Christ and believed that only the soul was saved. He believed that the Savior from above came to liberate the elect from the power of those wicked creator angels.

16

Engraving from an Abrasax Stone

This Savior is the *Christ*, the firstborn Nous (mind or intellect) of the unoriginate Father, who descended upon the human *Jesus* at baptism and displaced His human soul. According to Basilides, this same Christ was also a shapeshifter (think Harry Potter's Animagus or *Star Trek*'s Odo) and transformed Himself into the form of Simon of Cyrene (see Luke 23:26). Then it was Simon, not Christ, who was crucified, and Jesus (now in the form of Simon ... yes, it all gets very confusing) stood by laughing, mocking those who crucified the wrong man!

Christ then ascended on high. But before He departed, He taught a select few in secret that those who believed in the crucified man were blind to the truth, while those who had knowledge of the unoriginate Father would find salvation. Salvation, then, is completely realized after death when the body decays and the soul ascends to the heavens. There's more. Unfortunately for us (and any of his other detractors), Basilides also held to a strict determinism, so that only those who possess this special knowledge are saved, and those out of the loop are out of luck.

Application: Basilides's teaching reminds Christians of the importance of establishing clear expressions of the true doctrines of Christ and salvation. Christ is not merely a spiritual entity floating about in heaven or even one great angel among a number of other angels; He is the true God incarnate. Christ did not merely appear to be a man, nor did God transform Himself into a man for a time; rather, God was and is incarnate in the single, singular person of Jesus Christ.

When it comes to anthropology, Christians should not fall into the trap of rejecting the importance of the physical body in salvation. In the beginning God created the whole person, body and soul, to live in relationship with Him. Therefore, salvation includes redemption of both body and soul. As Paul argued, if there is no resurrection of the dead, we are still dead in our sins with no hope (1 Cor 15:17). But Christ has indeed been raised from the dead as the firstfruits of resurrection for all who believe in Him.

S.P.

Carpocrates and the Carpocratians

Irenaeus, Opponent of
Carpocrates

Date: ca. 140

Synopsis: Carpocrates believed he was better than Christ and the apostles, and he claimed to have the pictures to prove it.

Biography: Carpocrates and his followers, the Carpocratians, did not suffer from carpal-tunnel syndrome, nor were they crates o' carp, nor did they *carpe* anyone's *diem*, but they were another of the infamous Gnostic sects that popped up like the proverbial pseudo cent in the second century. Carpocrates was a native of Alexandria, Egypt, a city known in the ancient world for attracting sophisticated, tea-sipping types who frequented local bistros and pontificated on philosophical problems. Carpocrates seems to have been a charismatic figure, attracting a good bit of attention. He wanted to make sure everyone knew who his teammates were, so he branded the back of his disciples' right earlobes. No doubt this made for awkward greetings when they looked for the Carp marks.

churchfail: In Alexandria, Carpocrates soon founded his own school and invented new tales about the wicked god who created this world. It's difficult to define Gnosticism in the early church because every new teacher wanted to stand out and attract a following. In a classic game of one-upmanship, each Gnostic teacher invented new characters and new beliefs to outdo their predecessors. Like other Gnostics, the Carpocratians believed the world was created by a band of inferior, incompetent angels. They also believed that Jesus was a natural good ol' boy born to Mary and Joseph. The man Jesus did, however, have a special divine spark inside that was completely pure. Carpocrates believed the law of the Old Testament was a way to discipline this special soul. According to him, Jesus's special soul had a misty memory of the true nature of the wonderful regions of the unbegotten Father above, where the soul

18

had existed previously. This memory was all He needed: it empowered Him to reject the evil aeons who created the world (including the God of the Jews) and vanquish their ignorance.

But Carpocrates did not stop there; he actually claimed that he and his followers were stronger and wiser than Christ and His disciples—the Carps had a greater degree of power to accomplish even greater things. Thus, while Jesus might have been a swell guy who first revealed the knowledge of the unknown Father, those after Him superseded Him in every way. They also claimed to possess ancient artifacts and relics fashioned in the image of Christ by Pilate while the Messiah was still alive (and if you buy that, they have ocean property in Arizona for sale). These images (so they claimed) carried special powers, and they worshiped the images of Christ as well as of philosophers such as Plato and Aristotle. Like some other Gnostics, their licentious lifestyles led them to participate in love feasts and rituals that involved magic incantations, spells, and potions.

Application: The account of Carpocrates serves as a helpful reminder of the authority and sufficiency of the teaching of Christ. Carpo's claim to be greater than Christ and the apostles elevates his teaching above the authority of the Word of God and the teaching of Christ expressed in the Scriptures. Like other Gnostics, Carpocrates was not satisfied with following the Scriptures and believed he needed to correct or add to them. But in fact the final authority in all matters of the Christian life and doctrine is the Bible. We should not elevate our own views or personal convictions above the teaching of Christ. He did indeed say the apostles would do greater things (John 14:12), but that only meant they would establish the church and spread the gospel after He ascended to the right hand of the Father. He did not say that Christians would *be* greater. Moreover, Christians are to humble themselves as Christ did and acknowledge that only Jesus Christ is Lord (Phil 2:11).

At the same time, the Carpocratian fascination with representations also raises the problem of idolatry and imagery among the followers of Christ. As Christians we must think carefully about the use of images in the church and about the way we represent our Savior. The pictures and images are only illustrations and should not serve as any kind of authoritative portrait of Christ. Images can be helpful for understanding Scripture, but they also can distract our worship away from the true and living Christ.

S.P.

Marcion of Sinope

Date: ca. 144

Synopsis: This knucklehead rejected the Old Testament and most of the New Testament, keeping only what supported his beliefs.

Biography: Marcion was born about AD 85 in the town of Sinope. He was a bishop's kid—a BK burgher. Sinope is modern Sinop, at the northernmost point along the Turkish coast of the Black Sea.

churchfail: Marcion was a dualist before "dualing" was outlawed—cf. Manichaeism. He insisted that there were two Gods: the Hebrew God of the OT was a wrathful "demiurge," inferior to the all-forgiving God of the NT—cf. yin and yang. The NT God was represented by Jesus of Nazareth, a spiritual being who only appeared to have a physical body—cf. Princess Leia ("Help me, Obi-Wan!"). Thus Marcion held that Christianity was distinct from Judaism; in fact, it was diametrically opposed—cf. the Nazis, who divorced Christianity from its Jewish roots to create "Positive Christianity."

Like many heretics, Marcion had to be selective in his citations to teach such tommyrot. By the time he was hatching his heresy, all the books of the NT had been written and were circulating amongst the nascent congregations. Marcion was the first to bring together certain Christian books and call them the official writings of the church. So you could say that he invented the canon. But it backfired. He seems to have decided that Paul was a good author because he liked Paul's synthesis of Christianity; so far, so good. Then he noted that Luke was a pretty good book and, therefore, Paul must have written it. Can you say "non sequitur"? He then crossed out anything in this Gospel of Paul that he

Marcion

20

didn't like—such as anything that connected Jesus with Judaism. He also accepted ten of Paul's Letters into his list, but he omitted the other Gospels, the Catholic letters, and Revelation. In response, the church excommunicated him in 144. Later, Tertullian and other early church fathers slapped the "heresy" label on Marcion's ideas.

Thomas Jefferson embarked on a similar journey, beginning with what he presumed to be true and making the Bible affirm it. Marcion presumed that only Paul's theology was valid and assumed nothing else could be authentic; Jefferson presumed that there are no miracles and assumed no reports of miracles could be authentic. Jefferson literally cut the paragraphs he preferred out of various Bibles and pasted them together to create a "Bible" to his liking, finishing in about 1820 (Bill Gates didn't invent cut and paste). In 1985 the Jesus Seminar started from the same assumption: they denied the possibility of miracles, thus eviscerating the virgin birth, expunging exorcisms, forswearing the feeding of five thousand, and rejecting the resurrection. Literally voting on words and phrases in the Gospels, they blackballed any words that didn't fit their preconceptions, taking Jesus the Messiah, Son of God, blessed Savior, risen Lord, and reducing Him to a radical Jewish teacher and faith healer. And like Marcion, some atheists today consider God, as described in the OT, to be capricious, vengeful, and genocidal.

Application: Though Marcionism, per se, died out in the fifth century, many current churches and some denominations are "practical Marcionites," picking and choosing portions of the Bible they accept. Many churches hardly ever preach from the OT, and some even imply that the love of Jesus saves us from the vengeful God of the OT. In fact, it is not that way at all: we can learn much about the patience, grace, and mercy of God in the OT. Augustine said, "The new is in the old contained; the old is by the new explained." The OT and NT are not antithetical; they are complementary parts that make up a coherent whole.

Jesus is the Messiah, the fulfillment of the gracious promises of the gracious God of the OT to Abraham, Moses, and David, among others. The Bible is the account of the loss and restoration of mankind's relationship with God, starting with Adam and Eve getting kicked out of the Garden of Eden in Genesis and ending with the church, the Bride of Christ, reigning in the new heavens and new earth in Revelation. Furthermore, every major turning point in the Bible has been accompanied by miraculous signs. The Jews play an undeniable key role in this narrative, from near the beginning all the way to the end. No book, no miracle, and no nation in the Bible should be left out of our message; the whole plan of God should be preached (Acts 20:27).

D.S.

Apelles

Date: 150

Synopsis: Apelles taught there were four gods (one good, three bad) in the Bible and that Christ had super flesh.

Biography: Apelles was the famous disciple of the infamous heretic Marcion (p. 20) and, just to be clear, not the same Apelles whom Paul mentioned in Romans 16:10. For years, Apelles was Marcion's teacher's pet in Rome and absorbed his teaching religiously—literally. At some point, however, they had a falling out. No one is quite sure what happened, but it must have been bad because Apelles packed up and moved from Rome to Alexandria, Egypt. There he tried his own hand at a little teaching and philosophizing, and around this time he encountered a prophetess named Philumene, who intrigued him with her special utterances and nifty sayings. She convinced him that she was truly inspired, so he collected her words in a book entitled *The Revelations*. In order to try and outdo his teacher, Apelles developed quite the elaborate theological system. After Marcion's death, he eventually made his way back to Rome to try to profit from Marcion's passing and filch his followers. After his own death, his teachings were carried on by a group of disciples called the Apelleians, though it appears that they were not nearly as gifted at magic, so their shows were short-lived.

churchfail: Like Marcion, Apelles thought the writings of the Old Testament were ludicrous. He wrote as least 38 books dedicated to discussing the contradictions and fallacies of these accounts. Basically, he said everything the Jews wrote was nothing more than a big bag of worthless lies and fairytales. He often read the familiar Old Testament stories in unfamiliar ways. For example, he thought that Adam and Eve's desire to pursue wisdom and eat from the tree of knowledge of good and evil was the right thing to do.

But Apelles departed from his teacher Marcion in several ways. He didn't think it was fun enough to only have two gods (one good and one bad). He threw two more into the mix and came up with four gods. One good god, he believed, got a bad rap for all the havoc that three lesser angels were creating. These lesser angels had created all earthly things and liked to just roam around and bother people. One of them, who had an especially hot temper, called down fire from heaven to destroy a bunch of unassuming people and later spoke to Moses in the burning bush to lead him astray. Finally, when Christ showed up on the scene in the New Testament, He taught all about the true good God above and the false gods of the Old Testament.

While Apelles believed that Jesus took on flesh, suffered, and died, he also taught that Jesus's body was not born from natural birth. Instead he believed that Christ formed His body from magical heavenly flesh when He descended from the eternal realm above. This special type of super flesh had no connection to the present world and so, when He died, the spiritual particles of His body slowly ascended back up to the heavenly realm where they belonged.

Application: Marcion is by far the most famous heretic of the early church, but the account of his famous disciple Apelles reminds Christians that errant views of God are often handed down and recycled from one generation to the next, like that yellow Formica®-top table with the matching chairs. Even after one false teacher is gone, there are often others who will pick up their beliefs and habits and take them in new directions. The church should always be vigilant against false teachings in every genera-

Marcion Teaching

tion and against the way that one false teacher's influence spawns others.

At the same time, Apelles's views of the Old Testament and Christ teach us the importance of connecting the person and work of Christ back to the Hebrew Scriptures. In many ways the Old Testament prepares Christians to confess that Christ is a fully human Servant (Isa 42:1) and yet also "God with us" (Isa 7:14). Moreover, our Lord taught that only by reading and understanding the Law and the Prophets could we appreciate His work, because Moses wrote of Him (John 5:46-47; cf. Luke 24:27). Christ is not some super human or the revealer of a new god that was previously unknown. He is true God from true God, who offers salvation to all who believe in Him.

S.P.

Ebionites

Date: ca. 150

Synopsis: This "poor" sect taught that Jesus was only a natural man, not born from a virgin and not divine.

Biography: The Ebionites were a Jewish-Christian sect that sprang up in the mid-second century like kudzu in Carolina. Their beliefs were a jumbled compound of Judaism and Christianity—they couldn't decide whether to celebrate Christmas or Hanukkah. Their name derived from the Greek *ebiōnaioi* meaning "the poor," which likely stems from the emphasis on humility and poverty in Jewish piety. The Old Testament is chock-full of passages that talk about God's love for the poor. Some believe that the sect was founded by a heretic named Ebion, but this seems to be just a legend, and it's hard to imagine anyone with that name anyway. (His mama was going to name him "Filthy Rich," but she didn't want to put that kind of pressure on the little fella.) Among the early church fathers, the Ebionites were known for their rejection of the virgin birth, which is why Eusebius interprets the reference to poverty in their name ironically, saying they had "poor and mean opinions concerning

Eusebius, Opponent of the Ebionites

Christ."[4] The doctrines of the Ebionites were evidently rather influential, though, because they were being discussed and debated into the fourth century. Several early fathers of the church even suggested that the Ebionites preferred the Gospel of Matthew since it reflected just the right Jewish–Christian balance they preferred.

---

[4] Eusebius, *Ecclesiastical History*, 3.27.1.

24

churchfail: While the early church also rejected the Ebionite insistence that all believers must keep every jot and tittle of the Mosaic Law, the real issue was their views of the divinity of Christ and the virgin birth. Ebionites believed that while Jesus was probably a capable carpenter and great at entertaining people at weddings, He was not divine—at least not at first. Instead, He was a natural man who was born by a natural birth to natural parents named Mary and Joseph. He was just an average boy from the backwater burg of Nazareth, and there was nothing noteworthy about His nativity or early life.

The Ebionites were willing to confess, however, that something special did happen to Him at his baptism. At the moment John baptized the *man* Jesus, the *Spirit-Christ* descended and took possession of Him. Thus, for the Ebionite, "Jesus" and "Christ" were two separate beings that only became united for a period of time after Jesus's baptism. Obviously, after Jesus was possessed by Christ (who is also the Spirit), things changed. He became the Jesus Christ that Christians know and love. He was a wonder-worker and wisdom-teacher who brought the true and good knowledge of the Father everyone needed to hear. The Spirit-Christ remained with the man Jesus until His death on the cross, when (at the last moment) He abandoned Him and ascended back to the heavenly home. The Ebionites even appealed to the description of Jesus giving up His spirit in Matthew 27:50 as evidence of the moment when the Spirit-Christ departed. This view, known later as Adoptionism, rejects the virgin birth and the full divinity of the person of Jesus Christ, preferring instead to say that the man Jesus was adopted by the Spirit-Christ.

Application: So they're saying God—who said He would never leave or forsake His children—abandoned His most famous follower at the moment of His greatest need. 'Scuse me if I don't hang my hat on that hook.

The Ebionite heresy of Adoptionism is recycled in various systems and styles throughout the history of the Christian tradition. While the technical language of Christology was later worked out in the early creeds of the church, the immediate rejection of the Ebionites shows how the church was already repudiating those who did not affirm the full deity and humanity of Christ. The divinity of Christ is essential to the Christian understandings of salvation and justification. In order for Christ's sacrifice to be sufficient, He must be both fully God and fully man, and the divinity of Christ encompasses the virgin birth. Christ had a special and unique birth that is beautifully expressed in the words of Luke 1:35: "The Holy Spirit will come upon you, and the power of the Most High will overshadow you. Therefore, the holy One to be born will be called the Son of God." The Ebionites are far from the last group in church history to question the virgin birth, but their views show that the early challenges facing the church were not all that different from those facing our contemporary Christian churches.

S.P.

Justin Martyr

Date: 155

Synopsis: Justin was the early Christian apologist who found Christianity to be the true philosophy and thenceforth put on the Socratic stole like a caped crusader to evangelize, catechize, and (at times) antagonize professional Roman cynics. Those cultured enemies ratted him out to the emperor, who had this pesky preacher scourged and beheaded to silence him, which of course guaranteed that JM would be almost as famous as the Bieber.

Biography: Justin (100–165) was born to pagan parents in Nablus, ancient Shechem, famed as the location of Jacob's well. He converted from pagan philosophy in about 130, when, if his own rather poetic version is historically intended, Justin set out like a dogged Diogenes to dig up a doctrine he could drive his dentures into. Picking the pockets of Stoic philosophers and finding little more than lint, this Samaritan seeker also pooh-poohed his Peripatetic tutor as pathetically impassioned about student fee payments. He also criticized the Pythagorean curriculum's prerequisites in music, astronomy, and geometry as time-wasting tuition inflation. Finally, he matriculated into an online degree in Platonism because its upgraded version of the Greek classics "gave wings" to his thoughts. Then a crusty Syrian Christian plucked his Platonic poultry claiming that the Greek wiseguys stole their best proposals from the Old Testament prophets, whose wisdom came by revelation and was more reliable than Archimedes's lever. Those biblical prophets pointed Justin to Jesus, the Word become flesh, and his soul was set on fire and his tongue loosed to preach.

Justin now donned the philosopher's pallium to preach the true philosophy—the gospel. In Ephesus, this caped proclaimer had his famous disputation with Trypho (Tarphon, of Talmud fame?) the Jew in 135, which he turned into *Dialogue with Trypho* sometime after 155. Like a moth attracted to a fatal flame, the soon-to-be martyr moved to Rome and opened a Christian school where he trained apologist 2.0 Tatian (p. 32) even as he completed his own *First Apology* (155), which was addressed to Emperor Antoninus Pius and his adopted sons. This defense of Christianity argued that merely claiming to be a Christian was not a criminal act. It presents one of the earliest descriptions of Christian worship, baptism, and communion.

The *Second Apology* was likely written about 161, shortly after Marcus Aurelius put on the imperial purple. In 165, Tatian tattled that Justin and some of his students had been denounced to the authorities by the Cynic philosopher Crescens. Whereas the professor never answered any critic with angry indignation, his teaching assistant Tatian quite happily took the low road and called Crescens an avaricious money grubber and a lust-defiled pederast. When the prefect asked Justin to renounce his faith,

Justin Martyr

he replied, "No one in his right mind turns from true belief to false." Justin's conversion had been energized as he saw how Christians met martyrdom and faced the fears that all men fear. Thus, he and his students refused to sacrifice to Caesar. An official court report of their scourging and beheading still survives, like some disturbing ISIS video.

churchfail: Justin taught that the Greek philosophers had plagiarized their elemental truths from teachings found in the Old Testament. But he did the same thing when he copped the Stoic doctrine of the "seminal word" in his proposal that John 1:9—"the true light, who gives light to everyone"—meant that Christ was the "germinative word" as the seed of truth in all men. He did not blush to declare that Socrates and Heraclitus were Christians because they possessed this seed of the Word, while Christ of course was the whole Word. Justin was baptizing his dead pagans' society, like the way the Mormons baptize for the dead, in a vain attempt to sustain a philosophic bridge between Socrates and the Savior. Tertullian, who liked barriers better than bridges, denounced any continuity in thought between pagans and preachers: "What has Athens to do with Jerusalem, darkness to do with light?"

Justin went further into darkness when he asserted that the Word was numerically second after the Father and that the genesis of the divine Logos (Word) was as a voluntary act of the Father at the beginning of creation. Such subordination of the essence of the Son to the Father was condemned at later ecumenical councils.

Application: Great apologetics builds bridges and barriers. However, false bridges compromise the very gospel we wish to share by overstating what Christianity has in common with other religions or worldviews.

R.D.

Priscilla and Maximilla and the New Prophecy

Date: 156

Synopsis: New Prophecy in the late second century threatened to scuttle both episcopal authority and the New Testament. Two women in white robes and dark eye shadow declared ecstatically that Jesus had come to them as a woman. He declared their town was His choice as the touchdown site of the New Jerusalem.

Biography: In the year 156 in Pepuza, Phrygia, two women in white jumped up during the church worship as if shocked. In an ecstatically pitched timbre, Priscilla declared that Christ had come to her as a woman in a dream and had lain down beside her and informed her to tell everyone that a new prophecy had come: Pepuza was selected by the Divine Planning Department to be the site for the New Jerusalem. In that moment, authority in that Turkish church shifted from the horrified pastor to the two prophetesses, whose manner and accessories looked like topline Mary Kay. And since Jesus was already revving His heavenly chariot, the new prophetesses declared that marriage was passé. Montanus, watching this charismatic moment unfold, offered himself as manager—Paraclete to the pair (p. 210). The girls liked the smell and dyed color of his hair and the fact that he was one of those liberated believers who could mix God and the gambling tables.

Montanus made two quick moves to propel New Prophecy and the Prophetesses up the charts: he booked them into a second gig at the nearby church in Tymion and then wrangled the Roman Google Earth into renaming both towns "Jerusalem." His social media strategy had two immediate responses. First, hundreds of Christian women rescheduled their annual

The New Jerusalem

meetings to these new Jerusalems, bought white chiffon gowns, and headed north for a touch of the Spirit. Second, all bishops from Byzantium to Carthage went ballistic when their congregants began chanting for the New Prophecy and wondering when the Priscilla and Maximilla World Tour would come to their town selling T-shirts.

Bishop Claudius Apollinarius of Hierapolis, after stewing in the local hot springs, and Bishop Serapion of Antioch wrote against these new kinds of prophetesses, who left their husbands after their first experience of ecstatic speech and prophesied for money and haute couture. For her part in this dispensational debacle, Maximilla habitually prophesied of pending wars marking the advent of the New Jerusalem. Over a century later, Eusebius dryly observed that no wars were to be seen even decades after her death.

When the supposedly imminent millennium of the New Prophecy failed to make an entrance, the false teaching faded until the promotion genius of Montanus rebooted fans with a call to increased asceticism. No second marriages. No running from persecution. It was this Phrygian 2.0 bandwagon that reached North Africa and even turned the teaching of Tertullian, the famous converted attorney (p. 178).

churchfail: Most scholars consider Priscilla and Maximilla to have been in conformity to the core creeds of the church. However, the early New Prophecy phenomenon was exceptionally schismatic in the same way that the early Charismatic Movement of the 1960s and '70s divided churches and even denominations. Priscilla and Maximilla's ecstatic exhortations moved churches from eschatological hope to apocalyptic alarmism.

Apocalyptic notions often dismantle biblical ethics in the name of the nearness of the millennium. Jesus's words that there would be no giving of marriage when the kingdom comes (Matt 22:30) was taken as immediate license to walk away from the old ball and chain. Their charismatic prophecies were taken as evidence that the kingdom had come. Although Jesus specifically said that no man knows the date (Matt 24:36), Priscilla and Maximilla abused their gifts and experiences to claim a fresher knowledge than the words of Christ in Scripture. Paul warns of this in 1 Corinthians 14:32-33 with the injunction that the spirit of the prophets is subject to the prophets, meaning that ecstasy and prophecy are acceptable if assimilated into the direction of the church by the pastoral leadership, and if evaluated according to the norming norm of biblical revelation.

Application: Without the canon of Scripture there is no way to evaluate the level of authority and influence that individual spiritual experiences should have on the church as a whole. Enthusiastic and spontaneous experiences are to be checked against Scripture and maintained in alignment with the accepted confession of the faith. So maybe it really doesn't matter how high you jump, if you walk straight when you hit the ground.

R.D.

Valentinus

Date: ca. 165

Synopsis: Valentinus divided humanity into three varieties with distinct capacities and ultimate destinies.

Biography: Valentinus was a big dog in early Christianity. After Marcion (p. 20), he was probably the most influential Gnostic "thinker" (if he was really thinking clearly, he wouldn't be a Gnostic) in the second century. He received the best education in the renowned philosophical schools of Alexandria. He made his way to Rome, where he set up shop and taught religion religiously from 135 to about 165. He must have been a charismatic leader because he gathered quite a following of Gnostic disciples. A number of mystifying monographs are attributed to him, including the *Gospel of Truth* (neither a Gospel nor true), which may have been written by Valentinus himself. Other works from the Valentinian school of thought include *The Tripartite Tractate*, *The Interpretation of Knowledge*, *The Exegesis on the Soul*, *Treatise on the Resurrection*, and *A Valentinian Exposition*. The ominous influence of Valentinus carried on long after his death and filtered into many ensuing Gnostic texts and traditions.

churchfail: Valentinian beliefs are a bewildering web of theological and philosophical speculations.

His convoluted theological system began with a heavenly realm called the *plērōma* and the Supreme God, who is wholly distinct from the God who created the world. This *plērōma* (rhymes with sarcoma) consisted of 30 divine emanations called *æons* (rhymes with Klingons). According to this myth, everything was fine and dandy in the *plērōma* until the youngest of all *æons*, named Wisdom (*sophia*), committed the most heinous and egregious of all sins, the most depraved thing an *æon* could do: she actually attempted to understand the Supreme God . . . gasp! Then, to make matters worse, she attempted to create something on her own without her consort (i.e., her eternal male partner *æon*). These indiscretions set into motion the appearance of the Creator God described in the Bible, who was born of her error and, as a result, inherently evil. Everything that the Creator formed and did was also naturally evil. These fatuous fairy tales of Valentinus erected a theological dualism that oozed over to many of the other Gnostic thinkers and writers.

One distinct aspect of his theology is his realized view of salvation and election that apportions all humanity into three classifications: "psychics" (from the Greek word *psyche* meaning "soul"), "pneumatics" (from *pneuma*, "spirit"), and "hylics" (from *hylē*, "matter"). Each of these particular populations had their own qualities, capacities, and eternal destinies. The psychics were the everyday class of Gnostic laity who endured the humdrum of daily life. The pneumatics, on the other hand, were the elite and branded themselves the truly "spiritual ones." They were the upper crust of religious society, morally and intellectually superior to any psychic. Of course Valentinus believed himself to be a pneumatic; he was, after all, more spiritual than everyone else. The hylics, on the other hand, were a sorry lot. They were the lower class, purely material and the very

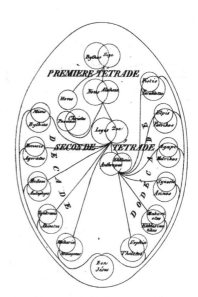

The Valentinian Plērōma

opposite of the pneumatics. The pneumatics were the only ones by nature guaranteed salvation, which is fine and dandy if you happen to be one. The psychics could achieve salvation in the present age if they realized the truth of the Gnostic teaching. The hylics . . . well, they had no hope and could do nothing to overcome their natural ignorance. (I encounter hylics every day on my commute.)

Application: Valentinus's views on anthropology remind the church of the importance of a comprehensive view of salvation that includes the body and soul of anyone who believes in the gospel. While Christians may debate the doctrine of election, we have always confessed that the work of salvation is not fully realized until the return of Christ, when He will raise the faithful to new life. Anyone who confesses Christ and believes the gospel is justified before God and enjoys the blessings and promises of God in the present life. But believers are also waiting for Christ to return again to destroy sin and death ultimately and finally (Rev 19–20).

Still, we who have confessed Christ and received the blessings of the Spirit of God and the hope of eternal life should not become so prideful that we view ourselves as more spiritual than others. The fruit of the Spirit is not pride and arrogance, but love and gentleness. May Christians continue to bear the fruit of the Spirit and preach the gospel of Jesus Christ, so that the Spirit of God might work and bring many more to repentance and faith.

S.P.

Tatian the Assyrian

Date: ca. 172

Synopsis: Tatian was a Gnostic who innovated the notion that Adam was beyond salvation.

Biography: If we compared early Christian disciples to NFL draft picks, Tatian would have certainly made the list of the top ten biggest draft busts. He had the potential to be the MVP, having the right education and pedigree, but his pride and lack of commitment to the Christian faith led him astray not long after his rookie year.

Tatian's story begins in Assyria, but like many contemplative young people he left home at an early age in search of the meaning of life and answers to life's more perplexing questions. Like an indecisive patron at an ice cream shop, he enjoyed sampling the arguments of all the theological and philosophical schools of the ancient Greco-Roman world. But he never found any of them satisfying until he encountered the writings of the Christian Scriptures. He studied the Bible carefully and eventually converted to Christianity. According to the church father Irenaeus, he studied under Justin Martyr (p. 26) in Rome in the 160s and quickly became a key leader in the Roman church. He is still known for a tome that harmonized the Gospels, the *Diatessaron*, quoted by many church fathers. But his only extant writing is *Address to the Greeks*, which defends Christian belief and solicits tolerance for Christian worship. Despite studying the Scriptures and even defending the Christian faith, after the death of his mentor Justin (ca. 165), Tatian quickly became captivated with his own academic capacity and started entertaining Gnostic notions, which got him excommunicated.

Tatian

churchfail: Tatian's heresy is a complex mixture of Gnostic cosmology, anthropology, and soteriology. Tatian became enamored with Gnostic notions on creation. But even this wasn't enough. He had to create his own system of belief, so he invented a version of Gnostic myth that rejected the salvation of Adam (a bad deal for Adam—no doubt he would have objected).

After his dishonorable discharge from the church, Tatian enlisted with the Encratites. The Encratites, like other Gnostics, rejected the physical world including their own bodies, because they believed the Creator of the world was a lesser, evil god. So basically everything this evil god made was bad by association. While the rejection of the material world led some Gnostics to become licentious (like crazed college kids on perpetual spring break), the Encratites went the other direction. They became highly ascetic and abstained from all the good blessings of creation—such as marriage, since that would only result in more evil people. They were also vegetarians; they did not want any association with animals, since those too had been created by this evil god.

While participating in all this fun, Tatian tried to make a name for himself by inventing the view that Adam was beyond any hope of salvation. He reasoned that Adam was so perverted by sin through his original act of disobedience that restoration was impossible. There was no hope for someone who had given himself so freely to sin and evil and had not withstood the pleasures of this world. Tatian was saying, "Adam was weak, not strong like me."

Application: Assessing where Tatian went wrong involves scrutinizing not only his theological perspective but also his spiritual life. Tatian lacked the humility that should characterize someone who is fully committing to follow Christ. Certainly Tatian was interested in the intellectual and theological discussions of the Old Testament and the person and work of Christ, but his pride got the best of him.

Tatian's story is, unfortunately, not nearly as uncommon as it should be. Christian leaders all too easily begin reading their own press releases and become enamored with the number of followers they have on social media. But the gospel calls us to humility, not pride. Tatian's pride led him to invent this heresy about Adam's salvation. While Tatian sanctioned many other theological problems within the Gnostic system, his erratum in re Adam should prompt all Christians to affirm with personal gratitude and humility that no one is beyond the grace of Christ. Adam's sin resulted in separation between God and His people. But just as all have sinned, so also salvation is available to all who believe (Rom 5:19). For God's desire is that no one would perish, but that all would come to repentance and faith—beginning with Adam.

S.P.

Adoptionists
(aka Dynamic Monarchians)

Date: ca. 190

Synopsis: The Adoptionists rejected the divinity of Jesus; they considered Him a mere man who was adopted into the divine.

Biography: Dynamic Monarchianism might sound like it refers to a group of charismatic royalty, but in reality it was an early Christian heresy involving errant views on the Trinity. Dynamic Monarchians are also known as Adoptionists, not because they liked to give homes to orphaned children, but because they believed that Jesus was a mere man whom God adopted at his baptism. Theodotus of Byzantium (aka Theodotus the Tanner or Theodotus the Shoemaker because of his leather trade) became the main exporter of Adoptionism. In between tanning and cobbling, Theodotus theologized about the nature of God and wanted to make absolutely sure that everyone affirmed monotheism and rejected tri-theism. His views, however, led him to reject the doctrine of the Trinity as one nature in three persons. Eventually Pope Victor I (p. 36) excommunicated Theodotus at the end of the second century.

Several others, including Paul of Samosata—the gregarious bishop of Antioch (260–68)—picked up the slack. According to the church fathers, he was a highly indulgent self-promoter who really enjoyed the limelight, so he had no trouble teaching things that were a bit controversial. He was often seen sauntering about the square dictating theological treatises to a horde of his groupies gathered around him. And like Theodotus, the main issue with his teaching was his unwillingness to accept the deity of Christ.

churchfail: To the Dynamic Monarchians, the church had lost its emphasis on monotheism. They reasoned that if there is only one God, as the Old Testament makes abundantly clear, then the Son and the Father cannot both be God. Once Christians started talking about Jesus being God and the Father being God, the Monarchians got all confused and rejected this talk as incoherent mumbo jumbo and jumbled mumbling. In fact, they believed that people who talked this way were really polytheists who rejected the one true God.

Baptism of Christ

This emphasis on monotheism is why they also taught that Jesus was not fully divine at His birth, but instead just a regular guy born in Bethlehem—though they are willing to concede that He was a superior moral person. They said that Jesus's formal adoption process began at His baptism when the power descended upon Him and enabled Him to perform miracles and speak profound wisdom. Adoptionists were strict Unitarians (not Trinitarians), so the Logos (Word) and the Spirit of God were not distinct persons from the Father, but impersonal attributes of God that empowered the man Jesus to accomplish miraculous deeds. Thus God imparted to Jesus special powers in order to command what He willed through the person of Christ. The divine powers working in Christ gradually deified the man Jesus, making Him worthy of honor and respect, though He must not be called "God" in a technical sense. Finally, after the resurrection, God adopted or absorbed Christ into the divine to become part of the one true God, which completed the act of adoption.

Ultimately the church rejected the Adoptionists at the Synod of Antioch in 268 because they refused to confess Christ as fully God and fully man from birth.

Application: In one sense, we might be tempted to sympathize with the Adoptionists. They appear to be adamant supporters of monotheism. Since God Himself taught the existence of only one God (Deut 6:4), they shut their ears to any debate or discussion about the number of persons in the one God. But in their sincere passion for the unity and uniqueness of God, they gave up the deity of Christ, which has important implications for the doctrine of salvation. If Christ is not fully God, then His death could not serve as an eternal sacrifice for sins, once for all (Heb 7:27). That would mean the people of God are still dead in their sins with no hope of salvation and eternal life with God.

The Apostle John, conversely, made it clear that the Son of God, the Second Person of the Trinity, became man and dwelt among us (John 1:14). It was this God-man who sacrificed His life for the sake of His people as an atoning sacrifice for sins and, as such, is worthy of all worship and honor (1 John 2:2).

S.P.

Quartodecimans vs. Victor I

Pope Victor I

Dates: ?–199

Synopsis: Victor was into intolerance before intolerance was in. He excommunicated the quartodeciman because they considered one day to be above another day.

Biography: Victor served as the bishop of Rome (i.e., the pope) from about 189 until his death in 199. He rightly excommunicated Theodotus of Byzantium (p. 34) for teaching Adoptionism: that Jesus was a mere man. (The Greeks taught that Triton was a merman. But I digress.)

churchfail: Quartodecimans are fourteenthers—not fourteeners, as in the average age of the crowd at a One Direction concert, but as in the fourteenth day of the month of Nisan. While Nisan might sound like a car, it is really the month of the Jewish lunar calendar when they celebrated the Passover (typically around March or April). The fourteenth could fall on any day of the week. This practice was handed down from a bishop in Smyrna named Polycarp (I wonder if his name means "a mess of fish"). Tradition holds that Polycarp had been a disciple of Apostle John and followed John's practice with regard to Easter. Before Polycarp died in 155, he and Anicetus, bishop of Rome, discussed the matter. They agreed to disagree and left it at that—neither thought it worthy of excommunication.

Then in the last decade of the second century, synods were summoned, discussions were discussed, and names were named. All bishops outside Asia argued that Easter really should be celebrated on the Lord's Day, Sunday, as purportedly promulgated down by Apostles Peter and Paul. However, only Victor deemed that the difference deserved disfellowship. Indeed, Irenaeus and others castigated him for his intolerance. So while you might think it was the Christians in Asia, whose worship was different from everyone else's, who were the heretics here, actually it was only Pope Victor I who failed at this time.

By 325, at the Council of Nicaea, Victor's version of viciousness was de rigueur, and the quartodecimans were the whipping boys. Again it seems that the antiquarto-decimans were the real churchfails.

The Council said the Christians of Asia honored the wrong day, but in Romans 14:1-13 Paul said we should not pass judgment on one another if "one person considers one day to be above another day" (v. 5). The Council claimed they had received their tradition from Peter and Paul, but Polycarp's practice was equally ancient and authoritative, since he had received it directly from John.

The Council also argued that they shouldn't look to the Jews to determine the date of Christian celebrations. They said the Jews killed Jesus, forgetting that Jesus died for sinful humanity; so, in fact, *they* killed Jesus. According to Eusebius, the Council said Jews were sinful, base, of ungoverned passions, and most wicked, and thus they had blind souls and could not perceive any truth. In this the Council seemed to consider all Jews irredeemable. They apparently forgot that Moses, David, Mary, Peter, and Paul were Jews—not to mention Jesus Himself! They also forgot that Peter's first vocation was missionary to the Jews.

The Council believed their celebration to be in line with the teaching of Christ. But Jesus did not specify any particular day. Moreover, Eusebius records that the Asian churches similarly argued from antiquity, saying that because they continued the ancient celebration of Passover (which God called "a permanent statute" in Exod 12:14), they observed the exact day—neither adding, nor taking away. The Council insisted that Easter should be held after the vernal equinox and it was scandalous if the Jewish calendar sometimes had Nisan 14 while the sun was in the twelfth sign of the zodiac. Looking back, it seems the canonized Council was paying way too much attention to heathen calendar elements.

For the Council at Nicaea to emulate Victor was a defeat. Better to have a nice touch like Anicetus or to be irenic like Irenaeus.

Application: De Dominis said, "In necessary things, unity; in non-necessary things, liberty; in all things, charity." There are myriad matters that might merit marching orders. For example, Paul warned that no one should preach another gospel. The resurrection is clearly key to the true gospel. But the color of the carpet in the narthex, the use of a Stradivarius or a Stratocaster in worship, and the particular day on which Easter is celebrated are not among the crucial questions for communicants. It is interesting to note in this context that the people of Asia Minor, whom the councils supposedly brought into orthodoxy, are now mostly Muslim.

S.P. & D.S.

Bardaisan

Date: ca. 222

Synopsis: Bardaisan loved pagan astrology and read his horoscope as often as he read his Bible.

Biography: Bardaisan (or Bardesanes, for the Greek speakers among us) was an ancient poet and songwriter from Edessa, located on the Southern border of modern-day Turkey. His name derives from the Daisan river (*bar*=son, so "son of Daisan") that flowed through the heart of the city. Born into the privileges of aristocracy, Bardaisan enjoyed a rich education. He spent his days like most aristocrats, learning archery and composing grandiose philosophical treatises. Bardaisan composed around 150 hymns, a few of which hit number I on the Byzantium top XL charts and became some of the greatest hits from Syriac Christianity. You may have heard of some of them: *The Dialogue of Destiny*, which set a new record for consecutive days at number I, and *The Laws of the Land*, which had a nice beat and was easy to dance to. Bardaisan was the Elvis Presley of Syriac Hymnody—even naming his son Harmonius, who turned out to be quite the musician himself.

Bardaisan

Bardaisan didn't always choose the best company. Before he converted to Christianity, he frequently hung out with the Valentinians (p. 30), and he further blended Valentinian thought with stargazing. Then he converted to Christianity and even became a priest in the local Daisan congregation. But eventually he became enamored with his own thinking and went back to the Valentinians. All this fickleness led Bardaisan to a synergistic variety of Gnostic, pagan, and Christian perspectives. He and his followers regularly met in caves to discuss pagan and Gnostic writings and, of course, to compose a few hymns. He eventually died around 222, but a community of his devotees—called the Bardaisanites—went right on singing well into the fifth century.

churchfail: Bardaisan's theology had a variety of issues, including the belief that God created all things from preexistent matter (not "from nothing"). He also argued that the Trinity was the union of the Mother and Father of Life who brought forth the Son, and he rejected any notion that Christ was born of a virgin. But a peculiar feature of his theology was his fascination with astrology. He loved horoscopes and would regularly introduce himself saying, "Hello, my name is Bardaisan, and I am a Sagittarius." His view of anthropology included a spirit-soul-body triad. The spirit was completely free and deposited from the divine world. The soul was completely bound by the movement of the planets and determined by a person's birth horoscope. The body was completely corrupt and destined for destruction. For this reason, Bardaisan rejected the bodily resurrection as absurd.

One church father, Ephrem the Syrian, dedicated an entire hymn to refuting the Bardaisan heresy. In the last few lines he reflected on Bardaisan's high view of his own intellect and his rejection of the true God:

> Whoever would destroy his life,
> Opens his mouth to speak concerning everything.
> Whoever despises himself,
> And would not circumscribe God,
> Holds it great impiety that one should think himself over-wise.
> And if he thinks he has said the last thing
> He has reached heathenism,
> O Bar-Daisan, son of the River Daisan,
> Whose mind is liquid like his name![5]

And so the hymn-writing heretic met his match in a heretic-rebuking hymn. These lines express how the ancient church rejected Bardaisan's conflation of astrology and Christian theology. He strayed into areas of cosmology and astrology that proved inconsistent with Christian understandings of creation and anthropology.

Application: Christians should not become fascinated with astrology or have anything to do with psychics or fortunetellers. It is all too common, even in our own day, for Christians to glance at horoscopes and wonder about the predictions of self-professed psychics. Certainly it is a challenge to walk by faith and not by sight (2 Cor 5:7), but God has asked believers to trust Him and to rely on Him no matter what happens. The example of Bardaisan demonstrates that these kinds of interests can lead a Christian away from the faith and from true understandings of God and God's interaction with the world.

S.P.

---

[5] A. S. Duncan Jones, "A Homily of St. Ephrem," in *Journal of Theological Studies*, vol. 5 (1904): 546–52, 551. Some of the language has been updated.

Patripassianists (aka Modalistic Monarchians)

Date: ca. 222

Synopsis: The modalistic monarchians argued that God the Father *is* the Son, but with a younger and hipper persona.

Biography: In the early church there was a group of thinkers called the modalistic monarchians, which is a fancy alliteration for a cast of characters named Noetus, Sabellius, and Praxeas. All three of these stooges taught similar divergent views on the relationship of the Father to the Son. Noetus came first, and the church quickly realized that he was not talking about God or Christ in the same way as everyone else. He argued that no distinction existed between the Father and the Son; they were one and the same person. When he was called to confess his curious creed before the congregation in Smyrna, the presbyters excommunicated him.

Then came the more-(in)famous Sabellius, who taught the same ideas as Noetus; in fact, modalism is called Sabellianism, especially in Eastern churches. (Ask Lou Gehrig whether it's an "honor" to have something named after you.)

Finally, a guy named Praxeas expressed some of the same ideas in the Western churches, and his views became known as patripassianism (which is a highfalutin' way of referring to the suffering of the Father).

churchfail: These modalistic monarchians, or modalists, identified Jesus with the Father in every way. It was not unusual for them to say that the Father was born of the Virgin Mary or that the Father died on the cross—expressing no distinction

Crucifixion of Christ

40

between the Father and the Son. Modalists did not deny the Incarnation but merely argued that Jesus was a different mode or manifestation of God. The reasoning of the modalists was simple: If Christ was God, He must be identical with the Father; otherwise He would not be God.

Modalists did not hesitate to speak of God as Father, Son, and Spirit, but for them these were just names attached to different modes of existence. God is a monad—or a single unitive principle—who expressed Himself in three operations or functions. The terms *Father*, *Son*, and *Spirit* do not reflect any real distinctions but rather names applied to the same God who appeared in different times and locations. These distinct roles or "modes" of God functioned according to the purpose and plan of God within the history of salvation. So God revealed Himself in the mode of Creator in the Father, the mode of Redeemer in the Son, and the mode of Sanctifier in the Spirit. So, when the Son suffered and died on the cross, the Father also suffered and died.

Modalists often used analogies to explain the nature of God: For example, the sun, as a single object, radiates both warmth and light. The Father is the form (i.e., the sun) and the Son and the Spirit are the modes of expression (warmth and light). They also used the idea of a human person being composed of body (i.e., Father), soul (i.e., Son), and spirit (i.e., Spirit). The church fathers describe how these stinker-thinkers liked to confuse those who have little knowledge of the Scriptures by arguing that if the Father is God, Jesus is God, and the Spirit is God, then the church is teaching everyone to believe in three Gods.

While some of these modalists were well meaning, the church has always rejected modalism and affirmed that God exists eternally as one nature in three persons.

Application: The early debates with modalists helped the church explain the doctrine of God as eternally existing as one nature in three persons. Even today, when some Christians use the terms *Father*, *Son*, and *Spirit*, it does not mean that they view them as separate persons. It is important to be clear about what we mean when we use these titles and when we talk about the unity of the nature of God and the uniqueness of the persons.

Christians should also be careful when using analogies to explain the nature of God (see p. 186). There are many popular analogies including the egg analogy (shell, white, and yolk), the water analogy (water, ice, and steam), or the man analogy (father, husband, and brother). All of these are modalistic, as they do not make a distinction between the particular persons of God. The best way to use the analogies, then, is not to explain what God *is* (because they almost always end up in modalism) but to explain what God is *not*. God eternally exists as one nature in three persons, which is not like any of these analogies.

S.P.

Hippolytus of Rome

Date: 170–235

Synopsis: Hippolytus of Rome, whose name perversely means "unleasher of horses," was a preacher imprisoned in the Sardinian mines only to be drawn and quartered by horses in 235. Naturally some sick puppy made him the patron saint of prison guards and horses (sick ponies in the Middle Ages were brought to the Church of Saint Hippolytus in Hertfordshire, England). Hippolytus never met a pope he agreed with, and some consider him the first antipope. He also became the first chronographer to work out an exact date for Christ's return.

PONTIANVS·I·PAPA·ROMANVS

Pope Pontian

Biography: Hippolytus was born and buried in Rome. One Catholic legend suggests Rome's most famous deacon, St. Lawrence, led him to saving faith. Because Hippolytus wrote his theology tomes in Greek, the Latin West didn't do much to preserve his commentaries, homilies, apologetics, and ecclesiastic law compendiums. While his principle book, *Against All Heresies*, was quite well known, until recently most attributed it to Origen, who had at least once come to Rome to hear Hippolytus preach.

Having both a brilliant brain and a quick quill, Hippolytus was supposed to possess an impeccable pedigree of discipleship—being mentored by Irenaeus, who had been mentored by Polycarp, who had been trained by John the apostle. Nevertheless, that lineage did not prevent our presbyter from disliking every pope he met, and he met five. He labeled Pope Zephyrinus a modalist like the proto-Unitarian Sabellius (p. 40). Hippolytus was horrified when Pope Callistus, whom Hippolytus called a sorcerer, lowered the bar for repentant adulterers and other stained saints and lowered it again for the many pagans seeking entrance into the church. Hippolytus's *Apostolic Traditions* called for three years of catechism prior to baptism, unless of course you were an infant and your parents were big givers. Hippolytus even allowed himself to be named and elected by the Puritan Party as a rival pastor to Callistus, thus making Hippolytus the first antipope.

42

Hippolytus continued his feuds with the guys in the tall hats right through Urban I and Pontian. The fuss with Pope Pontian was just getting interesting when Emperor Maximinus the Thracian declared a local persecution of Christians in 235 and punted Hippolytus and Pontian onto the next prison barge bound for the mines of Sardinia. Apparently, using a pick axe is a great setting in which to kiss and make up before you are martyred because Pope Fabian, the converted teen idol, brought back both in the same hearse (though no one is sure all the pieces of Humpty Hippolytus were recovered from the wild horse drawing and quartering). Whether ironic or iconic, Hippolytus and Pontian were both canonized and now share the same Feast Day, August 13, and get along pretty well, unless it's Friday the thirteenth.

churchfail: Hippolytus had an addiction to chronography, the setting of the events of history in a precise sequence, with his calendar covering the span from Creation to his contemporaries. Because the Scofield Bible was not available in Greek, Hippolytus went with the Septuagint's creation date of 5500 BC. And since his own commentary on Daniel identified biblical days with millennia, six thousand years after creation means AD 500 must be the Second Advent. So our chronographer became the first theologian to name the exact date of the Maranatha (cf. Montanus, p. 210), and, of course, the first to be wrong.

Two other false firsts deserve mention. Hippolytus was loony about liturgy; he wanted it right, "like it's always been done," and so he became the first to mention the Virgin Mother Mary in the order of service for the ordination of presbyters. I am not sure how she fits in with ordination, but she was very good at procuring extra wine when it ran low. If he is the rightful author of the *Apostolic Traditions*, Hippolytus also became the first to try to make infant baptism look like it was apostolic practice. Not only did he make the unbiblical case that converts must have three years of training prior to splashdown, he also insisted that babies can get dunked not only before they believe but even before they are potty-trained.

Application: Beware of developing an adversarial personality, being known only for whom you are against and being fully alive only when you have an adversary. Also beware of eschatomania, the demented mindset that attempts to do what Jesus said we cannot—namely, date His return.

R.D.

Donatism

Date: ca. 311

Synopsis: Donatism taught that a minister had to be perfect to baptize someone . . . which basically meant that no one would ever be baptized.

Biography: Donatus was from North Africa. He lived during the fourth century, when serious persecutions broke out against Christians at the hand of the ever-cantankerous emperor, Diocletian. Diocletian ordered that all sacred Scriptures be destroyed and all citizens demonstrate their loyalty to the state by burning incense to the Roman gods. As you can imagine, a good number of Christians didn't want to cause a stir, so they handed over their family Bibles and offered a little incense to the pagan gods. Then they just continued on their way, minding their own business—no harm, no foul. However, not everyone was willing to deny Christ so easily and give up the Good Book. Some gave their lives. When the smoke cleared, the issue essentially became one of mediating between the incense-offerers and resisters/martyrs.

churchfail: The issue created rival factions within the church, especially in North Africa. The Christians who relinquished their texts or sacrificed to Roman gods were branded *traditors* ("the ones who hand over"). Of course, even the least pew-sitter doesn't want to be branded a traitor (or *traditor*), but it was an especially serious point of contention when a church leader denied Christ. I mean, it was one thing for John the baker to pinch a little incense and worship a false god, but what was a person to do when a deacon or a preacher rejected Christ one day and then showed up to lead worship the next? Many Christians felt it was completely unjust to accept *anyone* who had committed such a grievous act back into the fold of the church, much less a *pastor*.

Things came to a head at the consecration of Caecilian of Carthage in 311 when one of the three presiding bishops over the rite, Felix, bishop of Aptunga, reportedly had given up copies of the Scriptures to the Roman authorities. When word of this spread through the rank and file of the bishops in attendance, 70 of them angrily declared the ceremony to be null and void.

While Caecilian's ministry was allowed to resume, after he died Donatus became bishop of Carthage and took a hard stance against the *traditors*. He demanded that every priest should be morally spotless and even even went so far as to state that the effectiveness of the sacraments depended on the moral character of the minister. So, for example, if a priest was guilty of a serious indiscretion (such as the sin of denying Christ) while performing a baptism, that baptism would be rendered invalid. Donatus's demand eventually resulted in two separate churches: those that allowed lapsed priests and those that did not.

The emperor Constantine tried to settle the matter in 314 at the Council of Arles, where they determined that the sacrament was effectual regardless of the moral character of the priest. They argued that baptism and the Lord's Supper depended on the ministry of Christ, not the sanctification of the priest who administered the rites. Augustine composed several works against the Donatists that essentially followed the same line of argumentation. As the parable of the wheat and tares teaches (Matt 13:24-30), until that day when the Lord returns in glory,

Emperor Diocletian

the church will be populated with saints and sinners together—and it's not easy to tell them apart. Eventually the anti-Donatists won the day, though Donatism remained well into the seventh century.

Application: The matter of pastors with temporary lapses was a hard one for the church, and the struggle against persecution is not going away anytime soon. As our Lord reminded His disciples, in this world Christians will face troubles, but Christ has left the faithful His peace that will help them endure (John 16:33). For the contemporary church, the lesson of the Donatist controversy stresses the importance of the graceful pas de deux of preaching the grace of Christ while calling for sanctification and repentance. The Donatists were caught up with concerns over moral indiscretions and neglected to preach grace.

At the same time, Christians must remember that salvation is the work of God and not dependent on the piety of a particular preacher. Unfortunately, news headlines repeatedly report pastors falling into sin. While this might disqualify them from holding a ministry position, it does not disqualify them from the grace of Christ.

S.P.

Arius and Arianism

Date: 325

Synopsis: Arius said that the Son of God was a great guy, but not really God.

Biography: The Arian controversy was one of the more important debates in early Christianity because it confirmed that Jesus Christ was more than just your run-of-the-mill Savior.

Arius was originally from Libya and learned theology from Lucian of Antioch, who emphasized Jesus's humanity to the point that he considered Him altogether inferior to the Father. Arius became a presbyter in Alexandria and began spouting the same drivel. The smoldering congregation conflagrated when Alexander became bishop. Alexander decided it was time to try his hand at unifying the church in Alexandria (don't worry, it is easy to get confused with all the Alex's involved!), so he began asking some of the local presbyters a few basic theological questions. His confab with Arius on the relationship between the Father and the Son left him a tad troubled to say the least. A contentious conflict ensued over the deity of the Son, and the debate only reinforced the rift in the church in Alexandria. Arius worked his angles and garnered some support from a pair of power brokers both named Eusebius (one from Nicomedia and the other from Caesarea). But Alexander had supporters as well.

The Emperor Constantine caught wind of the developing discontent and did what all good leaders do where there is a dispute: Get everyone into the same room and let them duke it out until they come to an agreement. This meeting was called the Council of Nicaea, and ultimately the anti-Arian bishops won the day. The Council declared Arius's views heretical and excommunicated

Arius

him. Some of his supporters, however, wouldn't let the issue die, and over the next few years Athanasius (who succeeded Alexander; see pp. 48, 52) found it necessary to defend the decision of Nicaea. Gradually, both the churches of the West and the East came to formally condemn Arius's views.

churchfail: It is hard to overestimate the importance of the Arian controversy for later theological discussions. In many ways Arianism became the archetypal heresy. Nobody wanted to be compared to Arius or be labeled . . . gasp! . . . an "Arian" (cue ominous music: *don . . . don . . . don*). Nevertheless, a few church leaders came to Arius's defense. He was, after all, a good presbyter just trying to read his Bible and understand what on earth Jesus meant when He said, "the Father is greater than I" (John 14:28). Arius pointed to this and other similar passages, reasoning that God the Father alone was eternal and unbegotten. The Son, then, was God's very best and brightest creation. Arius conceded that the Father brought forth the Son first, just to prove that He was best and show how much He loved Him. So, according to Arius, the Son had a beginning and was begotten, while God the Father did not have a beginning and was unbegotten. Arius's view became known by the axiom, "There was a time when He [the Son] was not." In other words, there was a time when the Son did not exist with the Father.

Much to the chagrin of Arius and his friends, the council of Nicaea determined that the Father and the Son are *homoousios*, which is a fancy way of saying "of the same substance." So the Son is, to use the language of the Nicene Creed, "true God from true God." Since then, the church has always affirmed the Son being equal and coeternal with the Father.

Application: While pockets of Arianism have resurfaced occasionally throughout church history, the Arian controversy proved helpful for clarifying the full deity of Christ. While Jesus indeed exalts the Father and glorifies Him, as Arius pointed out, He also states clearly, "The Father and I are one" (John 10:30). The Son is not subordinate to the Father, nor is He some kind of super-special angel; He is God. When we speak about the incarnate Christ, it is important always to worship him and honor Him as God. At the same time, believers should take care to speak clearly and carefully about the Son as God in our prayers and corporate worship times. The Son— who humbled Himself and became incarnate—suffered and died for the sins of His people, and He is worthy of all praise, honor, and adoration.

S.P.

Athanasius Contra Mundum

Date: 325

Synopsis: Athanasius became the public face of what historian Phillip Jenkins has called the "Jesus wars" of the fourth century. What started as a staff squabble quickly became an empire-eviscerating controversy that drew the attention of the Roman emperor Constantine. When other means fell short, the emperor called a first-ever council of the bishops at Nicaea in 325. (Who would turn down a month at the five-star imperial beach resort on the emperor's credit card?) At stake was how the church would express the mystery of the dual nature of the Son of God in the incarnation. This council set the precedent of the state church, which would not be successfully challenged until Luther started nailing theses to church doors in the sixteenth century.

Biography: In Athanasius's time, the megachurch at Alexandria was presided over by Bishop Alexander, and this multi-staff church operated with priests serving satellite churches in the greater metro area. The pastoral staff included a tall, fair, and articulate-but-arrogant songster named Arius and a short, dark (his enemies called him the "black dwarf" and the Emperor Julian labeled him a "little manikin"), and adversarial-to-the-point-of-violence academic named Athanasius.

By the time the controversy broke out, Athanasius had already distinguished himself in the Greek-speaking world as a thinker and writer. He probably had already written his main work *On the Incarnation* and may have penned the biography of the Egyptian desert monk, Anthony. Athanasius became alarmed when he heard Arius proclaim subordinationism in the Godhead—that the Son was not fully divine with the Father (p. 46). Athanasius ardently averred the full equality of divine nature (consubstantiality) between the Father and the Son. Whenever he saw that biblical truth at stake, Athanasius barked and bit. He became known as Athanasius *Contra Mundum* (against the world) because he spent 46 years of ministry defending the Nicene faith against emperors, bishops, Roman divas, and any and every kind of heretic. Someone apparently tried to persuade Athanasius to pacify his pontificating perch, petitioning, "Don't you know that the whole world is against you, Athanasius?"

"Then Athanasius is against the world," the diminutive diocesan retorted.

Four emperors tried to silence this mighty mouse by banishing him from his cathedral soapbox for a total of 17 years (p. 52), but the little Coptic curmudgeon cranked

Athanasius

out Greek words like hollow point bullets. His scathing wit refused to call his enemies by name, especially the Arians; instead they were dogs, lions, hares, chameleons, hydras, eels, cuttlefish, gnats, and beetles, which sounds like the name-calling Jude does in his biblical call to contend for the faith. When his great enemy, Arius, died, Athanasius shot off a letter to his friend Serapion giving all the details: how the heretic had howled in the house of prayer when he was promised communion the next day and was suddenly "compelled by a necessity of nature to withdraw to a privy where he fell headlong and burst asunder" (invoking the Acts 1:18 account of Judas's splat down from the tree by which he had hung himself) and was thereby dispossessed of the Eucharist and existence.

churchfail: Athanasius was a bit of a dirty fighter, and some reckon his multiple emperor-mandated exiles as the just desserts of an inveterate troublemaker. The famous Athanasian Creed,[6] which is addressed to "whosoever wishes to be saved," varies in one protruding point from the Nicene and Apostles Creeds: it heaps so many anathemas onto Arians and other heretics that Vatican II (1962–65) finally decided to suppress its use in the Catholic Church lest the abusive application of assorted anathemas appall even ardent attendees. Enough is enough for most, but when it came to attacks on the apostate, Athanasius had no "off" button. When Christian rebuke is too acidic, the delinquent will never become the repentant.

Recent scholarship also notes that Athanasius, like sand in the skivvies, has the desert anchorite notion that physical existence has little trustworthy goodness. He pictures Christ in the manner of the monks and not the monks in the likeness of the Master. For him, the élan of asceticism is the only path to purity. This misses the biblical mark that Christ alone is the path, the truth, and the life.

Application: Wherever and whenever false doctrine is taught, the mature in the faith must contend for the truth so that error can be refuted and the immature instructed. However, contending is not being corrosively contentious. On a happier note, one way to triumph over your enemies is to outlive them.

R.D.

---

[6] Probably not written by Athanasius, but nevertheless inspired by his message and method.

Empress Helena

Helena

Date: 327

Synopsis: Helen (ca. 250–330), also called Helena, was the mother of the Emperor Constantine She is venerated as a saint in five Christian denominations for making pilgrimage in her 70s to Palestine—resulting in her purported discovery of the cross on which Christ was crucified—and for construction of basilicas there on Golgotha and in Bethlehem. She is the patron saint of new discoveries, archaeologists, difficult marriages, and divorced people.

Biography: The place of Helen's birth is debated; either she was from Britain and the daughter of King Cole, "the merry old soul," and there are 25 holy wells in England named after her, or she was born in lowly circumstances in Depranum on the southwest side of the Black Sea, which city was renamed Helenopolis upon her death. Either way she caught the eye of the up-and-coming Constantius Chlorus and bore him a son, Constantine, in 274. Eusebius, the biographer of Constantine, tells that in 292 Constantius—who probably should have been named Inconsistentius—abandoned Helen to upgrade to the daughter of his mentor, Maximian, and rode Theodora's wedding train into the big house on the hill. Helen meanwhile was dispatched to the court of the eastern emperor and deserted by all except her boy, Constantine.

In 306 Constantius died and his troops declared Constantine as Augustus Caesar. By 312 Constantine remembered his momma and brought her first class to Rome and set her up in her own palace, where she immediately oversaw the renovation of the plumbing. Constantine's newfound Christian faith coupled with his devotion to Helena soon led her to faith as well. While Helen was pretty much fireproof in regard to palace intrigue, her beloved grandson, Crispus, not so much. When rumor reached his father in 326 that Crispus was trying to work a reverse Potiphar's wife seduction on his young stepmom Fausta, Emperor Constantine dispatched the upstart to a parallel universe. Grandma gained revenge by whispering to her son that it was actually

Fausta whose seductive perfumes were repulsed. So Constantine, who apparently had been skipping his morning devotions for some time, took a page from Machiavelli rather than Matthew and cancelled Fausta's role as stepmomma. Now Helen was First Lady of the empire, and Constantine realized she needed something to do, preferably way out of town. So Helen, in her 70s, was sent on a holy pilgrimage to seek and preserve holy sites in Palestine, now that Constantine had unified the western and the eastern empires. Helen jumped at the opportunity to use the imperial credit card to walk—OK, in her case be carried around—where Jesus walked. In no uncertain terms, the emperor told her watchdog guards, "If Momma ain't happy, I ain't happy, and you're dead."

According to Eusebius, the empress was responsible for construction or beautification of the Church of the Nativity in Bethlehem and the Church of the Mount of Olives. Helen packed two hats for the trip. She used her Indiana Jones fedora to find the site of the holy cross and then put on her construction hard hat and had the Temple of Venus bulldozed away so the site could be excavated. Three crosses were discovered, and using scientific methodology—like making really sick people touch the crosses—one was "conclusively" revealed as the true cross of Christ, which of course meant that Helen hid it in her suitcase to smuggle it through customs and put it in her chapel. Despite having the true cross in her chancel, Momma Constantine died at about age 80, with her son ordering coins to be minted in her honor.

churchfail: Preachers love telling good stories even if they are possibly false. Bishops Ambrose and Chrysostom loved telling the story of the Empress Helena and the three crosses. The story of Helen's pilgrimage and discoveries is one of the greatest sources of idolatrous worship and practice in Christianity. While pilgrimage can make healthy contribution to one's devotional life, it can never have saving or cleansing effect. Grace alone saves and purifies. Luther once declared that there were enough reputed reliquary pieces of the "true cross" in Germany to build Noah's ark. Tourists getting rebaptized in the muddy waters of the Jordan are not getting saved or cleansed; they are rededicating themselves at best and might be just getting wet. Touching sacred relics is more likely to yield splinters than sanctification.

Application: It is not what Momma wants but what Jesus wants that makes us truly happy.

R.D.

Athanasius's Pink Slips

Date: ca. 295–373

Synopsis: Athanasius was fired from his job as bishop of Alexandria five times, by five different chowderheads, but he kept getting rehired.

Biography: Athanasius was born about 295 to Christian parents in Alexandria and advanced quickly through the academic and ecclesiastical ranks in that city. At the Council of Nicaea (325) and later as the bishop of Alexandria (328–73), he clarified and defended an orthodox doctrine of the Trinity against the tenacious heresy of the Arian party (p. 46). His opponents called him the "black dwarf" because of his dark skin color and his inability to dunk a basketball.

"Should I Stay or Should I Go?" Despite being a staunch defender of theological orthodoxy and being greatly loved by his congregation in Alexandria as well as the majority of the bishops throughout northeastern Africa, five times Athanasius was ejected from his bishop's seat, as if it were James Bond's Aston Martin with a faulty switch. Altogether he spent 17 of his 45 years as bishop working from home. In part, this is what you get when you put secular political leaders in charge of local churches. Emperor Constantine capriciously consented to Athanasius initially but then booted him out. When Constantine died, Athanasius returned, but Constantine's sons— Constantine, Constantius, and Constans (I detect a pattern here, by George)—disagreed on whether or not Athanasius should stay. He returned under an emperor known as "Julian the Apostate," but when his boss had a nickname like that, you know Athanasius was out of a job again within a year. When Julian died, Athanasius returned, only to be ousted one more time before returning for his last seven years in Alexandria.

Athanasius

52

In part, Athanasius's yo-yo employment record is also the result of influential heretics run amuck. Arius himself had written songs to promote his beliefs in Alexandria, reaching high positions on the hoi polloi hit parade. Arius's followers were also quick to pick up on any rumor about Athanasius. One time Athanasius was accused of killing a man named Arsenius and chopping off his hand for use in magic—a grisly version of a "hired hand." A hand supposedly belonging to Arsenius was actually circulated around various churches, which emboldened the Arians to foist formal charges on Athanasius at a synod in Tyre (335). Unfortunately for the Arians, their plan backfired when Athanasius brought Arsenius, live and in person, before the synod draped in a cloak. Athanasius raised one of Arsenius's hands from under the cloak—fully attached, of course, and then paused dramatically before revealing Arsenius's other hand—again, fully attached. Athanasius then asked his opponents to show where Arsenius's third hand had been cut off! Apparently Arsenius had been hiding in a rival monastery the whole time, and, like Mark Twain, reports of his death had been greatly exaggerated.

Athanasius's forced sabbaticals were not a total waste of time, as can be seen from three things he accomplished while he was out of the office. First, he spent some quality time in Rome, during which he established significant contacts among the Western church leaders and wrote extensively against Arianism. Second, in his absence from his congregation in Alexandria he wrote them letters, which became authoritative on the controversy of when Easter should be celebrated (p. 36) and which specific books of the Bible belong in the New Testament. His *Festal Letter* was the first formal writing by a church leader in which all 27 books of the New Testament canon were specifically named. Third, he met a desert monk named Anthony in Egypt and was so impressed by Anthony's godliness that he wrote a book about him, *Life of Anthony,* which spent 27 weeks on the *Pharos–Seven Wonders Book Review* best-seller list and sparked a widespread movement of desert monks and monasteries for centuries to come.

Application: Athanasius's persistence in the face of all these ill-advised adversaries leaves us with a great example of following God's calling for our lives at all costs. When Athanasius was ordered by Emperor Constantine to re-admit Arius to fellowship with the Alexandrian church, Athanasius refused, preferring exile to ethical and theological compromise. When he was exiled, he spent his time productively, and he shrewdly responded where a response was most needed. Proverbs 24:16 says, "Though a righteous man falls seven times, he will get up, but the wicked will stumble into ruin." The Black Dwarf demonstrated this well throughout his life, even if he never got to dunk a basketball.

K.C.

Pneumatomachians
(aka Macedonians)

Date: ca. 373

Synopsis: The pneumatomachians tried to fight the Spirit, but were KO'd in the first round.

Biography: The pneumatomachians, which means "Spirit-fighters," win the award for the coolest name of any Christian heresy. They were a ragtag gang of mid-fourth-century Christians who were down on the deity of the Holy Spirit. Really, many were skeptical about the deity of the Son as well, but their main problem was with the Spirit. After all, the issue between the Father and Son had supposedly been settled at the Council of Nicaea, and while there were a few who continued to question the decisions, most just moved on to other issues. In some early cases the pneumatomachians were called the Macedonians, followers of Macedonius of Constantinople, who was reputed to have rejected the divinity of the Spirit (though some dispute this connection). But that name was not nearly as catchy as "Spirit-fighters." The group was condemned by Pope Damasus in 379 and the Council of Constantinople in 381, which helped to solidify the church's teaching on the full deity of the Spirit.

churchfail: The pneumatomachians were by no means a unified group, and questions surround their organization and identification. Among their ranks were some more conservative scholars who were on board with the deity of the Son and who could say *homoousios* with the best of them, but they stopped one person short of "Tri" in Trinity. Eustathius of Sebaste led the more radical thinkers of the group. These pneumatomachians continued to doubt the deity of the Son, though they were willing to concede some similarity with the Father. But the real sticking point for them was the Spirit. Eustathius expressed their views on the Spirit aptly by arguing that the Spirit was neither God nor a creature. Instead, Eustathius argued that He occupied a middle place. The Spirit was more like an impersonal force of divine energy (think *Star Wars*: "May the Force be with you") who helped accomplish the Father's will.

The pneumatomachians simply could not conceive how to make room in the Godhead, which was really starting to get crowded. If the Spirit was God, they reasoned, He would be something like the Son's brother, and Scripture didn't say anything about God having more than one Son. Besides, there are hosts of other spirits mentioned in Scripture, and the Holy Spirit could not be any more divine than any of them. He was just another spirit doing God's bidding. And of course, like all good heretics, they were reading their Bibles and citing a whole collection of passages that (they believed) demonstrated the Spirit's subordination to the Father (and the Son).

A piquant response to the pneumatomachian and Eustathian potpourri of perspectives came from Basil (the bishop of Caesarea and future saint, not the herb), who challenged them on several fronts. Appealing to the baptismal formula in Matthew 28:19, Basil cooked up an argument that the Spirit should be afforded the same glory given to the Father and the Son. Clearly the Spirit is unique and personally invested in all the divine activities of the Father and the Son. Basil pointed specifically to the power of the Spirit's operations and the work of the Spirit in sanctification. He summed up his theology of the Spirit with a doxology that says, "Glory be to the Father, with the Son, together with the Holy Spirit." The confession affords each person equal status and glory. With the deity of the Spirit clearly affirmed, the church's doctrine of the Trinity became cemented in place.

The Holy Spirit

Application: The discussion of the deity of the Spirit helps modern believers who are not quite sure what to do with the Spirit. Sometimes the Spirit is seen merely as a special force or blessing that is only imparted to the super-spiritual. In other cases the Spirit is set aside in preference for the worship of the Father or the Son. From the time of the pneumatomachian controversy, the church has always affirmed that the Spirit is God and should receive the same adoration and respect given to the Father and the Son. The Spirit is not some kind of super force or divine energy. The Holy Spirit has been active from creation, giving life, inspiring the prophets, and indwelling believers.

S.P.

Apollinaris

Date: 376

Synopsis: Apollinaris (310–390), bishop of Laodicea, was a Facebook friend with the cream of the Nicene crop in the fourth century until he began teaching that the Second Person of the Trinity was not human, He just wore a really cool human suit. Cautioned, corrected, unfriended, and then condemned, Apollinaris was anathematized at Constantinople in 381.

Biography: Apollinaris, son of a Beirut grammarian, was an active advocate of orthodoxy against Arian subordinationism (p. 46). He became a close friend of Athanasius and provided him refuge in 346 during one of his many exiles (pp. 48, 52). For most of his ministry, Apollinaris remained orthodox and texted regularly with the likes of Athanasius, Basil, and Jerome. He was a busy blogger, and Jerome credited him with many commentaries on the Scriptures and two apologetic defenses of Christianity. Apollinaris even coded a theological formula that became embedded into creeds. When the office of bishop of Laodicea became vacant, Apollinaris was a shoe-in, with references tweeted in from the Cappadocian clerics and Athanasius in Alexandria.

The trouble started in the 370s as Apollinaris tried to solve two problems. Ontologically, he could not see how the incarnate Word of God could both receive worship as God deserves and give worship as humanity should. Psychologically, he worried over the impeccability of Christ. If Christ was truly human—flesh, soul, and mind—how could He ever remain sinless? The theological solutions that Apollinaris devised and blogged immediately caused concern; they were a dilution of Christ's humanity. The pope reached for the "delete" button on St. Peter's keyboard.

Apollinaris battled back with proof texts, like John 1:14, "The Word became flesh," in an attempt to show he was right in saying that the Incarnation added only the flesh of Christ to the Word and nothing more. His BFF Athanasius and "Uncle" Gregory of Nyssa unfriended him and began posting extensive blogs against his teaching. Gregory self-published a devastating line-by-line refutation of Apollinaris's white paper on the Incarnation.

The Council of Constantinople condemned the writings of Apollinaris in 381, and he was anathematized. However, he had already begun issuing false teachings through forged website addresses like those of Pope Julius, the Emperor Jovian, and even Athanasius!

churchfail: Apollinaris doubted that two perfect beings could be authentically one. Since the Nicene Creed forbade anyone tampering with the deity of the Son, Apollinaris, like a Dr. Frankenstein, proceeded to tinker and truncate Christ's humanity. He believed that at the Incarnation the Word of God, the Second Person of the Trinity, nestled down and took up residence inside a human-like body of the man Jesus. Human nature is composed of flesh, soul, and mind, so the divine Word just sort of took over the mind part. Jesus looked like a man, but He had a super special divine mind that allowed Him to speak with great wisdom and to understand the deep mysteries of life. Therefore, Jesus was not fully human, but merely the fleshy creature that housed the divine reason.

Council of Constantinople, 381

But in John 1:14, John was not using "flesh" in the Neoplatonic tripartite sense of flesh, soul, and mind; he was using "flesh" as a figure of speech in which a part stands for the whole. John was, in fact, emphasizing the completeness of the incarnate union between God and man in Christ.

Application: When it comes to orthodoxy, it is possible to affirm some aspects of essential Christian beliefs and deny others. Just because someone says, "I believe in Christ," does not mean that they believe in the true biblical and historical view of Christ. This is why Scripture warns us to "test all things" (1 Thess 5:21) and to "test the spirits" (1 John 4:1) to see if they confess that Jesus has come in the flesh. While Apollinaris confessed belief in the Trinity, he denied a true understanding of the person of Jesus as fully God and fully man.

The gospel and salvation hang on Jesus's humanity. If Jesus was not fully human He could not save humanity. His sacrifice would be insufficient, and we would still be dead in our trespasses and sins. Apollinarianism never won the day or captured the hearts of believers because it offered a view of Christ that was woefully insufficient and didn't actually deal with the problem of sin. But we give thanks to God for Christ who is both fully God and fully man, through whom we have redemption and forgiveness according to His grace (Eph 1:7).

R.D. & S.P.

Priscillianists

Ambrose

Date: ca. 380

Synopsis: These Spanish Gnostics enjoyed their secret meetings.

Biography: Priscillianism was an early Christian heresy that sprang from the teachings of a passionate man named Priscillian of Avila. Priscillian's career began as a layman with a freaky fascination for spiritual mysticism and the teachings of the Gnostics and Manichaeans. Asceticism became wildly popular in his day—maybe because they didn't have supersized fast food—and Priscillian jumped on the bandwagon. He attracted such a substantial following of devotees that he later became bishop of Avila.

However, several bishops and church leaders in Spain were not taken in by his charisma, and they looked askance at his stance. In a move to settle the issue and stir up sympathy, a posse of Priscillian's supporters ventured to vindicate their views before Pope Damasus and the popular Bishop Ambrose. They thought these sophisticated church-leader types would surely understand their perspective and settle the disputes. But there would be no explanation or understanding. Instead, things moved rapidly toward rejection and execution. The Council of Saragossa condemned Priscillian and his followers in 380. Not long after, Emperor Maximus executed him and six of his associates on the charges of heresy and dabbling in the magical arts. After the death of their founder, the Priscillian devotees retreated into hiding and not much was heard of them, with only a few scattered references to Priscillianism into the sixth century, then nada.

churchfail: Priscillian took a page straight out of a Gnostic notebook when he devised his theological system. Various church fathers, including Vincent of Lerins, even invoked the reputations of other Gnostics like Simon Magus to explain his views and refute him. In other words, Priscillian was the contemporary manifestation of the infamous magician (p. 6), here again to haunt the holy saints.

Like the Gnostics before them, the followers of Priscillian held to a strict dualism. They believed that souls are the special part of humanity that fell from the divine realm and became imprisoned in human bodies. As a result, Priscillian advocated an ardent adherence to asceticism that exceeded many of his contemporaries. He viewed the spiritual life as an all-out, lifelong fight with the Devil and his demons. The one way to win in this mortal matchup was a life of strict self-denial including vegetarianism, celibacy, and teetotalism. The human body must work hard to conquer the kingdom of darkness through rigorous self-denial and abasement.

Priscillianists did not associate with anyone who had even the remotest taint of sin. Rumors circulated that they fasted even on Sundays, and that they gathered in mixed company to study the Bible as well as other unsanctioned apocryphal authorities. Of course, these secret meetings only fueled more speculation about their doctrine and covenants. There was much debate and discussion about what went on in these secret meetings, especially given that they included (gasp!) mixed company. But eventually the church broke up the party and sent the mixed multitude on its way.

Priscillian's death remains an infamous footnote in church history because he is one of the earliest figures of the church put to death for heresy—though this execution was executed by secular executives.

Application: The example of Priscillian and his followers teaches several lessons. First, heretical views rarely die. More often than not, they are recycled in new generations with new figures and new followers. The teaching of the Gnostics of the second century reappears in the Priscillianists of the fourth century. This is why pastors and church leaders need to be students of history. We should know where and when the church has made the most important theological decisions, so when the same ol' bad theology resurfaces in new forms and teachings we will be prepared, poised, and primed to refute it.

Second, we can learn a lesson about secret meetings. Many churches' small group Bible studies meet in homes, and this can be an effective way to build community. But it also comes with the risk of isolating the small group from the rest of the corporate body. In the case of Priscillian, off-campus gatherings led to off-credal blatherings that strayed from the common faith and life of the church. Instead, as Hebrews 10:24-25 exhorts us, the people of God should not be in the habit of avoiding general worship gatherings, but should encourage each other to worship the Lord together.

S.P.

Eunomius

Date: 381

Synopsis: Eunomius (334–393) was an anti-Trinitarian super-Arian and briefly bishop of Cyzicus in Cappadocia. This second-generation carrier of the future Jehovah's Witness subordinationist heresy was considered so disruptive that multiple "Against Eunomius" books became best sellers.

Biography: The neo-Arian sect that bears his name has long been extinct and his personal letters and commentary on Romans burned. However, his name persists for three reasons. Two of the great Cappadocian theologians, Basil and his younger sibling Gregory, have Eunomius on their list of churchfails. Basil's refutation of Eunomian subordinationism is so thorough that nearly all of Eunomius's lost "Apology" in defense of anti-Trinitarianism is fully recoverable. Those polemical refutations also led to Eunomius being immortalized and anathematized in the official proceedings of the Council of Constantinople (381), not to mention all those who unfriended him on Facebook.

Gregory of Nazianzus

Eunomius studied his extreme Arian theology with his co-conspirator, Aetius. Anomeanism asserted that the Father and the Son did not share a divine essence. During the reign of Emperor Julian the Apostate (361–363), Eunomius and Aetius—the latter had been ordained as a roving bishop, with a church credit card no doubt—worked to stage an Arian comeback in Constantinople by consolidating and consecrating bishops in support of subordinationism. Eunomius himself was appointed in 360 by his Arian-leaning mentor, the Archbishop Eudoxius, to the vacant bishopric at Cyzicus, northern Cappadocia. Poor Cyzicus already had a patron saint (Tryphaena); now they would have a patron heretic.

From the cathedral pulpit, Eunomius immediately advocated the subordination of the Spirit to the Son and the Son to the Father. The congregational objections to his doctrinal deviance grew by decibels, and they reached a fever pitch and the emperor's ears when Eunomius altered the baptismal formula. He refused to baptize in the name of the Father, Son, and Holy Spirit, baptizing instead into the death of Christ. Emperor Constantius II summarily ordered Archbishop Eudoxius to depose Eunomius from his bishopric. This anti-Trinitarian baptismal practice was so repugnant to orthodox Christians that recanting Anomeans were rebaptized correctly, even though rewetting was not required for repentant plain vanilla Arians.

Denounced, deposed, writings destroyed by imperial edict, deported from Caesarea, and delivered to the extreme of western North Africa, Eunomius was later only marginally restored to spend his last days at his birthplace in Dakora, Cappadocia.

churchfail: Eunomius was both a philosophical and a theological churchfail. Philosophically, he was a linguistic essentialist, touting that to name a thing is to know it fully. Eunomius and Aetius foolishly asserted that they possessed as much knowledge of God as God had of Himself. Claiming to know the inexpressible Mystery, these fatheads plunged over the precipice from common sense and humility, with Basil, Gregory, and others pushing.

The orthodox theologian Basil had no problem with the idea of God the Son submitting Himself to the Father in the Incarnation and on the cross in order to fulfill the plan of redemption, but he did object to the assertion of Eunomius and company that the Unbegotten God had never, even before the Incarnation, shared essence with the Son or the Spirit. Eunomius did not like to use the name *Father* since it was logically difficult to see how the Father could ever be the Father without the Son. But *Unbegotten*, his favorite referent, had no such inference attached. If the Unbegotten shared essence via begetting or generation, that would diminish the divine simplicity and would result in a loss of deity, reasoned Eunomius.

Whereas the Council of Nicaea had affirmed shared essence or substance between the Father, Son, and Spirit (*homoousios*), the defeated Arian party had moved from holding that the Son had a like but not the same substance as the Father (*homoiousios*) to a post-Nicene anomean position, which asserted that there was no shared substance between the Unbegotten and the Begotten (*heterousios*). The Son was ever subordinate in function and nature to the Father, just like the Jehovah's Witnesses now declare. "No!" roared back the bishops at the Council of Constantinople, "We believe in one Lord, Jesus Christ, the only-begotten Son of God, ever begotten of the Father . . . true God from true God." The Father is eternal and the Son is eternal, for the Father is not the Father without the Son.

Application: Before hiring shepherds, test their teaching. It is too common for deceiving doctors with deviant doctrine to hide their views until safely ensconced in a pastoral position. Let the flock beware.

R.D.

Bishop Ambrose and Emperor Theodosius

Date: 390

Synopsis: What happens when the pastor dies and a church fight spills into the streets over whether the next preacher should be Arian or Nicene? The city manager, Ambrose, intervened and some kid in the crowd yelled, "Ambrose for Bishop!" Ambrose went from being city administrator to lead pastor in warp speed— eight days from catechumenate baptism to bishop consecration—and Emperor Valentinian put his imprimatur on it. As bishop, Ambrose would have multiple staring contests with the next emperor, Theodosius, over which would have its way—church or state?

Biography: Ambrose (339–397) was raised by Christian parents, his father being a praetorian prefect and possibly a perfect parent because all three children would be canonized as saints. His oldest son rose quickly in a similar administrative path and became consular governor in northern Italy. Ambrose was 35 in 374 when his career took its famous sideways move. When nominated for bishop by an adolescent, he went from baptism, to ordination, to consecration in eight days. Though he had no theological training, Ambrose quickly reached the higher levels of the game through the coaching of a Roman professor and by using his rare mastery of Greek to read Origen (p. 180), Athanasius (pp. 48, 52), and Gregory of Nazianzus, with whom he exchanged e-mails routinely. Ambrose became a persuasive preacher. Milanese matriarchs started keeping their marriageable maidens home because Ambrose was hypnotic when propounding the virtues of perpetual virginity; according to him, true love waits forever. He specialized in using classical allegorical hermeneutics to interpret tough Old Testament passages, and this intellectual skill encouraged young hipsters in Rome, like Augustine, to seriously check out the gospel.

Arian Christians were crushed as the newbie bishop used his insider understanding of imperial procedure to orchestrate a lasting pattern, namely, the church using the state to suppress deviant faiths. It was the bishop's hand that influenced the "Theodosian decrees" of the 390s, which legislated persecution of paganism, removed non-Nicene Christians from the payroll, made the Vestal Virgins get real jobs, closed and demolished temples, made witchcraft and divination prosecutable, and basically took all of the fun out of being pagan by declaring their holidays were now workdays.

Agreeably, Theodosius I (reigned 379–395) pursued the religious policy of his predecessor Gratian and moved Rome toward a pagan no-fly zone (no Arians either). Then something went terribly wrong in Greece. When the mayor arrested their favorite charioteer for attempted rape of a stadium hawker, the people rioted like Manchester United fans. Rioters killed the mayor, so Emperor Theodosius dispatched the death star legion and seven thousand Thessaloniki citizens died. Bishop Ambrose then tweeted his sometime parishioner, "The pastor reserves the right to refuse to serve communion to mass-murdering sinners." When Theodosius showed up where Ambrose was cel-

Ambrose Bars Theodosius

ebrating communion, the bishop straight-armed the potentate at the door. Theodosius knew when to fold 'em, and as evidence of repentance issued an imperial decree that all future royal execution orders would be subject to a 30-day cooling-off period so that investigation could actually occur.

Ambrose again used the imperial e-mail address on the occasion of the burning of a Mesopotamian synagogue, likely lit by the local bishop's Zippo. Ambrose encouraged clemency since, after all, had not Jews torched churches first? An eye for an eye and a pew for a pew! Desperate to drink the cup and eat the cracker, the crown caved in and pardoned the bishop.

Theodosius the Great died in 395 with the eulogy delivered by Ambrose. The bishop died two years later on Good Friday, having just had communion.

churchfail: Ambrose got it right when he disciplined the emperor about the massacre at Thessaloniki but missed the mark in advocating abuse of alternative adherents, in blocking the rebuilding of the Jewish synagogue, and in defending the episcopal arsonist. The clash between bishop and emperor offers an instructive case study of church-state relations when the status of the church becomes so privileged by the state that the church becomes corrupt and can no longer hear Jesus saying, "My kingdom is not of this world." Everybody needs Jesus. Christian celebrities and authorities need spiritual accountability within a congregation just as much as nurses and garbage collectors. But when church discipline gets confused with religious persecution, then the church goes Taliban, and ISIS is us.

Application: Keep in good faith with your preacher; he will have the last word at your funeral.

R.D.

Simeon Stylites

Date: 423

Synopsis: Christian hermits are a weird bunch by anybody's measure, from Julian of Norwich plastering her mud hut up against the town cathedral to Anthony making the thorny bushes of the Egyptian desert his domicile. But Simeon Stylites, the pillar dweller, literally stands above them all. In 423 he climbed up a pillar in the name of Christ and to distance himself from his growing popularity as a super monk who might have a miracle or two up his sleeve. He stayed perched there for 37 years. He was ultimately rewarded with sainthood by the papacy and in two Eastern Orthodox traditions. Simeon spawned a movement of extreme monasticism, drove up the price of pillars, and precipitated an avalanche of satirical critics of asceticism ad absurdum. Lord Tennyson pilloried Simeon in a 220-verse poem, and Mark Twain put a praying and tailoring columnar cleric into King Arthur's Court along with the Connecticut Yankee. After Simeon's time, the popes became soft touches to buy paintings of the Syrian monolith monk or of any of his imitators.

Biography: While still a teenager, Simeon said bah to his shepherding career and entered the monastery in Antioch, Syria. His penchant for extreme acts of asceticism, like standing and fasting for the 40 days of Lent, put his colleagues to shame and eventually got him expelled from the monastery for not playing well with others. However, his over-the-top antics of self-sacrifice became the talk of the town, and word of his miracles caused his Twitter feed to go viral. To escape this unwanted attention, Simeon did something guaranteed to make him a household word throughout the fading Roman Empire.

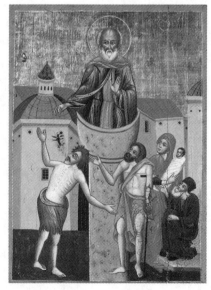

Simeon Stylites

In 423 Simeon climbed up a nine-foot pillar with the intention of staying, but six cubits was not a sufficient height to keep his growing audience from interrupting his morning quiet time. He started upgrading, literally, his pillar penthouse until it eventually surpassed 50 feet, with a small platform and parapet on top so he wouldn't roll off if he dozed during his devotions. Imagine the Antioch planning department debating Simeon's application for a building permit: "Where are the plumbing fixtures and the electrical outlets?" Those wanting Simeon's wisdom, intercession, or blessing had to do so at their own peril by ascending a shaky, non-OSHA-approved fifty-foot ladder, often to receive something like the words of W. C. Fields to a pesky child: "Go away, you bother me."

From atop his pillar's porch perch, Simeon did do some good. He was a champion for Chalcedonian orthodoxy and urged, by carrier pigeon or distance shouting, the Byzantine Emperor Leo I in Constantinople to stay the course of Trinitarian and Christological orthodoxy.

Simeon's saintly antics soon made his pillar a destination that every ancient tour guide had to have on his itinerary. Eventually the obelisk was encircled by a church, which was then expanded to four basilicas radiating outward like points on the compass. Their ruins are visible to this day along with the bottom of what may have been Simeon's last sky pulpit.

Over the centuries, Simeon has found many imitators and detractors. About 120 years later, Simeon the Younger homesteaded his own pillar in Antioch for 23 years, and another pole-sitting saint stayed atop his column for 57 years. (Ann Landers also had a column for 57 years, but that was a tag-team affair.) Pillar dwelling as a practice was never as popular in the West as in the East, maybe because it was easier to find good pillars in the East among the abandoned Greek and Roman ruins.

churchfail: Simeon transformed Christianity into a curiosity. Discipleship became falsely measured by extremist antics rather than by continuing in Christ's teaching and Spirit. Tennyson's 1842 poem satires Simeon's "life of death" as an attempt to out-martyr the martyrs and thereby extort sainthood from God. When did Jesus ever say that we are to take up our pillar daily and perch for Him? In an effort to separate himself from the world, Simeon made himself a prime time reality show. In explaining the gospel to the lost afterward, Christians have had to commiserate, "Well, every family has a crazy Uncle Simeon."

Application: Extraordinary asceticism always captures the popular imagination. People uncritically imitate whomever they put on a pedestal, even if the person supplied the pillar himself. Beware the damage when such false idols fall.

R.D.

Pelagius and Celestius

Date: 431

Synopsis: Pelagius, the namesake of the grace-diluting Pelagian heresy, was the British lay ascetic who immigrated to Rome and, with his compadre in corrupt doctrine, Celestius, attempted to sideswipe the gospel of grace with a self-help, will-worship, buck-up message that attracted lots of wealthy Christians and angered more bishops than a hive has bees.

Biography: History has smudged the birth and death certificates of Pelagius (ca. 354–418). Historians record him as British, tall and portly, but Jerome describes him as a Scot who loves Irish porridge. At any rate, this British/Scotch/Irish monk pops up on the Roman scene about 380 and immediately makes a stylish splash because of his dexterous bilingualism in Latin and Greek, for his articulate advocacy for practical lay asceticism, and for plopping a huge wad of dead Caesars into the offering bag. Pelagius quickly attracted two kinds of followers: graduate students like Celestius, who wanted to turn his teacher's practical proverbs into theological theorems, and rich Christian disciples.

These influential toga-wearers liked Pelagius because his was a biblical-sounding doctrine of self-made souls infused with the Stoic perspective of captaining your own salvation.

Pelagius and Celestius loved to pick apart the concept of original sin as inherited from Adam and to deny the human necessity for salvation by divine grace. Increasing cries of "mad monk" and "Irish idiot" were rudely interrupted in 409 by Alaric and his Goth army approaching Rome on massacre mode. Everyone with an African Express gold card boarded the next yacht for Carthage, where the conservative bishops were ready to take a bite out of Pelagius and Celestius.

Seeing the lay of the Libyan land, Pelagius revised his playlist to include some

PELAGIUS

Accurst Pelagius with what falfe pretence
Durft thou excufe Mans foule Concupifcence :
Or cry down Sin Originall, or that
The Loue of God did Man predeftinate .

Pelagius

lyrics from "Grace Greater Than Our Sin" and clarified that he liked baby baptisms as much as the next Catholic. Because he was fluent in Greek and Latin, whenever he was subpoenaed on charges of heresy (which was pretty much an annual event until his death), Pelagius maneuvered out of the charges by calling for doctrinal confessions in whichever language the bishops were incompetent. Celestius, on the other hand, retracted nothing and put the teachings of his professor in such heterodox clarity that bishops loved calling conciliar barbecues with him as the main entrée.

Augustine stayed out of the fight until 415, when one of his priests, Orosius, publically charged Celestius with heresy. Augustine stood up for Orosius, bought a Costco-sized vat of polemical ink, and started writing books, letters, and sermons on original sin and human depravity. Then in 418, when Celestius got Julian of Eclanum to charge out of his Pelagian closet, the bishops of Hippo and Eclanum began shelling each other with barbed and bitter books until Augustine's battleship sank with his death in 430. Also, in 418 more than 200 bishops assembled in Carthage to condemn Pelagianism, with the pope and the emperor playing the anathematizing chorus of bishops. Pelagius lost interest in the struggle and disappeared from history. Young Celestius, however, continued betting on losing horses like Nestorius, whom he hoped would intercede for him with the pope. Instead, both got voted off the Council of Ephesus Island in 431 and were condemned and exiled.

churchfail: This infamous fifth-century heresy undercut salvation by grace by diluting the doctrine of depravity.

- Pelagius and Celestius asserted that Adam would have died even if he had not sinned. Augustine and the bishops answered back, "You are denying that death is the wage of sin" (see Rom 6:23). Death came to Adam because of his sin, not out of physical necessity.
- Pelagius and Celestius asserted that Adam's sin harmed only himself and not the whole of humanity. Augustine and the bishops answered back: Paul proclaimed that, in Adam, all fell and all have come so short of the divine glory as absolutely to need the saving intervention of the cross.
- Pelagius and Celestius asserted that children are born with a slate as clean as Adam's before his fall. The fifth-century Catholics responded that newborn children must be baptized on account of original sin. Protestants respond that baptism does not wash away sin. It is grace alone through faith alone that apprehends salvation. Baptists further aver that baptism is the first step of the disciple. In mercy, God extends the grace of the cross to all who are unable by age or capacity to be accountable for their sin.

Application: There is a way that seems right to the self-made man, but the end thereof is death.

R.D.

Nestorius

Date: 431

Synopsis: Nestorius nestled up to the view that Jesus was actually two separate persons.

Biography: Born in Germanica, Nestorius served as the bishop of Constantinople—at least until people caught wind of his unusual perspective on Jesus. He sat under the teaching of the famous bishop of Antioch, Theodore of Mopsuestia (yes, this is as hard to pronounce as it looks). Nestorius took Theo's views to an extreme and rejected the essential unity of the person of Jesus Christ. Nestorius's fiercest opponent was the bishop of Alexandria, Cyril. The arguments between them became so bitter that the church called a comprehensive confab (aka ecumenical council) in Ephesus in 431. Nestorius, though, sat out because he feared that a few might toss tomatoes at him, and he was right. Several of his supporters put up an admirable defense, but the synod sided with Cyril. There were attempts to reverse the council's decision, and at one point Emperor Theodosius II got involved; but in the end Nestorius's views were condemned. After his excommunication, Nestorius eventually made his way to Egypt where he lived until about 451. Not long before his death, Nestorius—as a result of the Council of Chalcedon—once again, received the bad news that he could just stay in exile, because his views were still anathema. Through it all some, especially in the Eastern church, were willing to stand by him and never accepted his excommunication. Like hardy nasturtiums, some Nestorians persisted for many years.

churchfail: Nestorius and his followers taught that Christ was two separate persons, or at least that is what his opponents understood him to

Nestorius

teach. Jesus was just a man who was born from Mary, suffered, and died; but the Son of God, on the other hand, was divine, eternal, and unbegotten.

Things really heated up when Nestorius refused to say that Mary was *Theotokos* ("bearer of God"), a sophisticated way of saying that Mary's child was also God. For some, refusing to say *"Theotokos"* was tantamount to an out-and-out denial of the Incarnation. But Nestorius would submit that it is better to say that Mary was *Christotokos* ("bearer of Christ"). Now some might be thinking that saying "Christ" and "God" were synonymous, but other church fathers didn't think so. They thought Nestorius meant that Mary gave birth to a mere man who was simply a temple inhabited by the *Logos* (the Son of God). Mary basically gave Him a human suit in which His divine super powers could function.

Now when it came time to explain his views from Scripture, Nestorius basically sounded like he diagnosed Jesus with split-personality disorder. Whenever Jesus acted like a man, that was the human body, but occasionally the *Logos* that resided inside Him took control of His mind and body and did miraculous things.

Cyril responded by affirming that the *Logos* was preexistent but became united with human nature, thereby creating what is called the "hypostatic union," a single essence. The Incarnation was a union of both God and humanity that could not be divided or separated in any substantial way. So in this sense, it is proper to affirm that Mary gave birth to the God–man, Jesus Christ, who was both fully God and fully human. The contrary views of Nestorius helped reaffirm and clarify the church's understanding of the union of God and humanity in the one person of Jesus Christ.

Application: The lesson of Nestorianism communicates the importance of the understanding of the person and work of Christ for the doctrine of salvation. If Christ was just a man who died on the cross, how would this sacrifice atone for sins? On the other hand, if the Son of God was not human, how could He redeem people when He was not one of them? It is necessary for Christ to be fully man and fully God in order to accomplish the atonement.

At the same time, the lesson of Nestorius reminds pastors and teachers of the need to describe the work of Christ carefully. We should not speak of Christ sometimes acting in His divine nature and sometimes acting in His human nature. Instead, every act of Christ was performed by the God–man, and no particular act can be said to emphasize one person over the other. Ultimately, the hypostatic union of Christ is a mystery that demands our faith and adoration, because it is only in this God–man Jesus Christ that believers find salvation.

S.P.

Eutyches

Date: 448

Synopsis: Eutyches (ca. 378–454) was an ecclesiastical infighter who lost his faith and his dream job in the imperial capital when he was found guilty of teaching that Jesus doesn't save. Eutyches had made his theological boxing reputation at the Council of Ephesus in 431 when he helped beat down Patriarch Nestorius for the latter's schizophrenic Christology. But 20 years later, attempting a rope-a-dope move against the new but aging Patriarch Flavian, Eutyches slipped on the soap at the Council of Chalcedon in 451 and was buried in Pope Leo's Tome.

Biography: Eutyches first appears in the ecclesiastical boxing ring at Ephesus. There he and other envious bishops jabbed at Nestorius, the Patriarch of Constantinople, for failing to preach the union of God the Son's two natures in one person via incarnation. The real motive for the doctrinal gang war at Ephesus was that Nestorius seemed to insult the dignity of Mother Mary by arguing that if Mary is the mother of God then she also must be the mother of man. No one messes with Momma, but that's a story for another time.

Eutyches lacked self-awareness that his theological acumen was subpar for the conciliar level. His motor mouth was insufficiently wired to a sufficiently equipped brain, which is not too dangerous if you have humility. Eutyches didn't, so he gleefully rose to the level of his incompetence by brokering himself into a sweet job just outside the imperial walls of Constantinople as the abbot of a mass of 300 monks. No doubt his bribe-loving godson, Chrysaphius (working as a eunuch in the emperor's bedroom), pulled the strings to make this happen. Now Eutyches had his own hooded gang, and he would need them.

Who would've thought that only two decades after thrashing Nestorius, Eutyches himself would receive a papal slapdown for Christological heresy? Apparently, sometime after his pugnacious success at Ephesus, Eutyches began preaching to his monks that, after the Incarnation, the Son only had one nature and was also no longer consubstantial with humanity. Eutyches had dropped his guard and lost his Savior. Two bigtime bishops accused him of heresy, and his Patriarch, Flavian, deposed him in 448.

However, Eutyches could take a licking and keep on ticking and talking. A great infighter, he called on his secret weapon, that highly-placed emasculated godson,

Chrysaphius. Eutyches's condemnation and deposition were successfully appealed to Pope Leo in Rome, the monks of Egypt rallied for their fellow monk master, and the Byzantine maneuverings by his fight-promoting godson got Eutyches restored in 449. But the clock was running out for both Eutyches and his godson. Their final round had begun, and the hammer was about to hit the bell.

When Emperor Theodosius II—who loved having the baby-faced Chrysaphius around—died in 450, Pulcheria and Marcian ascended to the imperial throne. Both were personal enemies of Eutyches's godson, who quickly was terminated in every understanding of the word. The doctrinal charges against Eutyches were reinstated when a Council at Chalcedon convened. Though Pope Leo did not participate in the rematch in person, he turned against Eutyches and created the brass knuckles, famously called Leo's Tome (a fancy word for a long letter written because he couldn't come in person), that knocked Eutyches out.

Fourth Ecumenical Council of Chalcedon

churchfail: Jesus saves? Not so much, said Eutyches. The fastest way to be called a heretic is to devise a theology that makes Jesus no longer able to save. Eutyches taught the Christological heresy of Monophysitism, that Christ after the Incarnation had only one nature, not two. For him, the Incarnation was a divine blender that conflated Christ's divinity and humanity so profoundly into a new third composite that Christ was no longer consubstantial with humanity. This contradicted the teaching of Hebrews 2:14-15, which asserts that because Christ shared in our humanity, He was able by His death to break Satan's power and free us who live in fear of death. What the Son took up in His human incarnation is what He redeemed. Eutyches proved here that he was one punch-drunk heretic.

Application: In the words of the Hollywood theologian, Dirty Harry Callahan, "A man's got to know his limitations." Eutyches failed here, and his pride precipitated his plunge. More importantly, Eutyches failed to follow Jesus in Scripture. If Jesus was not fully God and fully human, then we cannot be fully saved.

R.D.

Medieval churchfails

If middle age is when men famously act infamously, the Middle Ages lived up to (or down to) that stereotype. Francesco Petrarch called them "Dark Ages," since middle-agers let classical Greek and Roman erudition atrophy, while having no smarts of their own. J. M. Roberts notes that even kings were illiterate in those days. But Thomas Cahill applies a dubious honor: "It is seldom possible to say of the medievals that they *always* did one thing and *never* another; they were marvelously inconsistent."[7] We will look at some inconsistencies. First, a warning: In the late eighteenth century Georg Christoph Lichtenberg cautioned, "Perhaps in time the so-called Dark Ages will be thought of as including our own."[8]

There is some evidence the information age will be labeled dim if not dark, and the feeble light of our electronic devices will have been an important portent of impotence.

---

[7] Thomas Cahill, *Mysteries of the Middle Ages: And the Beginning of the Modern World* (New York: Anchor, 2008).

[8] Georg Christoph Lichtenberg, *The Reflections of Lichtenberg* (London: Swan Sonnenschein, 1908), 48.

Paulicians

Date: ca. 675

Synopsis: These medieval Gnostics preferred their contemporary service to the boring traditional worship.

Biography: The Paulicians were an early medieval sect, though no one is quite sure which "Paul" they invoked—the apostle Paul, the infamous Monarchian Paul of Samosata, or just some Armenian hombre named Paul. Whichever, it started with a guy named Constantine—no, not the famous emperor; a mule driver. A passing stranger gave him a copy of the New Testament, and he devoured it like a dachshund on a dinner table. He became enamored with the writings of the Apostle Paul, and in an act of solidarity and devotion, changed his name to Sylvanus, after one of Paul's trusted companions. Likewise, his followers took on the other names of Paul's companions, like Timothy or Titus.

The true sacred text of the Paulicians was called the "Key of Truth," a systematic treatise that apparently unlocked all the mysteries of the Bible and explained the true nature of God and humanity. They struggled to form their own established church. In reality, most of their practical theology was built on what they rejected—the institutional church—rather than on what they affirmed—any basis of formal church governance. The Paulicians met a bloody end before the rise of the Middle Ages, as most of their ranks were either disbanded and relocated or killed.

churchfail: There are wide-ranging disputes about the beliefs and practices of the Paulicians, especially among modern baptistic traditions. On the positive side, they anticipated later free-church traditions such as the rejection of infant baptism and traditional ecclesiastical offices. They also repudiated the use of icons and most other sacramental practices, such as communion, praying to the saints, and the general holy days in the liturgical calendar. Their spiritual lives involved simple dedication to preaching, prayer, and the study of Scripture (especially Paul and Luke). Whatever other views they held, these kinds of convictions would become decisive issues for later Protestant traditions.

But the problem with the Paulicians was not necessarily their practical theology, but their views of the Bible and Christology. It is not easy to pin down the theological connections with earlier heretical views. They have been accused of ripping off various dualistic or docetistic groups including Gnostics, Marcionites, and Manichaeans. The Paulicians merely recycled the radical dualistic views. They would have loved the Star Wars movies, since they believed that good and evil were two great opposing forces engaged in an unending struggle. They believed that there was one god who made the world, which turned out to be a rather dank and dark place, and another God above in the heavens, who is the one true God and deserves all honor and glory.

Persecution of Paulicians

Like Marcion (p. 20) and other Gnostics, they rejected the Old Testament and were infatuated with the Apostle Paul. They also rejected the Incarnation and taught that Christ was merely an angel sent into the world to do some good things. Thus Mary was not really the mother of Christ because He descended directly from the heavenly realm. His basic teaching was that people only needed to believe in Him to escape judgment.

Unfortunately—and ironically to some degree—the theological disputes with the Paulicians took a bloody turn, and many of them suffered greatly at the hands of the Nicene Christians.

Application: The example of the Paulicians shows that later Protestants were not the first to raise questions over religious rites. Other ancient groups had already wrestled with the tension between authentic saving faith and religious rituals and practices. But where the Paulicians veered off course began with the rejection of the Old Testament. Like Marcion and other Gnostics before them, they considered it a fictive work of a lesser, evil god. Instead, Christians should affirm that the whole Bible, composed of both Old and New Testaments, is the work of one true God. As Christ Himself affirms, everything in the Old Testament points to Him (Luke 24:25-27).

The Paulicians also failed to recognize the nature of Christ as fully God and fully man. While this has been a consistent point of contention in the church, there is no place in orthodox Christianity for confusion concerning the person and work of Christ.

It is tragic, though, that the Paulicians had to suffer at the hands of Christians, which reminds believers that regardless of the beliefs of others, we must always strive to speak the truth of God in love.

S.P.

Saint Boniface

St. Boniface

Date: 722

Synopsis: Winfrid, better known as Boniface, was the Oak-of-Thor-chopping, eighth-century apostle and archbishop of the German parts of the Frankish empire. He partnered with Charles "The Hammer" Martel to save Europe from the Muslim invasion in 732. Patron saint in both Germany and his native England, he was martyred by Frisian terrorists on the eve of Pentecost while on mission in the Netherlands.

Biography: Winfrid or Wynfrith (675–754) was born in Wessex, England. Willibald, his earliest biographer and nephew, writes that Uncle Winfrid attended a monastery school at an early age and later traveled to Utrecht where he joined Willibrord, "the Apostle to the Frisians," who had been working there since the 690s. He spent a year preaching in the countryside with Willibrord until war interfered as the Frankish king, Charles Martel, decided to hammer the Frisians and their red-bearded king, Radbod, into submission.

In 718 Winfrid hopped a wagon with Anglo-Saxon pilgrims headed to Rome. There, Gregory II commissioned him to evangelize pagans east of the Rhine, and most particularly to use the Roman liturgy during the mass and not the loosey-goosey Celtic one. After four years on that mission, Winfrid returned to Rome for his performance evaluation, got promoted to bishop, and was given the name Boniface. The new bishop zeroed in on Hesse as the best organizational center for the work, and in 722 he and Charles Martel sharpened a plan for Boniface to wield an axe against the sacred oak of Thor and to baptize a legion of Hessian soldiers into Martel's army. Everything worked according to their script: The oak fell without any lightning from Thor, the soldiers were sprinkled, Boniface got a statue on the stump, and King Charles Martel—fortified with slightly damp Hessians—stopped the Arab and Berber tour de force at Tours in 732.

Meanwhile, Boniface caught a bullet train back to Rome to meet the new pope, Zacharias. The oak-slayer was enthusiastic about the future of the Church in Germany because the Benedictine monasteries in England kept supplying the work with prayers, letters of support, and new missionary talents, including his own niece. Returning to Germany, Boniface created a nucleus of four monasteries, organized the Church in Bavaria with its own bishop, and named and mapped a number of dioceses still in use today. In 743 Boniface, with the help of the Frankish co-regent, Karlmann, held the first ever Vatican-approved Germanic Concilium.

In 746 Boniface was assigned as Archbishop of Mainz and in 751 he helped St. Sturm, yet to become one of the X-men, found the famous Benedictine monastery at Fulda. This rapidly became one of the leading monasteries in Franconia and would be the final resting place for the bones of St. Boniface. Two years later, longing for more mission and less administration, he resigned from Mainz, sharpened his axe, and headed north to Frisia, only to meet martyrdom at the hands of brigands in 754 while reading to neophyte believers. The CSI investigation afterward found a bloody copy of St. Ambrose's "On the Advantage of Death" lying next to Boniface.

churchfail: This reformer of the Frankish church was the catalyst for the alliance between the papacy and the Carolingian family. The orchestrated confrontation at the Oak of Thor was on the surface either cultural genocide against indigenous centers of pagan worship or spiritual warfare—the dark forces of divination and witchcraft against the light of the gospel and Church.

However, the subtext was the immediate need for Charles Martel to amplify his Christian army with the vaunted Hessian veterans if he was to thwart the Arab and Berber invasion coming up from Spain. In the minds of the Hessians, watching Boniface face the sacred oak with his axe, they anticipated swift retribution from Valhalla as the thunder of Thor's hammer came down on the bishop's head. The Hessian soldiers were impressed that Boniface came in the name of Charles "The Hammer" Martel, and they billed the event as axe against hammer, man against oak. When the oak fell without divine vengeance, their allegiance switched to Martel, and they willingly underwent baptism to get on his payroll. This was a classic case of axe evangelism where political expedience is substituted for faith experience, where people are buried alive in baptism by sprinkling them without their having been born of the Spirit.

Application: When mission is paired with politics, conformity to ideology supplants biblical theology. Expedience is no excuse for not insisting on a gospel experience.

R.D.

Marozia

Dates: 890–937

Synopsis: When Pilate asked Jesus about His kingdom, He answered that it was not of this world. Power can be a great temptation. Marozia tried to stage a coup and turn God's kingdom into her own personal fiefdom.

Biography: A century after Charlemagne unified much of Western Europe, his Holy Roman Empire was neither holy nor Roman. With the Roman-bishop backed empire weakened from within and challenged from without, local rulers gained increasing influence over political and religious activities. This was particularly true in Rome, which was controlled by powerful political families.

Marozia was a member of the robust Roman Crescentii clan. She was noted for her boundless beauty and potent political pugnacity. At the tender age of 15, she became the mistress of her father's cousin, a man who would become Pope Sergius III (904–911). They had a son who would later become pope. This began a 60-year period of sex, thugs, and Peter the Rock rolling over in his grave. It became known as the *Saeculum Obscurum*, meaning the Dark Age of the papacy. This perverse period is also known as the Pornocracy (904–964). It began with a pope who was Marozia's lover and ended with the pope who was her grandson.

In 909 Marozia married Alberic I of Spoleto, with their first son, Alberic II, arriving a couple of years later. When Sergius died, Marozia and her mother, Theodora, heavily influenced papal

The Wedding of Marozia and Hugh of Italy

selection. Two short-lived papacies led to John X (914–928) assuming the papal throne. He became Theodora's lover (it is even rumored that Marozia joined her mother as one of the pope's lovers).

Over time, Marozia had confrontations with the cavorting cleric. After the death of her mother (916), father (925), and husband (925), the opportunity arose to put her own mark on events. Marozia married Guy of Tuscany to stem the pope's influence. Shifting political winds suddenly provided an opportunity, and Guy had John X imprisoned in Castel Sant'Angelo. There is some dispute about whether the pope died of neglect in prison or was smothered with a pillow by either Guy or Marozia. We don't know. There's no pillow talk.

Guy died in 929, and Marozia immediately negotiated a marriage with her late husband's half-brother, Hugh of Arles. The fact that he was still married at the time was no hindrance at all. He had his first marriage annulled, and the new nuptials proceeded despite the fact that this marriage violated canon law. When Hugh tried to circumvent the law by killing his siblings from his mother's second marriage, Marozia's teenage son, Alberic II, led a successful revolt. Hugh was driven out of Rome, and Marozia was put in the same prison where she had kept John X. (It seems ironic that Marozia should finally be deposed by somebody who was revolting.) She died there five years later, but not until she arranged for her illegitimate son by Pope Sergius III to be elected Pope John XI (931–935).

The rotten apple did not fall far from the tree. Alberic's son (Marozia's grandson) became Pope John XII (955–964). He ascended to the papacy at the wise age of 18 and died not quite nine years later. It was rumored that the young pope became paralyzed in the act of breaking his vows of chastity, dying a few days later. Marozia's prodigious progeny populated the papal palace for a prolonged period after her passing. Over the next century, a total of six popes descended from her activities. It is said that the hand that rocks the cradle rules the world. Marozia's hand rocked not only the cradle, but also the papacy itself.

churchfail: Marozia used sex, treachery, and deceit in order to gain political power. This is nothing new. Using the church as a vehicle for violence and debauchery certainly fails to comprehend the true nature and purpose of God's kingdom.

Application: There will always be those who see the church as a platform for procuring power and prestige, rather than a community of committed converts. When given influence, they will wreak havoc and bring disgrace.

L.H.

The Great East-West Schism

Date: 1054

Synopsis: The church schism that had been brewing for centuries finally boiled over in 1054 when the representatives of the Roman Catholic Church, led by papal trouble-shooter Cardinal "Not Humble" Humbert, exchanged anathemas with representatives of the Eastern Orthodox Church, primarily Patriarch Michael "Not Hilarious" Cerularius, in a scandalous spectacle of ecclesiastical tit for tat. The Western church rubbed rock salt into that deep wound when the fourth Crusade went rogue and they raided Constantinople, robbed revered relics from the Orthodox basilicas, and replaced the patriarch with a Vatican-loyal Latin speaker.

History: The great ecclesiastical earthquake of 1054 eventuated because multiple fault lines between the Eastern and Western churches had been growing since the rapid spread of the gospel during its first three centuries. Six fault lines as big as the San Andreas can be identified:

First, the linguistic fault line of church bilinguality, Greek and Latin, spiked as the gospel spread: Latin came to predominate in the West while Greek governed the East. In some doctrinal disputes, one simply could not understand what the other was saying.

Second, the geo-political divide grew when in 330 Constantine declared Constantinople to be the "New Rome" and then in 476 the Western Roman Empire functionally ceased to exist. Caesaropapism developed as the popes sought to fill the political vacuum fusing tiara and crown, spiritual and political authority; the papal primate pursued primacy in all particulars. The Eastern megachurch patriarchs agreed that the Roman pontiff should have the honor of marching first in parades, but honor and authority were definitely two distinct issues.

Third, the one thousand-plus miles between St. Peter's Basilica and the Hagia Sophia inevitably led to alienating liturgical practices like the use of tasteless, Old Testament unleavened flatbread in the West and tincture (dipping the bread and dirty fingers into the wine) in the East, with each finding the other's practices strange and indigestible.

Fourth, ecclesiastical jurisdictional debates over who decides the hymns in the Balkans festered and fulminated through the centuries with the long arm of the pope often reaching east to get a hand on the patriarch's steering wheel.

Fifth, the pretend doctrinal fissure was the half-millennial-old complaint that when the Third Council of Toledo (589), held with nary a Greek speaker, added the Latin word *filioque* ("and the Son") to the Nicene phrase "the Father [and the Son] sent the Spirit," it did so in direct violation of the seventh canon of the Council of Ephesus (431) against adding anything to the Nicene Creed. The patriarchs and Eastern monks objected in very loud Greek. *Filioque* festered into a foul, fighting phrase with occasional fistfights flaring up at Catholic–Orthodox bingo conventions.

Pope Leo IX

Sixth, the ecclesiastical precipitating fissure was the patriarch's determination to upgrade his title to ecumenical patriarch, which the Latin westerners—who were woefully weak in Greek—mistranslated as universal patriarch. This, of course, looked like Constantinople was primping to poach papal priority.

When the Roman gunslinger, Cardinal Humbert, showed up for communion with the patriarch in 1054, name calling broke out and cursing escalated into mutual excommunication followed by a hasty recessional rendition of the Tammy Wynette classic "D-I-V-O-R-C-E." In 1204 rogue Crusaders sealed the schism by sacking (literally: the bones of Chrysostom and Gregory Nazianzus were bagged and tagged for Rome) Constantinopolitan basilicas, not to mention the installation of a Latin speaker as patriarch. No one understood the preacher at the next Sunday service.

churchfail: Heresy is a doctrinal dispute about matters of faith. Schism is a relational failure of love and peace. Doctrinal purity is pointless without relational unity, and truth is best shared in love (Eph 4:15). When the sun set on the anger expressed in 1054, Satan got a chokehold on the church's witness (Eph 4:26-27). When Cardinal Humbert and Patriarch Michael practiced mutual alienation, they failed to engage their identities as ambassadors of Christ and to practice the ministry of reconciliation (2 Cor 5:18-20). When Humbert dumped his umbrage on Michael, the whole Church had a great fall that persists to this day, even though Rome mailed the looted bags of bones back in 1965 and the patriarch came to the pope's funeral in 2005.

Application: Failure of nerve to speak the truth in love fosters offense and fractures the fellowship of Christ. Keep anti-schismatic survival supplies in the trunk of your church, so that you can practice reconciliation whenever angry words make people want to walk away.

R.D.

Urban II

Dates: 1088–99

Synopsis: As the prelate of Peter and a proponent of peace, Pope Urban II proclaimed a war for the glory of God.

Biography: The corks were popping about 1042 when Otto (Odo or Otho) was born in the Champagne region of France to a knightly family. He grew up to become a reform-minded monk at Cluny.

Jerusalem's fall in 1070 prompted an immediate call to reclaim it. Pope Gregory VII (1073–1085) wanted to drive the Seljuk Turks back out of the Holy Land and heal the schism of 1054 that split the Church into Eastern (Constantinople) and Western (Rome) factions (p. 80). His proposal in 1074 fell on indifferent ears. Continuing conflict with Emperor Henry IV prevented further action. In 1078 Gregory made Otto the Cardinal Bishop of Ostia, and he became one of the pope's chief advisors. Returning to Rome in 1083, Otto was imprisoned by Henry due to his support of Gregory, who had excommunicated Henry. In 1084 Henry marched on Rome and set up his own pope, Clement III, who then endorsed Henry as emperor. If at first you don't succeed, find a preacher who will do what you want. An advancing Norman army put the fear of God into Henry, and he retreated from Rome to Tuscany. The people of Rome, disgusted at the actions of Gregory's allies, the Stormin' Normans, drove him out of town as well. He went to Salerno where he died a year later.

Time and time again, armies either supporting or opposing Henry attacked Rome, with varied measures of success. By

Urban II Preaching the First Crusade at Clermont

1098 the castle of Sant' Angelo, the last of Henry's remaining strongholds, was in the hands of those supporting the Roman pope.

On March 12, 1088, bishops loyal to Gregory chose Otto, his designated successor, as the next pontiff. Otto took the name Urban II and announced his plans for Urban renewal by continuing his predecessor's plans to reform the Church, the main point of which was an insistence that priests not be married. Unfortunately, Otto could not drive into Rome because it was controlled by forces loyal to the rival pope, Clement.

Plans for Urban renewal soon turned to Urban warfare. The new pope promptly excommunicated his rival Clement III as well as the emperor who set him up, Henry IV. A cheeky response sometimes replaces turning the other cheek. Toward the end of the year, Urban was able to enter part of the city. After three days of pitched battle, Urban's forces were victorious. His rival fled Rome, and Urban entered St. Peter's Basilica in triumph. However, just a month later, the Roman populace pushed Urban to the suburbs on news that Henry's forces were gaining ground. For the next three years, he wandered in rural southern Italy before regaining a toehold in Rome. Urban finally entered the city center for good just before Easter 1094.

Over the next year, Urban campaigned for a crusade to help the Eastern Church push back the Seljuk Turks in the Holy Land. After the warfare in Italy, it was certainly in Urban's best interests to send thousands of knights to fight "over there" rather than to be taken into the employ of a rival. Excitement continued to build until the official call to war came in 1096. The assembled ensemble announced, "God Wills It!" The headlines for the next day's *Roman Rambler* could have read, "Prince of Peace Wants War!" Participants were promised complete pardon for all sins committed during the campaign. Hardly a call to restraint.

The pope, encouraged to lead the charge personally, elected to remain in Rome to keep the home fires burning. The call to arms galvanized support for Urban and weakened that of his rival. The Crusaders captured Jerusalem in July 1099. However, Urban died before hearing of the victory.

churchfail: As a purported parson of peace, Urban spent his entire pontificate at war, first with his rival for the Chair of Peter and then in launching the Crusades. Urban's plans for renewal fell victim to his preoccupation with fighting to defend his position.

Application: There are times when the weak need to be defended or a stand for what is right must be taken. In doing so, we must be certain that the means we use line up with the godly end we wish to achieve. The ends do not justify the means.

L.H.

Abelard and Heloise

Date: 1141

Synopsis: Peter Abelard (1079–1142) was a twelfth-century Parisian rock star philosopher whose penchant for pugnacious posing of questions disrupted the lectures of colleagues so thoroughly that two quit and became monks. In his prime, Abelard fell hard for a beautiful linguist, Heloise (1090–1164), seduced her by renting a room in her uncle's house, and became her very private tutor. Abelard's obsession led to the philosopher's double damnation—by ecclesiastical condemnation and actual castration.

Biography: Abelard was born in Brittany to a moneyed military man named Beranger. When the academic genius of his oldest son manifested itself, Beranger happily funded his budding boy to bigger and better things. Eventually Peter made his way to Paris and became first a star scholar in the school of William of Champeaux and then a pain in his professor's neck. Peter loved to pick a peck of practical puzzlers and impeach his professors in public. He liked to holster his ego on one hip and his IQ on the other and call pretenders into the street for an intellectual shoot-out.

By the time Abelard reached his prime, lecturing in Paris to packed halls with student fees flooding his purse, he decided to add romance to his life. Peter became smitten with Heloise, who was about 27 and had already acquired a scholarly reputation in Greek, Hebrew, and Latin literature. The professor's desire to pluck this peach knew no bounds, and inquiry revealed that Heloise was the pet niece of a canon priest of the Cathedral of Notre Dame. Abelard bartered for a room in Uncle Fulbert's manse in exchange for tutoring his nubile niece in medical science. The resulting moral meltdown went unabated for five months until Fulbert caught them playing doctor. The tutor had to move out, the affair went underground, and the bun went in the oven. Abelard hid her with his family under his sister's care, which turned out to be a permanent arrangement to raise baby Astrolabe. Canon Fulton forced the two to marry, Abelard obliged Heloise to become a nun, and reality reduced Abelard to love her by letters (which are still read with delight on the Internet).

He retired to the monastery of St. Denis until he was kicked out in 1121 for challenging the legend of their patron saint. He retreated then to an abandoned chapel. However, when his location was identified and posted on the Empire-wide web, university hacks from Paris to Marseille headed north to be as near the professor

Tomb of Abelard and Heloise

as possible. Abelard then used the location to found the Oratory of the Paraclete, which developed into a convent over which Heloise herself would later be prioress.

The details of the tragic romance are found in Abelard's famous auto-biography, *The History of Calamity.* Abelard's infamous *Sic et Non* ("Yes and No") points out contradictions in Scripture and in the theological works of the church fathers, purport-edly "to question unexamined faith." When Abelard published his theolog-ical magnum opus, *Theologia Summi Boni,* it was payback time for his many enemies. They condemned his doctrine of the Trinity at the Council of Soissons (1121) and made him burn the book.

The next condemnation came in 1141, when St. Bernard (p. 86) himself came down from Clairvaux and gave the council some midnight monkish straight talk about heretics, which resulted in Abelard being anathematized the next morning before he could even finish his Cheerios. Abelard's appeal to Pope Innocent II was denied, and the Vatican confirmed the condemnation. Only the intervention of the abbot of Cluny saved the philosopher from further humiliation and secured Abelard's reception into a Cluniac monastery. The abbot then went a second mile to get the papal condemnation rescinded and St. Bernard reconciled.

churchfail: Bernard successfully brought charges of false teaching against Abelard's writings. In his *Ethics,* Abelard had taken the subjectivist approach that sin and crime were to be measured by the motive and not the act itself. Bernard saw that as opening the door for Twinkie defenses instead of appeals to the price Christ paid on the cross. Bernard and others considered all the philosophical dialecticism and rationalism of Abelard as exalting reason over revelation, especially with reference to the Trinity.

Application: Greatness of gifts can blind a person to the need for moral and rela-tional guidance. The first rule of such guidance is, if your head is made of butter don't sit near the fire. "Make no plans to satisfy the fleshly desires" (Rom 13:14).

R.D.

Bernard of Clairvaux

Bernard

Date: 1146

Synopsis: Bernard of Clairvaux was the greatest preacher and monk of the medieval period of church history. His unfinished series on the love of God contained 86 sermons from the Song of Songs, yet when the Christian fort at Edessa in Asia Minor fell to the Muslims and Pope Eugenius issued a call for a Crusade— and offered get-out-of-Purgatory-free cards ("plenary indulgences")—Bernard preached the Second Crusade in the Name of Divine Love (of all things) with such ringing clarity that many mobilized to take up the cross. The resulting military failure and loss of life was an epic churchfail that still is in the top three reasons not to believe, right up there with priest pedophiles and adulterous and avaricious televangelists.

Biography: Bernard, best known as Saint Bernard (1090–1153), was born to be a monk and a preacher. Birthed to blue bloods near Dijon, the mustard capital of France, he entered the recently founded monastery at Citeaux 22 years later. Like a Benedictine pied piper, he brought along 30 other young noblemen of Burgundy, including his own brothers. Three years later he was asked by the abbot, Stephen Harding, to plant a new monastery at Clairvaux, which became one of the chief centers of the order of the Cistercian monks in white. He intended to form a movement of stricter Benedictine habit wearers who worshiped hourly and worked daily— Scripture and sweat in the truck farm being the prescription for perfection. Bernard had no truck with any monastery that did not live up to the ascetic ideal, and very soon you could recognize any Cistercian by their white hoods, tight belts, and green thumbs.

In 1129 Bernard helped launch a new order of monks with swords, the Knights Templar, perhaps even drawing up their Rule for faith and fencing. His Vatican stock went through the dome in Rome when Bernard sided with Innocent II against the rival antipope in the disputed election following the death of Pope Honorius II (1130). The triumphant pontiff showered privileges on the Cistercians, but the real downpour of Vatican favors fell when Bernard handpicked a former pupil to put forward as the next wearer of the pointy hat, Eugenius III (1145).

Before that white smoke had fully cleared from the cathedral, Bernard found himself preaching to conscript soldiers for Jesus for a second campaign against the Muslims. But like a smart recruiter, when the Second Crusade failed miserably, Bernard blamed the recruits—those who managed to limp home anyway—for their lack of faith. To his credit, this Cistercian did stand against most of his Catholic colleagues by opposing any persecution of the Jews. Bernard died in 1153, received sainthood in 1174 (otherwise the dog breed would just be called "Bernards"), and was made a Doctor of the Catholic Church in 1830—meaning that if Bernard said it, you can take it to the Vatican bank.

churchfail: Bernard knew his Bible as much as Luther, and he knew there was nothing in Scripture giving power to the pope, or anyone else in an alb, to grant plenary indulgence for going to war against the keepers of the Qur'an. Yet in the name of Christ, Bernard preached and preached falsely. His four-point sermon declared:

- Sinful men ought not refuse the papal get-out-of-purgatory-free card received by those buckling on their swords to go crusading. (But purgatory was just a medieval invention to make people mind priests and popes.)
- A terrible judgment awaited those who fail to take up the cross in the Crusade. (This nullifies Christ's shed blood on the cross.)
- This is a plan not made by man but coming from above, from the heart of divine love. (Is sheathing your sword in a Muslim stomach really what Jesus meant by "love your enemies"?)
- How can you not go on Crusade when the Muslims in Jerusalem say, "Jesus was not who He said He was"? If you win, you get glory; if you lose, to die is gain. (Bernard was abusing the word of grace to proof-text a foul papal promise to save patsies from a purgatorial fate that doesn't even exist.)

Application: Loving your enemies means giving good for evil, not evil for evil. It also means using the Word of God as the sword of the Spirit to share the gospel. Soldiers can follow the faith well, but not by being taught that God loves a high body count.

R.D.

Innocent III

Date: ca. 1160–1216

Synopsis: This megalomaniac usurped and asserted more authority over the Catholic Church and the empires of Europe than any of his predecessors.

Biography: Born to a wealthy and influential family in Italy, Lotario dei Conti di Segni was educated in theology in Paris and law in Bologna . . . and that's no baloney! He was elevated from cardinal-deacon to pope in the year 1198, skipping right over the step of being ordained as a priest. Through his aggressive work as pope he greatly enhanced the new monastic orders of Franciscans and Dominicans, called for the Fourth Crusade (1204), and supervised the creation of church laws in the famous Fourth Lateran Council (1215). Taking the name Pope Innocent III, he rose to—and exceeded—his papal potential.

His nom de papacy was a misnomer. For one thing, he had blood on his hands. He instigated the Fourth Crusade, intending to take hold of the Holy Land by marching north out of Egypt. However, the soldiers got sidetracked and attacked Constantinople instead of the successors of Saladin, the Sunni sultan of the Saracens. (Innocent was naïve enough to think the outcome might somehow improve relations with the Eastern Church. It did not.) Confirming his incompetence in controlling his commandees, his Albigensian Crusade of 1209 included the massacre of ten or twenty thousand men, women, and children at Béziers, including many Catholics. The abbot serving as CO was reported to have said, "Kill them all; God knows His own."

Innocent III also came up well short of innocent in his political machinations. Jesus told His disciples, "You will receive power when the Holy Spirit has come on you, and you will be My witnesses in Jerusalem, in all Judea and Samaria, and

Innocent III

to the ends of the earth" (Acts 1:8). Innocent procured power when the mood came on him, and he became a dictator in Rome, in all Italy and Hungary, and to the ends of the Empire.

churchfail: Innocent III believed that the future kingdom of God—proclaimed in the Bible by Jesus and the apostle John—was to be constructed by the church on the earth in Innocent's own day. This would, in his thinking, involve greater claims and actions by the pope than ever before. He insisted on four things to accomplish this goal.

- He sought the right to intervene in the lawful election of kings throughout Europe. Before a royal council was called to elect a new king, the pope had "the right and authority to examine the person elected." Open up, and say "ahhh"!
- Because the pope was the ultimate moral authority on the earth, and kings ruled justly by moral authority, the pope by default was the overlord of all royalty. This would make him king of kings. Wait, someone already has that title.
- Innocent claimed he was the "Vicar of Christ," as if Christ were not available to fill His position as head of the church (Col 1:18). This would be the position of every pope and his posse thereafter.
- He claimed to be Melchizedek, the incarnation of Jesus Christ as the head of the church and the head of secular society (Gen 14; Ps 110; Heb 7). His overreaching claims opened the door for future popes, who did not have as much actual power, to make even larger claims of authority and influence.

So Pope Innocent III, purporting to be Christ's representative on earth, modeled exactly the opposite of Christ's example of servant leadership (John 13:12-15) and humility (Phil 2:5-8).

Application: In the fourteenth century, John Wycliffe wrote against many of the abuses among church hierarchy of their authority, wealth, and influence. He pointed Christians back to Jesus Christ as the ultimate example of someone who used His authority and influence to serve and love people into and within the kingdom of God. Wycliffe did not disparage those who had authority, wealth, and influence but rather encouraged them to use what God had given them to serve others in humility. He reminded Christians of Jesus's teaching that whoever wanted to be great within the church should become a slave or servant to all (Mark 10:42-45). In other words, if God has given us authority, wealth, or influence, let us make use of those assets to be a channel of God's grace to Christians and to the world in all humility and love.

K.C.

Thomas of Aquinas

Date: 1270

Synopsis: Thomas of Aquinas was the greatest Catholic theologian ever. This Dominican scholastic wrote 60 tomes before he turned 50. He is the patron saint of publishers, printers, booksellers, pencil makers, CliffsNotes, Catholic schools, and students. At the 1545 Council of Trent, Thomas's magnum opus, *Summa Theologiae*, was placed on the altar between the Bible and the papal decretals. So influential is Thomas that when President George W. Bush was preparing to invade Iraq in 2003, his advisors cracked open the *Summa* to show him that "just war" theory was not the same as the Nike slogan "just do it."

Thomas

Biography: Thomas was born in 1225 into a large, aristocratic Italian family with a golden spoon in his mouth—OK, maybe a serving spoon. His father calculated that he was likely to be the biggest of the litter and might turn out to be smarter than he looked. So when he was five, his parents dropped Thomas off at the ritzy Benedictine monastery at Monte Cassino, where his uncle was the current abbot and where the expectation was that this pudgy kindergartner was a future abbot.

All went according to plan until Thomas became delighted with the Benedictines' cross-town rivals, the Dominicans, those black-and-white-robed monastic preachers and papal pit bulls who valued study more than sweat. Thomas vowed to take up the pen and not the plow, and in 1244 he left for the University of Paris to study with the Dominican scholar, Albert the Great. There his fellow students mistook Thomas's introverted quietness as intellectual ineptitude. But Albert corrected them: "You call him the dumb ox, but in his teaching he will one day produce such a bellowing that it will be heard throughout the world." Indeed, Thomas's hoof prints can be found in every Catholic and a good many Protestant works ever since.

Thomas proceeded to produce as prolifically as his professor had prophesied. He worked out his "natural theology," the truth that comes through human observation

90

and reason, in his *Summa contra Gentiles*. What was intended as a missionary hand-book, he delivered as four books and 1,207 pages. Dominican missionaries for centuries had to lug that tetralogy in their trunks.

Thomas had weak hands, so he relied on scribes, usually dictating to five scribes on five separate projects simultaneously—like Bobby Fisher taking on the whole local chess club. His *Summa Theologiae*, a compendium of all that is known of God and humanity's relations with God, is published in five volumes and 3,500 pages. Its two most famous pages contain five proofs for the existence of God.

Thomas stopped writing on December 6, 1273, when he had so profound a mystical experience that one witness described him as weeping and levitating before the portrait of Christ. No prodding from his faithful associate Reginald could get Thomas back into his writing routine.

Thomas stopped breathing three months later after a head injury. The clergy of the church breathed a collective sigh of relief because they were having a hard time reading all that Thomas had already written.

churchfail: What Catholics called true in the *Summa*, the Reformers called false. In actuality, it took the Catholic Church itself 300 years to decide if Thomas was right or wrong. Thomas had defined the doctrine of transubstantiation whereby, when the Roman Catholic priest elevates the bread and the cup during the Mass and utters the Latin words "Hoc est corpus meum!" (This is My body), the bread and the wine are transformed into the very flesh and blood of Christ. "The inner substance is changed but the outer accidence stays the same," wrote Thomas in his best Aristotelian accent. "Hocus pocus," snorted Martin Luther. The Protestant Reformation condemned the theology of Aquinas because it failed to make Scripture the norming norm for faith and practice. It also failed to trust in the finished work of Christ on the cross for salvation. Many Germans sold their *Summas* cheap to snatch up a copy of Luther's German Bible or Calvin's *Institutes*.

Application: Productivity is always impressive; Thomas is unmatched at six million pages. If intelligence is the ability to discern relationships, again Thomas has got to be top pick with or without levitation. But faith in search of understanding means that intelligence serves biblical revelation and not the reverse. Truth is not always logical and the church is not always right, but every word of God proves true.

R.D.

Dante Alighieri

Date: 1290

Synopsis: Dante Alighieri (1265–1321) was the Florentine poet, philosopher, and politico whose epic *Divine Comedy* energized the European Renaissance and captivated people's Catholic imagination about who's in damnation and how deep and who's in heaven and how high. As each of the one hundred *cantos* (chapters) was published, Italians snatched them up like the newest gossip from the grocery checkout stand. Clearly, Alighieri was the man going around taking names.

Biography: Dante Alighieri was born in Florence. At age nine he met his untouchable heartthrob Beatrice, likely the daughter of a Florentine citizen and wife of Simoni de Bardi. Nine years later he realized the best he could do was write her poems. He was betrothed to Gemma at age 12, lost his parents at 18, and married at 28. In the crisis of Beatrice's death in 1290, Dante vowed to write a poem for her such as "had been written for no lady before." The result was *The Divine Comedy*, Dante's sacred poem describing his Catholic vision of the three destinations possible in the age to come: *Inferno*, *Purgatorio*, and *Paradiso*. The poem consists of 14,233 eleven-syllable lines, rhymed in a cycle of tercets. Each of the three canticas has 33 cantos with the last word in each cantica being "stars"—which in a medieval allegory must mean, "keep looking up." Traditionally, poems dealing with so serious a subject as human redemption would be written in uppity Latin and called a tragedy, as opposed to Dante's decision to choose the low road of comedy and to use "vulgar" Latin, as did Jerome in the Latin Vulgate.

Dante's trilogy reads like *Bill and Ted's Excellent Adventure* meets the fires of Mordor. It begins the week of Easter 1300 with Dante lost hopelessly in a dark forest. Beatrice dispatches Virgil of *Aeneid* fame to lead Dante down the

Dante

rings of Gehenna to Lucifer, frozen horns-down in an iced lake—to cool his temper no doubt—then it's up the ten terraces of Mount Purgatory. Virgil, the symbol of human reason, has been the guide up into Purgatory, where Beatrice, who represents medieval Catholic theology, conducts her beloved rhymer up through the nine planetary and stellar spheres to the Empyrean. There the baton is passed to St. Bernard, who gets Dante a ticket in to see the Blessed Virgin Mary, whose intercession grants the poet a glimpse of the triune beatific vision. Can you say, "Most excellent"?

churchfail: In the Inferno, poetic justice prevails, as divine retribution is meted out as an eternal lip lock between the adulterous Paolo and Francesca, and as fortunetellers have their heads screwed on backward. The authority of the Catholic Church and the office of the pope are accepted in principle, but particular popes and churchmen do not receive get-out-of-hell-free cards—not the way Dante plays Monopoly. Reason, played by Virgil, is able to lead Dante into but not out of Purgatory, indicating that human effort to put away sin is necessary but insufficient for salvation.

The deceased but undamned enter Purgatory happily borne by angels, with everyone singing about exodus from Egyptian slavery. These crooning shades work out their sanctification with fear and trembling by working up the ten terraces of the cardinal virtues. Here, in brilliant rhyme, the poet sets sanctification before justification, progressive works before justifying grace, Ephesians 2:10 before 2:8-9. But biblically, salvation is by grace through faith, not by but unto good works. The biblical post-regeneration sanctifying work of the Holy Spirit through the Word is projected in iambic pentameter into a post-death purgatorial experience that has no genuine biblical basis. Purgatory is a fiction.

Finally, if you step back from the gaudy and graphic trifold vision of Dante's hell, purgatory, and heaven, you begin to see a worldview that has the Trinity so transcendent that you're on your own (OK, you get help from a dead Roman poet and/or your unrequited lady love) to climb a 99-rung ladder to get a final shove by a dead saint to pop your head into the glowing cloud to see the triune essence. This song of ascent fails to stir any imagination about the descent of God the Son in Jesus as the basis of God's mission of redemption.

Application: In words taken from the film, *Stranger than Fiction*, you must decide if you are in a comedy or a tragedy. The presence or absence of Christ in your life is the determining factor.

R.D.

Boniface VIII

Date: 1294–1303

Synopsis: This heretic had an ongoing feud with the French king until he lost his life at age 86 from the battle scars.

Biography: Benedict Gaetani was born in Anagni, a town just south of Rome that produced a passel of popes: Innocent III, Gregory IX, Alexander IV, and our beau Boniface. He was educated and served in various levels of ministry in Italy *(ciao!)* and France *(bonjour!)*. In 1294 he was elected to the papacy and adopted the name Pope Boniface VIII because "Boniface VII" had already been taken. Presuming a proportion of power claimed by previous popes in an era when he actually had no such clout, Bonny overstepped his bounds several times until it finally claimed his life in what many would call the worst treatment of a pope by secular authorities in the history of the Catholic Church.

In 1297 Boniface took sides in a feud within the Colonna clan, some of whom had supported his rival and predecessor, Celestine V. Jake and Pete Colonna presided over Palestrina, a town near Anagni. Boniface promised that the city would be spared if the citizens submitted. He lied. He razed the city and confiscated the real estate for the papacy, thus felling the fortunes of that faction of the family.

churchfail: Ever since Pope Leo the Great filled a secular power vacuum in the fifth century, several popes had yearned for a united Europe significantly influenced, if not ruled outright, by the pope. When Barbarians invaded the western Roman Empire, they had no aspirations of European unity, and their grandchildren were happy to rule local kingdoms rather than all of Europe. Because Catholics viewed the pope as the CEO of a united church in Europe, the manifold monarchs' individualistic nationalistic tendencies rubbed against the papal grain like fingernails on a chalkboard. Even though a thousand years had passed since the first emperor converted to Christianity and made it legal, popes and kings were still jockeying for position and waxing eloquent about their God-given spheres of influence.

The chest thumping between popes and kings finally came to a head with Philip the Fair of France and Pope Boniface VIII. The kings of England and France were having turf wars in northern France and sought to fund them by tweaking the tax brackets for the church. Bonny objected in his papal bull *Clericis laicos* (1296), in which he threatened to excommunicate any secular ruler who taxed their local churches without the pope's prior approval. Phil responded by stopping all money and valuables from leaving the country to Rome (including the tithes and offerings).

In 1301 the feud rekindled when Phil brought Bonny's papal representative to trial. Bonny retaliated with the letter *Ausculta Fili* (lit. "Listen, my son"), where he asserted the pope's authority over kings and their kingdoms and even summoned Phil to appear before the papal court in Rome. As if that wasn't enough, Bonny took it a step further in his papal bull *Unam sanctam* ("One Holy" Catholic Church), in which he claimed papal authority over every person and all creation—an assertion emulated

Boniface VIII

by Muhammad Ali after he defeated Sonny Liston: "I must be the greatest. I showed the world. I talk to God everyday. I know the real God. I shook up the world. I'm the king of the world. You must listen to me. I am the greatest! I can't be beat!"[9]

Phil had enough of smack talk! He sent William "Knuckles" de Nogaret and Sciarra "Scarface" Colonna with instructions to arrest Bonny. (Sciarra was Jake Colonna's nephew and Pete's brother.) But Billy amplified the accusations against the 86-year-old vicar, and Colonna smote the pope—a whack that would go down in history as the "Anagni slap." Following some further unfriendly persuasion they let Bonny go, but he died a few weeks later, physically and emotionally wounded beyond repair.

Application: Although Boniface VIII clearly overstepped the boundaries of ecclesiastical meddling in secular affairs, his struggles and their sad conclusion prompted much-needed discussion among leaders of church and state in the centuries to come. First in America then in Europe and around the world, formal and informal arrangements would be made to draw lines of demarcation between sacred and secular authority. While a true separation of church and state will never be possible where their spheres of influence overlap, they can learn to share their toys and play nicely on the same playground.

K.C.

---

[9] Muhammad Ali as quoted in Dave Kindred, *Sound and Fury: Two Powerful Lives, One Fateful Friendship* (New York: Free Press, 2007), 58.

Avignon Papacy

Date: 1309–77

Synopsis: For almost three quarters of a century, the French Bishops of Rome relocated to Avignon, France, a period referred to as the Babylonian Captivity of the Papacy.

History: Though Rome is often referred to as the "Eternal City," its population dwindled significantly during the Dark Ages after the Vandals sacked Rome in the fifth century. This is where we get the term "vandalism." With a population of more than a million at its height during its empire years, the population shrank to only tens of thousands in the tenth century—kind of like Detroit in the late twentieth century.

Since there weren't many people in and around Rome for a millennium or so, the Roman Bishop, aka the pope, sometimes found it difficult to convince other bishops and countries that he should still be in charge of the whole church everywhere. After all, why should the vicar of a broken down backwater burg rule the world's Christians? As long as Catholics continued to recognize the pope as their central authority, he'd still have a job with some income from those intercontinental coffers. However, the Papal States—the region in central Italy under the pope's control—weren't able to raise sufficient funds, so he had to do a lot of begging and pleading (as well as some ethical sleight of hand) to maintain the standard of living to which he was accustomed.

While Rome's power was falling, France's was rising. After some verbal ranting and legal raving between the French king and the pope in the early

Coat of Arms of Clement VI on Avignon's Papal Palace

fourteenth century (p. 94), the French king rigged a papal election and had his puppet, Clement V, installed as pope. Clement moved his headquarters to Avignon, a small town in southern France, where the French king could keep a close eye on him. For the next 72 years, the popes would be supporters of France and its kings. However, choosing to champion one country meant losing international support and the support of rival families in Italy. As flag-wavers in each country spurred on nationalism, there seemed to be less need for a central religious leader who stuck his nose into the secular matters of other countries.

So, how did the popes make it back to Rome? Well, so many Catholics teased the popes about being French puppets (*les fantoches, n'est-ce pas?*), and the popes had lost so much of their power to the French kings anyway, that they finally figured it would be best to pack their Gucci luggage and move back home. Imagine how much ridicule the US Presidents would face if 18 terms of them ruled from Acapulco, Mexico! ¡Ay caramba! A mystic prophetess by the name of Catherine of Siena felt called by God to go to Florence and France, tell the families to stop fighting each other, and beg for the pope to return permanently. In 1377 Gregory XI did return, but he died a few months later. That's OK: ever since then, there's been a pope in Rome.

Application: Throughout history there has been tension between two opposing political ideas: independence and cooperation. On the one hand, we want to serve, promote, and protect our own goals—free from outside interference. On the other hand, we sometimes feel the need to cooperate with larger and distant groups to accomplish our own agendas.

Church politics seems to work much the same way. We like many of the benefits of religious freedom and independence, but we are occasionally willing to yield in certain matters to build alliances with other Christian groups and even groups outside the church if it will promote our objectives. The existence of independent congregations and denominations and the exercise of free speech display our desire for independence. The existence of a pope displays our historically Christian tendency to want universal unity with our Christian cousins, and the practice of interfaith dialogues and humanitarian aid displays our desire to play nicely with our neighbors. Perhaps there is a healthy balance to be struck between independence and cooperation as we seek to follow the same Creator, Savior, and Lord of all.

K.C.

Urban VI

Urban VI

Date: 1378

Synopsis: Bartolemeo Prignano (1318–89) was elected pope on April 8, 1378, on the Pesto reform ticket when the Italians—after 70 years of the Avignon papacy—made an offer the electors couldn't refuse: the next man in the miter had better be Italian! Known for his austerity and dexterity in Vatican diplomatic affairs, the triple tiara must have gone to his head because Urban immediately began to conduct himself in such a violent and overbearing manner (five cardinals were tortured and six killed) and with such unmoving stubbornness that the French cardinals, who were in the majority, declared the election null and void and elected Robert of Geneva as antipope Clement VII. Within six months of Urban's election there were two opposing popes and two sets of opposing cardinals. The Great Catholic Schism had begun.

Biography: Bartolemeo Prignano, though of humble origins, avidly climbed the Catholic ecclesiastic pecking order from priest to bishop to Archbishop of Acerenza in 1363. He then took a lateral move to Bari in 1377 and an assignment to the chancery working out visas, passports, and the like for the Vatican. His acquired rep was as a seriously austere saint wannabe who knew how to get things done around the Sistine Chapel. When the Italian cardinals put the old mafia squeeze on the French cardinals, everyone settled for BP in the chancery office. Urban VI was proffered the pontifical pallium and crossed keys on Easter Sunday, 1378.

Urban was elected to undertake the reformation for which so many were calling, especially following the 70-year "Babylonian Captivity" of the Avignon papacy (p. 96). Zealous without prudence, Urban declared the bishops of his court to be traitors to Christ and perjurers, since they were absent from their pastoral field to attend papal politics. With equal imprudence, Urban moved to amputate the ostentatious lifestyle of his cardinals with the ultimate papal weapons, excommunication and expropriation.

Many scholars of the papacy assert that Urban VI was fraught with such a frightful anger management problem that he may have been mentally ill. He so alienated his inherited leadership that all the cardinals, even previously loyal Italians, withdrew to Avignon and elected a new pope. They preferred Charles V's Gaul to Urban VI's gall.

Meanwhile, Urban appointed 26 new cardinals from amongst his closest allies, including four nephews. For the first time in 1,300 years, there were two popes and two sets of cardinals. All western Christendom was forced to choose sides—croissants or pizza? Before this great schism was resolved a generation later in 1414, there would be four popes simultaneously competing for Catholic loyalties. It would be 200 years before another pope dared take the name of Urban.

The resolution of this impasse had come through a council, giving rise to the short-lived conciliar movement, which implied that an ecumenical confab of Christians might check and balance the papacy. However, within a century the pontifex had flexed his pecs, and by the nineteenth century he was officially infallible.

In 1606, while rebuilding St. Peter's Basilica, workmen found a trough and were about to dump the debris out of it so they could use it to water their thirsty workhorses. They were stopped by the church historian, Giacomo Grimaldi, who identified the "trough" as the sarcophagus of Urban VI and the "debris" as his remains. The workmen had to conserve the coffin and its cadaver, and were forced to find a different trough. Even posthumously, Urban was still impeding the improvement of the church in Rome.

churchfail: Urban VI functioned almost exclusively on the basis of his recently achieved status as pope of the Catholic Church. He assumed that because he had the position, he had the power to lead. He was wrong. Furthermore, he failed to discern and develop loyalty from his inherited underlings. He eventually forced even good soldiers to become deserters and organizational terrorists. Despite his assignment as the ultimate emissary of Jesus Christ on earth, he did not love his enemies and he did not wash anyone's feet. Even if he had actually held the keys of St. Peter to heaven's gates, Urban VI was much more interested in repulsing his rivals than in admitting anyone into the kingdom. Authoritarian leadership angers any fellowship until that ship finally and fatally sinks.

Application: Rise to the level of your excellence, not your incompetence. Maturity that matters is the ability to make and maintain friendships. If the way you are leading produces a high body count, think about other employment. Starbucks is always hiring.

R.D.

The Great Schism of Western Christendom

Date: 1378–1417

Synopsis: Is the Pope Italian? Not necessarily. In 1378 the Roman Catholic Church split over who would be pope—the Italian Urban VI or the French-elected Swiss claimant, Clement VII. Before the fight finished 40 years later, there would be three popes partitioning the one, true, holy catholic church.

Setting: Political intrigue in 1305 by France's King Philip IV resulted in the election of French-leaning Pope Clement V (1305–1314). Adding insult to injury, Clement moved the papal court from Rome to Avignon, France, and appointed enough French cardinals to ensure that future popes would be French. The Avignon papacy became known as the "Babylonian Captivity" because it lasted about the same length of time as the Jewish sojourn in balmy Babylon. In 1377 Pope Gregory XI moved the papacy back to Rome, dying a year later.

With the next election to be held in Vatican City, the Roman populace warned that the new guy had better be Italian or else. Taking the threat seriously, and even with a majority of the voting Cardinals being French, the red hats sent up the white smoke for the Italian insider reform candidate, Bartolemeo Prignano—Urban VI—who quickly alienated even his Italian allies (p. 98). The French cardinals declared the election invalid due to mafia-like duress and promptly elected one of their own as Pontifex not so Maximus, Clement VII.

The ever-faithful monarchs in Europe promptly threw their support behind the pope who would further their own political interests and thwart their rivals—largely along the shifting alliances arising from the Hundred Years' War (1337–1475). England and most of Germany endorsed Urban, while France, Spanish Castile, and Scotland championed Clement. The papal claimant lineage hardened so that in Rome only Italians were elected, while in Avignon, Clement was succeeded by the Aragonese Benedict XIII. Administrative disarray, jurisdictional dysfunction, and spiritual disease spread like the plague. Multiple attempted rapprochements failed. The loss of prestige and loyalty prefigured the Protestant Reformation a century later and can only be compared to the institutional shame induced by pedophile priest scandals of recent days.

Clement VII

But as is not unusual in a fallen world, bad things get worse before they get better. The best hope of healing looked to be the Council of Pisa in 1409. The assembled church leaders deposed the popes in Rome and Avignon and elected Alexander V as pope. Unfortunately, there was insufficient political backing for the decision, so now there were three popes—a veritable potpourri of popery.

Hoping to gain political influence by picking the right horse in the race and by helping to end the schism, the king of Bohemia threw his support behind the Pisan pope. His hopes went unrealized, but he was able to get John XXIII to call a council in Constance, a German town on the Swiss border. The council deposed the Pisan John and the Avignon Benedict and accepted the resignation of the Roman Gregory. The Council then elected an Italian as the one and only pope. Martin V returned to a Rome in miserable condition but was able to restore it rapidly through bestowing strategic honors on nephews and uncles, since blood is thicker than sacramental wine or liturgical oil. After this, the Italians made sure the papacy stayed in Rome. Apart from two Spanish and one Dutch pope, Italians controlled the papacy until John Paul II in 1978.

churchfail: Fear and distrust created a toxic church environment. Each region wanted to make sure its interests prevailed. Papal pride prevented a quicker resolution. They should have followed the pattern of Jesus in Philippians 2:5-11 to divest themselves of miter, tiara, and surplice to take the form of a servant in fulfillment of the Father's mission of redemption. Submission in obedience to serving Christ is no dishonor. Church fights are a call not to retrench or retreat but to engage in the hard work of listening and reconciliation. Whenever as few as two or three are gathered in the reconciling name of Christ, that dialogue apprehends the miracle of His presence.

Application: Fear and intimidation may be effective tools for getting one's way, but they fail miserably at leading people into a dynamic relationship with Jesus. Two heads are not better than one when there is only one hat. Submission and reconciliation are higher, harder, less traveled roads. Contrary to cellular biology, the church does not usually grow by splitting.

R.D. & L.H.

Geoffrey Chaucer

Date: 1387

Synopsis: Chaucer's decision to publish *The Canterbury Tales* in vernacular Middle English rather than the usual Latin or French established him as England's first poet and confirmed English as the land's first language. Chaucer was a career bureaucrat on the king's payroll, but it must have been one of those less demanding jobs that let him do his word processing on the clock because he produced an enormous body of work. Influenced by Dante, Boccaccio, and Petrarch, Chaucer's poem of 29 tales shared by pilgrims on holy pilgrimage to Canterbury Cathedral earned him the first statue of 29 more to come on Poets' Corner in Westminster Abbey.

Chaucer

Biography: Geoffrey Chaucer's (ca. 1343–1400) birth date is a bit fuzzy, perhaps owing to the fact that his father and grandfather were wealthy vintners. Nevertheless, his father was able to call on his contacts at court to land Jeff his first job as page to a countess at age 12. In 1359 he followed his duke, the countess's husband, into the early part of the Hundred Years' War in France and was captured in 1360 during the siege at Rheims. The king ransomed this future poet for £16, a royal sum in those pre-inflation days, and upon repatriation Chaucer was inducted into royal service for the next 30 years and even undertook several James Bond-like diplomatic missions. Incidentally (and probably arranged by Queen Philippa in 1366), the former page married the Pan, as Philippa de Roet was called for her role of keeper of the pantry. The royals gave the newlyweds a lifetime annuity as a gift. Four children would come from this union. The eldest, Elizabeth, became a nun at Barking Abbey, where presumably dogs were allowed. Thomas entered military service, and Lewis is the son for whom Chaucer wrote a scientific treatise on the astrolabe, the medieval star computer. The youngest, Agnes, went into the family lady-in-waiting business.

Chaucer's literary works are usually divided into three periods of production: the French, stimulated by his involuntary tutoring in his Rheims cells; the Italian, because of his exposure to Dante and company during diplomatic forays; and the English, when Chaucer matured as a self-defined Brit with a non-anxious awareness of the vernacular. The poet had begun work on *The Tales* in the 1380s, about the time he became a Member of Parliament and his wife died. Chaucer died on October 25, 1400, and will be remembered for centuries to come for three reasons: *The Canterbury Tales* and the asteroid and moon crater that are named after him.

churchfail: While Chaucer demonstrated his Latin skills by translating Boethius's influential sixth-century work, *The Consolation of Philosophy*, he seems to have drunk this Italian's Kool-Aid. Writing while awaiting martyrdom under the Arian king, Boethius baptized the Wheel of Fortune for medieval Catholic thinking. (Is Vanna White really Boethius's Lady Philosophy?) That Wheel rolled with Platonic providential inevitability, enriching some with windfalls and "overwhelming others with grief beyond bearing and deserting them when least expected." Boethius's *Consolation* blasted a philosophical predisposition into medieval scholasticism to consult philosophy before Scripture—both for the beatific vision of God and for wisdom to endure the vicissitudes of life.

In Chaucer's epic poem "The Monk's Tale," Vanna White rolls the tragic wheel of fortune over the great to bring them low, and in "The Clerk's Tale," Griselda is brutally and repeatedly tested by her "noble husband," as if running over her with a giant, studded wheel of divine providence, and then backing it over her again to see if she is OK. Chaucer unconsciously chants with Boethius a melody that proposes a much more Muslim fatalism (Allah wills it, so accept it) than Christian providence, with little to no remembrance of the Messiah who will not crush a bruised reed and knows how to rescue the godly from trouble. Christians are not called to endless suffering but to take up the cross with hope of the crown. Chaucer is so superb a story weaver that we can be hypnotized into the faithless fatalism being advocated, where a devoted wife is asked to endure incredible abuse by her husband's whim without justice or divine intervention.

Application: Beware buying a ticket to a Canterbury, where godliness means acceptance of meaningless, continual suffering for yourself and others. Bawdy tales may a distracting bedtime story make, but God gives renewing songs in the night that the morning may with love, hope, and faith be faced.

R.D.

churchfails in the Reformation

When Martin Luther posted his poly-pointed placard on the papist portal, he brought to a head various issues that had been fomenting for some years. But while he and others ostensibly rescued the universal Church from certain specific errors, they introduced new fallacies that Rome hadn't thought of. That is, Body of Christ 2.0 was buggy.

Girolamo Savonarola

Date: 1494

Synopsis: Girolamo Savonarola (1452–1498) was an Italian Dominican friar whose apocalyptic prophecies foretold civic glory for his beloved Florence, provided the citizens paid the price of repentance. Just two decades before the start of the Reformation, Savonarola was the last hope for Catholic reform from within, but his bonfires of the vanities and denouncing of clerical corruption so frayed papal nerves and angered Florentine muckety-mucks that they threw him and his friends a necktie party, burned their bodies in the city plaza, and dumped their ashes in the Arno River.

Biography: Girolamo Savonarola was third born of seven in Ferarra, Italy, in 1452. He displayed an early penchant for composing apocalyptic poetry, including such upbeat rhymes as the 1472 hit, "On the Ruin of the World," and its 1475 sequel, "On the Ruin of the Church." His dream of becoming a Dominican preacher was met with derision, but in 1475 Savonarola knocked on the door of the convent in Bologna and informed them that he wanted to be a knight of Christ. He took the vows of poverty, chastity, and obedience and one year later was ordained to the priesthood.

Savonarola studied, practiced preaching, and started complaining to the management about a decline in convent austerity. By 1478 a ticked-off professor managed to get rid of Mister Grumpy Pants by assigning him to an internship in Florence. There he taught logic, wrote manuals, composed devotionals, and prepared sermons, but his delivery was less than successful because his hayseed accent and style clashed with the Gucci tastes of the congregation. But that all changed when Savonarola suddenly stumbled on seven reasons why the saints were about to be scourged. He shared these apocalyptic themes when he preached at Lent in 1485 and got a return gig for more of the same in 1486. He hit the sawdust trail for several years, and his apocalyptic message of repentance and renewal found an audience. His letters home to Mama show his confidence and sense of mission growing along with his widening reputation.

In 1490 Girolamo returned to Florence, and the cathedral crowds responded to his preaching from Revelation with such emotion that onlookers took to calling them the "weepers and wailers." He made pointed allusions to tyrants, the rich, and corrupt clergy. Savonarola expanded his Salvation Army by commissioning adolescent Munchkin Mullahs to keep immodestly dressed divas or misbehaving misters

off the streets just like an Italian Taliban. In
1493 he began to prophesy that a new Cyrus
was coming over the northern mountains
to scourge the cities, renew the church, and
make Florence the spiritual navel of the
world. Prophetic fulfillment loomed on the
horizon in 1494 when King Charles VIII of
France crossed the Alps with a formidable
army. While Savonarola worked to successfully convince Charles to bypass Florence,
the populace overthrew the Medici dynasty
and declared Florence a republic.

Savonarola

In 1495 the Florentine Republicans
refused to bat in Pope Alexander VI's holy
league against the French Invaders, so the
Vatican demanded that Savonarola steal
home to Rome. Girolamo declined and
preached despite a pontifical ban. The pope
retaliated in 1497 by excommunicating him
and threatening to place Florence under
interdict, the papal i-bomb of eternal death. In 1498 a rival Florentine preacher challenged Savonarola to a trial by fire. When Girolamo delayed the game for hours by
debating the lineup, and the game got rained out, the crowd was furious with their
prophet's pitching, and attendance at the cathedral stadium plunged. The city authorities then grabbed Savonarola and two of his fellow friars. They imprisoned and tortured them until Savonarola divulged that his visions and prophecies were inventions.
On May 23, 1498, church and civil authorities gave Savonarola his trial by fire. They
condemned, hanged, and burned all three in the main square. (After that his followers
might have encouraged each other by shouting, "Remember Girolamo!")

churchfail: Savonarola never played well with others. Prophets often don't, but when
pastoral insights became intoxicated with apocalyptic fervor, Savonarola rejected all
accountability to others and plunged himself and his church into chaos. Savonarola's
fifteenth-century attempt to bring heaven to earth failed and became a living hell
because he tried to carve his cathedral pulpit into a political ark with himself as the
new Noah.

Application: It is sometimes easier to be right than effective. Prophetic insights
supercharged with apocalyptic vision must be coupled with patient political negotia-
tion; otherwise the preacher will just be a flashfire in a plaza pan.

R.D.

Johann Tetzel

Tetzel

Dates: 1465–1519

Synopsis: In the nineteenth and early twentieth century, snake oil salesmen hawked concoctions of uncertain origin as cures for anything that was ailing. In the early sixteenth century, Tetzel was the same kind of person— peddling pardon from perdition for all one's peccadilloes for a particular price.

Biography: Johann Tetzel was a Dominican monk who served as inquisitor for a time in Poland and Saxony. In 1503 he entered the profitable world of selling indulgences.

An indulgence promised God's forgiveness apart from the seven official sacraments. The practice of selling indulgences arose during the Crusades and became very lucrative. The Church based the franchise on the idea that Mary and the saints lived such holy lives that their good deeds outweighed their sinful ones. These extra good works were stored in heaven in a "Treasury of Merit." Since the pope has Peter's keys to the kingdom, he alone can open this treasury and transfer these unused merits to average Christians who finish their lives with a deficit. All it takes is the appropriate "contribution" to the church and the transaction can be made, reducing the tab that must be settled up in the afterlife.

Indulgences could be earned by going on pilgrimage to certain locations—such as Rome or Jerusalem—by fighting in the Crusades, or through observing certain objects, such as a rosary or relics. An entire accounting system was established to determine how much time in purgatory could be reduced by each action. Viewing relics on certain days, such as All Saints' Day (November 1, not when the New Orleans football team is playing) magnified the impact. The collection of relics in Wittenberg, home of Martin Luther, numbered 5,005 pieces in 1509, the viewing of which—accompanied by the appropriate donation—brought a reduction of 1,443 years in purgatory. By 1520 the collection had grown to 19,013 items, including a twig from Moses's burning bush and a piece of bread from the Last Supper. (The sale of "antiquities" was a booming business.) Viewing the entire collection could preserve the person, or his deceased dears, from up to 1,902,202 years and 270 days of pain in purgatory!

Johann Tetzel was one of the best in the business. "Do you love your Mama? Then don't leave her suffering in purgatory. Act today! For whenever a coin in the coffer rings, a soul from purgatory springs!" Only the pope could authorize the transfer of merit from saint to sinner. What a monopoly! It was a wonderful life selling indulgences. I can see Zuzu Bailey now as she drops pennies in the plate: "Look, Daddy! I'm freeing people from purgatory!"

Partial indulgences pulled a percentage of sin's penalty. A plenary indulgence was the Golden Ticket. It extricated the purchaser from the entire punishment due to sin. Go directly to heaven, do not stop in purgatory. Tetzel sold plenary indulgences. The cost was on a sliding scale—the more a customer could afford, the more Tetzel charged.

While the merits were stored in heaven, the money to access them had more temporal uses on earth. Albert of Brandenburg was an ambitious man. By age 23, he had become bishop of two regions. Knowing his ambition, the pope charged him almost double the normal price for buying the Archbishopric of Mainz, one of the most influential and lucrative sees. Albert had borrowed heavily. For his part, Pope Leo X wanted money to pay Raphael, the new architect renovating St. Peter's Basilica. The two men struck a deal: they would hire the most successful indulgence seller of the day and give him exclusive rights to Albert's concession. Half the profit went to Albert and the other half to Leo. Needless to say, this fleecing of the German people raised Luther's ire. (His 95 objections to the sale of indulgences is another story.)

churchfail: Tetzel was a talented salesman of religion. Unfortunately for him, and tragically for his credulous customers, there is no biblical foundation for purgatory, much less indulgences. The money he raised in God's name could not achieve what he promised; it was merely used by unscrupulous individuals for mundane purposes.

Application: A strong pitch that appeals to people's love of family or fear of the unknown always receives a response. Just send me three small installments of $19.99, and I will reveal the secret to being free of disease, achieving great wealth, bringing your loved ones through the apocalypse, and clearing up your acne!

A discerning steward of God's money will test the spirits of a cause before committing any currency.

L.H.

Pope Leo X

Dates: 1513–1521

Synopsis: Pope Leo X was born and bred for the papacy, enjoying the power and pomp of the office. He used the position to further his interest in Renaissance art and architecture, funding such notables as Raphael and Michelangelo, but he could not fathom the theological questions posed by Martin Luther.

Biography: The man who would be pope was born Giovanni di Lorenzo de' Medici in 1475. He was the second son of Lorenzo the Magnificent, ruler of Florence, an influential, independent country now part of Italy. The city took part in leading the Renaissance, and his parents financially backed education and the arts. As the second son, young Giovanni was to have a career in the Church. Toward that end, he entered the ecclesial community at age six and became an abbot at the age of seven. By age ten, he controlled the famed abbey at Monte Cassino. After strong lobbying (and financial contributions) by his father, Giovanni was designated cardinal-deacon at the mature age of 13, but was not allowed to vote in the papal elections until he was 16. The Church did have standards after all.

The family's political fortunes waned after Lorenzo's death in 1492. Just two years later, Giovanni had to escape Florence in disguise. For almost 20 years he lived supporting the arts, styling himself an amateur artist and mismanaging most of the money that came his way. His fortunes suddenly changed when he came into favor at the end of the reign of Pope Julius II. When Julius died, the way was paved for a move to Rome. At just 37 years of age, Giovanni was elected pope on March 9, 1513. Since the pope is also the Bishop of Rome, this presented a problem, for he was not even a priest. So on March 15 Giovanni was ordained a priest, consecrated as a bishop two days later, and crowned Pope Leo X two days after that. Let it never be said that spiritual maturity stood in the way of naked political ambition. Perhaps, though, the Church learned its lesson: Giovanni was the last non-priest to be elected pope.

Leo viewed the papacy as a platform for patronage of the arts. He famously declared, "Since God has given us the papacy, let us enjoy it!" He was also politically plugged in. When Henry VIII condemned Lutheranism in 1521, Leo gave him the title "Defender of the Faith." Henry would go on to defend his divorce as well, and to split from Rome in 1534.

In 1517 Martin Luther protested the fleecing of his flock with the selling of indulgences (see Tetzel, p. 108). Leo was using the money to finance the rebuilding of St. Peter's Basilica. To Leo, Luther's lament was an economic annoyance. To Martin, it was a matter of scriptural support for ecclesiastical praxis. Leo could not comprehend the Augustinian angst expressed by the German monk.

Adept at political maneuvering, Leo tried to have Martin muzzled. His efforts backfired. Luther bested his opponents in open debate and could not be bribed with the offer of a higher office. The strong-willed Saxon was spoiling Leo's spruce-up! So the perturbed possessor of the papacy kicked Martin out of the Church. Leo described Luther as a "wild boar" who was ruining the Lord's vineyard, and he threatened Luther's life. Luther's support-

Papal Bull against Luther's "Errors"

ers outmaneuvered Leo, allowing Luther to escape the fiery fate that befell John Huss a century earlier. Just six months after Luther's official condemnation, and ten days shy of his own forty-sixth birthday, Leo was called to account by the true Judge and King of all.

churchfail: Leo was a true Renaissance Man, but he was religiously clueless. In the jungle, the theological jungle, this Leo slept alright. He could not fathom why anyone would object to his papal plans. A more theologically aware person could have understood the true scope of Luther's concerns and might have acted more wisely.

Application: People of power and prominence can be presented with positions in the church because of their business prowess or financial influence. Sometimes such leaders are helpful and wise, sometimes not. Some power-hungry people view the church as a means of gaining prominence and prestige. They want the perks without actually being a proper pastor. The proverb about pride and a plummet should be heeded. Also, those whose responsibility it is to search for God-called leaders with adequate insight need to grasp the gravity of their assignment.

L.H.

Johann Maier von Eck

Dates: 1486–1543

Synopsis: Johann Maier, commonly known by the town where he grew up, Eck, was a brilliant scholar and debater and could maneuver any situation to his advantage. In debating Martin Luther he relied on his natural talents rather than on preparation. As a result, he talked himself into a corner.

Biography: Johann Maier was born November 15, 1486, just three years and five days after Martin Luther. His Uncle Martin, the pastor at Rothenburg am Neckar (where Anabaptist Michael Sattler would be brutally executed in 1527), took in the lad to begin his education. Johnny entered Heidelberg University when he was 12 and received his Master's degree at 15. It's amazing what can be accomplished without video games. By the time he reached the age of 24, John had earned his Doctor of Theology, had been ordained to the priesthood (he needed papal permission because of his youth), had joined the faculty at Ingolstadt, Germany, and had taken the name Johann Eck. He had studied Latin, Hebrew, Greek, law, physics, math, and geography and wrote books on science, philosophy, and theology. What a slouch.

Two hundred fifty miles to the north, a backwater Augustinian monk was causing a stir. The Incomparable Instructor of Ingolstadt would soon be on a collision course with the Wunderkind of Wittenberg, Martin Luther. By 1518 the hotshot theologians were in a running battle of words. This led to an academic showdown. Theological debate. High noon. At Leipzig. June 27, 1519. Leipzig favored Eck: it was staunchly loyal to the pope and not likely to be lured by Luther's newfangled notions.

The undercard event was Eck versus Andreas Karlstadt, Luther's colleague. They agreed to use the German method of debate

Johann Maier von Eck

in which each person would speak for a set amount of time, then the other would respond. Karlstadt relied heavily on his notes and was scoring points. Eck changed the rules in the middle of the game. "Did I say *German?* I meant *Italian.*" They would now use the Italian method of debate where they could interrupt each other and no books or resources were allowed. This was Eck's clear strength. He had a sharp mind, excellent memory, and was quick on his feet. Half-truths, innuendo, and sarcasm turned the tables in his favor.

Round two featured Eck and Luther. Eck was supremely confident that he could beat Luther to a theological pulp. The issue was the authority of the pope. Eck defended the pope as the Vicar of Christ. Luther responded that Jesus is the head of the church, not Peter or the pope. Eck landed a few jabs by quoting documents asserting the pope's prominent place. Luther countered by proving the documents to be fake. After several rounds it became clear that Luther's ability to quote large passages of Scripture from memory had exposed Eck's weakness because he could not. Realizing that he was in trouble, Eck tried to smear Luther by claiming Luther's views were just like the condemned heretic, John Huss. After reviewing Huss's works, Luther noted that some of Huss's views were, in fact, biblical. Guilt by association led Eck to claim victory on points, but it was clear that Luther outmatched him. Eck even apologized later for not being as prepared as he should have been.

churchfail: Natural talent is a God-given blessing. Eck trusted his talent while Luther memorized Scripture.

Application: Reading and memorizing Scripture will help anyone see the world through God's eyes and be a ready resource in dealing with the challenges of life.

L.H.

Zwickau Prophets

Date: 1522

Synopsis: Three prophets fanned the flames of Reformation too much, too soon.

Setting—Zwickau: The city of Zwickau, Germany, was an industrial town with a high population of weavers. A council of fat-cat merchant employers ruled the city, so labor riots broke out from time to time. Most of the weavers went to one church, St. Catherine's. In 1520 their pastor, Thomas Müntzer, along with weaver Nicholas Storch and scholar Marcus Stübner, developed some notions that were unorthodox for their day. Their ideas irked the elite, so they were kicked out of the city. Müntzer left for Prague, but Storch, Stübner, and their friend Thomas Drechsel heard about a new thing in Wittenberg called the "Reformation," so they crashed that party.

churchfail: These "Zwickau Prophets" held to some strange beliefs—very foreign to Catholics and too far in left field for their new Protestant friends.

1. They took the Lutheran emphasis on the priesthood of all believers to the point of anarchy. This spilled over into disliking all who held positions of authority in the church or state.
2. They claimed they had the Holy Spirit on speed-dial, which not only helped them properly interpret the Bible but also superseded its authority. This undercut any need for a formal education or church authority to tell them what Scripture really means.
3. They believed that the end was near. Jesus's imminent return would result in the death of all those priests who didn't get with the program, and a communitarian kingdom of God would replace all current political structures.
4. They preached against infant baptism and other "pointless rituals" through which, according to the Catholic Church, grace was conveyed.

In 2 and 3 they echoed Montanus (p. 210). In 1 and 4 they prefigured the Anabaptists.

Setting—Wittenberg: Kicked out of Zwickau, they took their show on the road and wound up in Wittenberg two days after Christmas, 1521. With Luther on the lam in Wartburg, Phillip Melancthon and Andreas Karlstadt were supervising the Reformation. They had already broken with the long-standing tradition of holding back the wine from the lay people during communion ("bottoms up!"), but now Karlstadt started preaching in casual Friday clothes (but no skinny jeans) instead of robes. Scandalous! When the Zwickau Prophets came to town, they contributed to the chaos. Karlstadt was a big fan of their zeal and led a movement of students and townspeople to rid the church of all its Catholic images, pictures, and crucifixes—anything that seemed to become an object of worship. They even prohibited music in church. With the Zwickau Prophets providing direct messages from the Holy Spirit, the town believed they had God on their side. Any priest who impeded iconoclasm was pelted with stones, mud, or even dung.

Iconoclasm

This was not the type or pace of reformation Luther had in mind! Hearing about all the chaos in Wittenberg, he reappeared from hiding, re-donned his monk's robe, and returned to the hood. Luther proclaimed, "Give me time. . . . Don't suppose that abuses are eliminated by destroying the object that's abused. Men can go wrong with wine and women; shall we then prohibit wine and abolish women? The sun, moon, and stars have been worshiped; shall we then pluck them out of the sky?" Altogether Luther preached eight fiery sermons against the riots.

The Zwickau Prophets requested a private meeting with Luther. They bet him they could read his mind. Seemed fair enough, but when they actually succeeded, Luther claimed their power was from the Devil and kicked them out of town—and booted Karlstadt as well.

Application: The doctrines of the Zwickau prophets do not sound that heretical—believer's baptism, the priesthood of believers, a separation of church and state, guidance from the Holy Spirit, and the imminent return of Jesus. However, these things along with the violence-induced reform efforts were too much, too fast for Wittenberg. Luther's Reformation required the backing of the state, so social and political rebels were not welcome. Historians have often noted that one form of tyranny often replaces another.

Karlstadt would later refer to Luther as the "Wittenberg Pope" because of his stern measures. We should credit Luther with this though: genuine reformation does not need to be forced. If the reforms are good and true, God's people will be convinced of them as the Spirit leads in God's own time and manner.

K.C.

Erasmus

Date: 1524

Synopsis: Erasmus was the prince of the humanists. His printed works in the 1530s accounted for 15 percent of all book sales in Europe, and his 1516 Greek/Latin New Testament was the basis for Martin Luther's German translation of the Bible as well as William Tyndale's English translation. Some acrimonious monks claimed that Erasmus laid the egg that started the Protestant Reformation and Luther hatched it; Erasmus countered that Martin hatched a different bird entirely.

Biography: Desiderius Erasmus (1466–1536) was born in Rotterdam, Holland, like a little cheese ball to a priest from Gouda named Roger Gerard and a physician's daughter named Margaretha. Though unmarried, the two loved Erasmus and his brother Peter until they perished from the plague in 1483. The brothers were boarded off to the best Latin school in the Netherlands, which was also the first pre-university school to offer Greek. A failure of funds forced the fledgling scholar to enter the priesthood in 1492, and he was ordained but never regularly practiced it. His normal rational temperament was derailed at Stein when he was passionately enchanted with another young canon and wrote several juicy letters to his heartthrob. Although nothing came of it, Erasmus later covered himself carefully by denouncing sodomy and praising sexual desire between husbands and wives.

Erasmus's superior Latin skills earned a temporary dispensation from his vows to serve as secretary to the bishop of Cambrai. Pope Leo X made the dispensation permanent because the Vatican needed some brighter bulbs working for St. Peter. In 1495 the bishop blessed his boy with tuition funds to attend the University of Paris, that bastion of Scholasticism and soon-to-be epicenter of Renaissance Humanism. Four years later, Erasmus accepted the invitation of the charming, young, handsome, and well-heeled (Do we see a pattern?) Baron William Blount to come to England, where the Dutch import became the first professor of Greek at Cambridge. Though he stayed from 1510 to 1515, Erasmus constantly complained of the weather and the wine, the latter doing nothing to relieve his gallstones. So he left the Thames for the Seine and better medicinal Madeira and to produce a new edition of Jerome's dusty Latin Vulgate.

Desiderius Erasmus

The Dutchman's revision of the Vulgate became a Greek and Latin side-by-side New Testament with textual notes. One of the footnotes may have started the Protestant Reformation, when he explained that Jerome had mistranslated the Greek word for "repentance" as "penance." When Luther got to that footnote, he burst out, "I love this guy!"—in German of course.

Erasmus had a habit of collecting proverbs from any of the multitude of works he read or consulted, and when he published them in the *Adagio* ("Adages"), first in 1500 and repeatedly through the years, he became a made man in the Western world. Desiderius received many prestigious invitations from royalty and universities to teach, but he preferred the posture of itinerant scholar—though it brought in less, it also had fewer intellectual restrictions for study and writing. When Wittenberg and Rome split, both sides wanted Erasmus as their intellectual cannon, but he saw himself as a preacher of righteousness and not of dissent, and he valued the ancient doctrines and wisdom of the Church too much to ever leave the shadows of St. Peter's. When he died of a sudden bout of dysentery in 1536 in his beloved Basel, he received a magnificent funeral service in the cathedral, though he did not receive the last rites from the Church.

churchfail: Erasmus abhorred violence, although he did commit drive-by satire. He avoided getting into the doctrinal dueling that broke out between Luther and the pope after 1517. He did get dragged into a dispute with Martin himself over the freedom of the will. Luther saw humanity so deeply in bondage to sin that free will was a farce with none seeking after God; rather, He is the Seeker and Saver of sinners. Erasmus did not see depravity so seriously and took the medieval Catholic approach of human effort cooperating with grace to bring salvation through sanctifying works. He so believed in reason and research that he presubscribed to Enlightenment optimism about human effort, despite the obviously corrupt kings and cardinals that he had so often made the subject of his scathing wit.

Application: Scholarship in the service of the gospel is a high and hard calling that needs to be well nurtured if the scholar is to walk worthy of said call.

R.D.

Münster Rebellion

Date: 1534

Synopsis: A gang of zealous Radical Reformers took over the town of Münster and imposed martial law while waiting for Jesus to return.

Setting: During the early years of the Protestant Reformation, certain Christians wished to pursue their beliefs without the help or approval of the state. These "Radical" Reformers were generally termed "Anabaptists" and lumped into one subversive category because they generally opposed the practice of baptizing babies. However, in those days baptism was not just a religious rite, it was also the official way in which people became citizens of the state. To stand against sprinkling your suckling, therefore, was seen as open rebellion against the established church-state. Opponents misrepresented Anabaptists' beliefs and actions to such an extent that eventually Anabaptists were not just insulted, they were punished and even executed.

For the most part, Anabaptists sought to live peacefully and work hard to share with others in need. However, there was one exception to this peaceful tendency that their opponents would always use against them.

churchfail: The Magisterial Reformation moved slowly and methodically—waiting for the approval of the state in everything. Sometimes the Radical Reformation lacked this patience. Such was the case with a young, fiery Dutchman by the name of Jan Matthys. He tried to help Jesus come back sooner by creating a communitarian state on earth to usher in the New Jerusalem. He sent out twelve apostles (sound familiar?) throughout the Netherlands to preach this good news.

Execution of the Leaders

In 1533 one of those apostles, John of Leyden, went down to the north German town of Münster, where he found an energetic audience among the peasants who were jealous of the political power of their local rulers. The impatient rabble called for help from Matthys, and down came a bunch of Dutch chums to stir the pot. Before long, they were kicking out any opponents of their radical reform and taking over the city by force. The most militaristic among other Anabaptists heard there was a cage fight in Münster, so its population swelled with the most hostile of Radical Reformers. When the burg's bishop hired two thousand troops to suppress the rebellion, the citizens took them on, and much blood was spilled in the streets. Once the Catholics and Magisterial Reformers (aka Protestants) heard about the bloodshed in the city, they sent their armies to lay siege, and the rebellion was in full swing.

The siege lasted about a year and a half. John of Leyden was crowned king, and a "Committee for Public Safety" served as enforcers. During the siege, anyone on either side who was suspected of spying was executed. The besieged city's communitarian ideals mixed with practical survival concerns, so meals, prayers, and property were shared. With so many men having died or abandoned the cause, that wasn't all that was shared. Many women who supported the Anabaptists' cause were content to be somewhat linked to a family as concubines—seeing biblical justification in the Old Testament.

As the siege wore on, King John allowed all who wanted to, to leave the city. Once they left, however, the Catholic and Protestant soldiers promptly executed them. One bad egg who chickened out saved his bacon by telling the soldiers where the wall was weak. On June 24, 1535, the Catholic and Protestant forces broke through, conquered the city, killed everyone they could—quickly or by slow torture—and reestablished Catholic control.

Peasants and Anabaptists across Europe gave their support for the Münster rebellion. Yet, when they were all by default designated among the dissidents, their reaction was to disown those militants by becoming strict pacifists. "Make love, not war!" as their 1970s flower-child counterparts would later exclaim. Anabaptists would remain staunchly pacifistic from this time forward, but they would earn respect as hardworking farmers and deeply pious loners.

Application: The book of Proverbs warns against inactivity on the one hand and foolish zeal on the other. Somewhere between the two extremes, prudent people actively seek the leading of the Holy Spirit as they wait on Jesus to return in His own time. Jesus will come when He is good and ready. He should find us prepared, but not by taking over towns! As God gives us zeal for following Him, let us put it to good use by loving God, telling people about God's love, and showing love to anyone who is in need.

K.C.

churchfails in Modern Times

Wise people learn from their mistakes; they don't repeat them. I seem to make every possible mistake, but generally only once. So, those condemned to repeat history aside, you'd think the church would eventually run out of mistakes. But there seems to be no end to the heresy and hilarity. So when it  comes to creative ways to be wrong, never underestimate the ingenuity of a fool—or the cunning schemes of Uncle Screwtape.

Elias Keach

Dates: 1667–1701

Synopsis: Preachers' kids have a notorious reputation. They often appear prim and proper but are in fact disobedient and defiant. Elias Keach helped reinforce this stereotype. He looked like the former while masking the latter, and the mask of his deception was pulled away in a peculiar way.

Biography: Elias Keach was the son of a preacher man—a prominent preacher man, no less. By the time E. K. left England for the new American colonies in 1686 at age 19, his father, Benjamin Keach, had already enjoyed fame as the author of books on Christian pedagogy, preaching, and poetry. He wrote in defense of believer's baptism by immersion and the laying on of hands for new members. Ben introduced the singing of hymns to English worship, an endeavor that took him 20 years to accomplish. (There was probably a lot of resistance to allowing lutes and sackbuts on the worship team.) He penned two popular allegories, the first preceding *Pilgrim's Progress*. Finally, Ben was the primary author of the *Second London Confession of Faith* (1677, 1689), an influential theological document with a profound impact on Baptist life in America. Hundreds of people came every week to hear him preach. Ben had scores of peers on Ye Olde Facebooke.

Growing up in the shadow of such a prodigious papa would be difficult for anyone. Those shoes seemed even bigger to fill for the one-and-only son of the noted pastor. Elias was the second child born to Ben's first wife. They had three more girls before her death in 1670. Ben remarried two years later and had an additional five children, all daughters. No other boys. No one else to carry on the family name. No pressure at all to follow in Daddy's footsteps. No wonder that 19-year-old Elias left England for the City of *Brotherly* Love.

Benjamin Keach

122

While he left England behind, Elias did not leave his past behind. After he arrived in Philadelphia, he began dressing like a preacher, wearing the clerical garb typical of the day: ministerial frock coat and white preaching bands. It didn't take long before someone discovered that the son of the prominent pulpiteer was in town. The handful of Baptists in the burg wasted no time in asking him to preach. And so it was that Elias Keach met with the gathered faithful to proclaim the Word of God. The service started well, but in the midst of his message, Elias stopped with an expression "like a man astonished." You see, when the congregation asked Elias to preach, they neglected to ask if he was a Christian. In fact, Elias was far from being a pious preacher, he just looked the part. He was actually in rebellion against both fathers—terrestrial and celestial. He had hoped to acquire a quick quid by preaching the things he remembered hearing his old man say. But the joke was on him: Elias Keach was converted under his own preaching!

Over the next two years, Elias helped organize the Lower Dublin or Pennepek Baptist Church (also known as Pennepack or Pennypack—seems the Lower Dubliners couldn't decide how to spell it). This congregation started dozens of other congregations, making Philly the original buckle of the Bible Belt. Returning to London in 1692, Elias founded a new congregation, baptizing some 130 people in a nine-month period. At the ripe old age of 34, Elias Keach died after a short illness. His famous father died three years later.

churchfail: Keach was guilty of hubris rather than heresy. He thought he could play the part of a preacher, proclaiming a redemption he did not have in order to make an easy buck—imagining that fake faith is a way to material gain. God does not play with eternity, and He turned the deception back on the deceiver—which was great gain indeed!

You can also look at the Baptists in Philly as failures. They did not check to see whether their supposed shepherd was really a wooly wolf.

Application: Abraham Lincoln is credited with saying that you can fool all of the people some of the time. That includes fooling yourself. Keach discovered that God will even use words of truth meant for deception to transform a life (see Phil 1:15-18). The power is in God's Word as illuminated by the Holy Spirit, not the eloquence or art of the speaker. So be careful little mouth what you say. The words you utter may catch you by surprise.

L.H.

Matthew Caffyn

Dates: 1628–1714

Synopsis: Some people are their own worst enemies. This can especially be true for people who are really smart, or who think they are. Matthew Caffyn was one of those people. He tried to figure out the doctrine of the Trinity, and when that endeavor failed, he gave up the doctrine altogether.

Biography: Matthew Caffyn was born on October 26, 1628, to a small landholding farm family in Horsham, in the southern English county of Sussex. About age seven, a neighbor recognized Caffyn's potential and supported the upwardly mobile urchin's education. Being the seventh son born into his family, this outside support was welcomed. Caffyn accompanied the neighbor's son to grammar school in Kent, and in 1643, at age 15, he went to All Souls College in Oxford to prepare for caring for souls in the ministry. Young Matthew spent considerable time plumbing the depths of spiritual mysteries and pondering the impenetrable. During the course of his studies, the questioning collegiate found himself in a quandary. Master Matthew came to doubt infant baptism and the doctrine of the Trinity (one God existing as three co-equal persons). As the civil war raged between King Charles I and Parliament, faith battled doubt in Caffyn's cranium. In the end, the selective 17-year-old scholar was given the boot by the college and returned home to farm.

The General Baptists in England believed that Jesus died on the cross for all sinners in "general"; their counterparts would be the Reformed or Particular Baptists. The small General Baptist congregation in Horsham asked Caffyn to preach. He was soon preaching throughout the county. Because he owned land, had some college education, and possessed a sharp mind, Caffyn exerted considerable influence

Billingshurst Unitarian Church, Horsham, Formerly General Baptist

over churches in the region. By the time he was 25, he served as a denominational leader among General Baptists.

Caffyn contended with the quirky Quakers in friendly dialogue. William Penn, who later founded Pennsylvania, grew up in the area. During the Restoration, aka the Return of the King, state authorities sent Caffyn to jail five times for preaching outside the state church during the reigns of Charles II and James II.

His inquiring mind needed to know the answers to questions that have confounded clerics throughout the ages. One observer noted, Caffyn "began to puzzle himself with endeavouring to explain inexplicables."[10] When the Trinity transcended his understanding, he decided the fallacy could not be in his figuring; the doctrine must not be true. Next, he tried to comprehend and defend Jesus's divinity by claiming that He did not receive His human body from Mary. This undercut Jesus's humanity. He later capitulated on Jesus's divinity as well.

Several detractors attempted to de-Caffynate the group, pointing out his errors. Caffyn shrewdly convinced his challengers that only Bible words could be used in discussing theology. Since the word *trinity* is not found in the Bible (although the concept clearly is) the term was not allowed in debating Caffyn's dubious dictates. While his objectors were thus obstructed, his inconsistent ideas percolated throughout southern England.

Caffyn died on June 10, 1714, at the ripe old age of 85. Five years later, the views he had spread would split Baptists, Presbyterians, and Congregationalists into those supporting the doctrine of the Trinity and those who had become Unitarians.

churchfail: Caffyn was young and smart, and his talents and circumstances thrust his theological thinking into prominence. Failing to fathom the Father's familiar connection with the Son and the Spirit, he concluded that the teaching of a millennium and a half was lacking. He failed to consider that he might be the one at fault.

Application: Intelligence does not automatically translate into wisdom. And even wisdom, once gained, can be lost. Solomon is considered the wisest man to have ever lived. And yet, he had 700 wives and 300 concubines. Who in their right mind wants one thousand mothers-in-law?!

One of the challenges really smart people face is the temptation to believe their own press releases. They assume God must have made them smart for a particular reason. That reason must be to fathom the foundations of faith and to explain the inscrutable. When that fails, they deduce the error must be with the doctrine, not the doubter.

Haughty arrogance regarding one's own abilities leads to one's downfall. Humility protects us from confusing our place as God's creation with being the creative God.

L.H.

---

[10] H. Leon McBeth, *The Baptist Heritage: Four Centuries of Baptist Witness* (Nashville: Broadman, 1987), 156.

John Gill

John Gill

Dates: 1696–1771

Synopsis: John Gill was an influential Particular Baptist—an adept student and staunch defender of orthodox theology. However, he took his understanding of God's sovereignty to such an extent that he omitted a key component of the gospel.

Biography: John Gill was born on November 23, 1697, to founding members of the Kettering Baptist Church. (Eighty-five years later, this church would be served by Andrew Fuller, a founder of the Baptist Missionary Society.) Gill was a bright student in the local grammar school. He spent hours in the local booksell-er's shop, reading a wide variety of authors and subjects—but maybe missed Isaac Walton's *The Compleat Angler*. His formal schooling ended at age 11 when attendance at Anglican services became a requirement for all students, including those from homes of Dissenters. However, by that time, he had already learned Latin and Greek.

Saved at age 12, Gill waited—because of his young age—to be baptized until he was 18. Soon after, he was asked to preach in the area, impressing his hearers with his insight and piety. After the untimely death of Benjamin Stinton, shepherd of the con-gregation founded by Benjamin Keach, the grieving fellowship invited Gill to be their pastor. His youth was both attractive and a concern. The congregation voted to reel the young man in, in spite of opposition of all the deacons. Perhaps the deacons knew something the others overlooked, for as soon as he arrived, the church split.

Gill's move to London came hard on the heels of the meetings at Salters' Hall in 1719—a gathering of Baptists, Presbyterians, and Congregationalists (Puritans) to discuss the doctrine of the Trinity. In the end, the Trinity fell four votes short. Though swimming upstream, Gill proved himself a staunch defender of this fundamental doctrine of the faith. He was also an able backer of believer's baptism by immersion. In addition to his responsibilities as pastor, he preached regularly at the doctrinal gatherings at Great Eastcheap. He produced an astounding 10,000 pages of theology and became the first person to write a verse-by-verse commentary of the entire Bible in English, his *Exposition of the Old and New Testaments*. In response, the University of Aberdeen conferred a Doctorate in Divinity on him, much to his surprise, since he did not seek the degree. Gill had become a very big fish in an ever-growing pond.

In spite of his increasing stature, there was something fishy about his views. The congregation adhered to a Reformed view of salvation, as had all its pastors. Gill took these views to a new level, contending that since God is sovereign in all things and the elect were chosen from the foundation of the world, no one needed to invite sinners to repent. That was God's job. Evangelism was at best a waste of time since human effort had no impact on God's actions, and was at worst an ill-advised foray into God's business.

After a decade in the pulpit, Gill replaced Keach's confession of faith with his own. Gill gutted all references to faith regarding justification and removed all statements on the necessity of providing a free offer of the gospel. The scales were firmly tilted in favor of sovereignty. By request, he wrote on justification in 1730, arguing that it precedes faith and belief. This meant that before one of the elect even believed in Christ or had saving faith, he was justified before God. By 1752 Gill was not coy; he clearly stated his belief that the Bible did not support a free offer of the gospel, but that it was part of the everlasting covenant of election. Gill preached the need for salvation, but never invited his hearers to accept it. Charles Spurgeon would later lament that Gill's theology "chilled many churches to their very soul, for it has led them to omit the free invitation of the gospel, and to deny that it is the duty of sinners to believe in Jesus."[11]

churchfail: At Pentecost, Peter and the other disciples instructed the crowd to repent and be baptized. Gill was proud of the fact that he never invited sinners to repent. But in order to fill a boat, the fisherman must cast his net into the water and haul it in.

Application: We get into trouble when truth is out of balance. Taking our understanding of God's sovereignty to an illogical extreme negatively impacts the kingdom.

L.H.

---

[11] *The Autobiography of Charles H. Spurgeon* (Chicago: Fleming H. Revell, 1898), 1:310.

Congregationalists vs. Mrs. Backus

Isaac Backus

Date: October 15, 1752

Synopsis: The authorities of Massachusetts Bay, where the Congregationalist church was united with the state, arrested an elderly widow for refusing to pay her church taxes. Epic PR fail!

History: In 1629 the Massachusetts Bay Colony received a charter that granted self-government in New England. For the Puritans, this was a godsend. After suffering persecution from the Church of England, they could now enjoy religious liberty, but only for themselves—not Anglicans, Presbyterians, Catholics, Quakers, or those upstart Baptists! The persecuted became the persecutors!

The Puritans established Congregationalism as the state church. Even worse, in 1718 Massachusetts Bay imposed a tax on every family in order to pay the salaries of Congregationalists. In other words, they taxed Baptists to support Congregationalist pastors. Baptists complained, "Taxation without representation!" Thirty years later, most colonists would take up this cry against England. (Three hundred years later, we've figured out that taxation *with* representation is no picnic either!)

Enter Isaac Backus and his widowed mother Elizabeth. They were among thousands of Congregationalists impacted by George Whitefield and the Great Awakening. These revived Congregationalists considered themselves "New Lights" with a different perspective on sin and grace, conversion and revival. The regular Congregationalists, or "Old Lights," opposed emotional revivalism. For example, Charles Chauncy, aka "Old Brick," pastor of First Church, Boston, once greeted Whitefield, "Sorry to see you back." Whitefield replied, "So is the Devil!"

Isaac and his mother cut ties with their Old Light church and joined a New Light congregation. Isaac was soon ordained as pastor and began his remarkable career as minister and advocate for religious liberty. He pointed out that, according to the Apostle Paul, the church is "a chaste virgin to Christ . . . subject to him in everything, as a true wife is to her husband."[12] But a wife who elevates the magistrate to the place of her husband is a harlot. To Isaac, the union of church and state was prostitution. This pastor called it like he saw it!

It didn't take long for Isaac to get thrown in the pokey for refusing to pay. He was released and threatened with more jail time, but he didn't stop lobbying against unfair taxation. In fact, prison was becoming a respectable pulpit for protesting parsons!

churchfail: Elizabeth actually fared worse than her son for her stubborn refusal to pay the church tax. On a dark and stormy night, October 15, 1752, tax collectors entered her home, finding her ill and wrapped in quilts, sitting by a fire reading her Bible. They hauled her to the hoosegow, where she languished for 13 days. She wrote, "Though I was bound when I was cast into this furnace, yet was I loosed, and found Jesus in the midst of the furnace with me. . . . Now the prison looked like a palace to me. I could bless God for all the laughs and scoffs made at me."[13] The magistrate probably was relieved when she was released!

A letter like this one, written from a mother to a son who was devoted both to her and to religious liberty, was like saying "Sic 'em" to a Rottweiler! Widow Backus's community respected her, and Isaac made sure that her arrest became a public relations fiasco for the Congregationalists and Massachusetts Bay.

Aftermath: Isaac Backus, his mother, and most New Light Congregationalists converted to the Baptist faith. Even before his mother's arrest, Isaac had been baptized as a believer by immersion, and in 1756 he founded the First Baptist Church of Middleboro, Massachusetts.

Baptists in Massachusetts and Rhode Island formed the Warren Association and its Grievance Committee—which functioned like a Political Action Committee—with Backus as their chief lobbyist. The state offered exemption laws for Baptists, but bureaucratic red tape was just as gnarly then as it is now. Furthermore, the exemption fee was just as steep as the tea tax that prompted American revolutionaries to throw the Boston Tea Party. Maybe Backus and other Baptists should have joined the party and dumped some Congregationalist clergymen into Boston Harbor!

Application: Isaac lived to see religious liberty established by the First Amendment. But he died in 1806, long before Massachusetts disestablished the Congregationalist Church in 1833. Antidisestablishmentarianism among Massachusetts Congregationalists proved to be almost as stubborn as Isaac and Elizabeth Backus! Fortunately for the cause of religious liberty, church and state finally divorced.

R.B.

---

[12] *An Appeal to the Public for Religious Liberty* (1773).
[13] H. Leon McBeth, *The Baptist Heritage*, 257–58.

Elijah Craig

Dates: 1743–1808

Synopsis: Elijah Craig lived his life as a Baptist preacher, church planter, and entrepreneur, but his legacy is the invention of bourbon whiskey.

Biography: In 1755 a group of evangelistic Baptists established the Sandy Creek Association in North Carolina. Seventeen years later, this association had planted 42 churches and ordained 125 pastors in a region that spread from the Carolinas, south to Georgia, north to the Potomac River, and westward to the Mississippi River. Church planting when church planting wasn't cool!

One leader of the Sandy Creek movement was Elijah Craig, who was born, saved, and baptized in Virginia. He and his brothers, Lewis and Joseph, became Baptist preachers at a time when the Anglican Church was the state-established church. Elijah was jailed at least twice for preaching without a license. His lawyer warned the court, "The Baptists are like a bed of camomile; the more they are trodden the more they spread."

Indeed, Baptists spread like weeds in spite of—or because of—the persecution of Baptist preachers, who were whipped, fined, beaten by mobs, exiled, and jailed. When in jail, however, they preached through the bars and attracted crowds of listeners much to the embarrassment of the Anglican authorities. In spite of such opposition, Elijah and other Baptists preached to congregations that included freemen and slaves, white and black. They worked with patriots such as Patrick Henry and James Madison to secure religious liberty in Virginia and in the United States.

Eventually, Elijah emigrated to the new territory of Kentucky and became the first pastor of the Great Crossing Baptist Church. A contemporary chronicler wrote that Elijah had a powerful voice for preaching and singing and that he brought many of his hearers to tears and to the Lord.

churchfail: In spite of his popularity and effective ministry, however, his parishioners could not pay him much of a cash salary, so they paid him in corn. It was not cost-effective to send the corn to New Orleans as a cash crop, so he turned it into corn mash. He aged it in charred barrels and thus is credited by some with inventing the process for bourbon whiskey, named for nearby Bourbon County.

Elijah became involved in a number of other entrepreneurial endeavors: land speculation, several mills, and rope works. A contemporary preacher criticized Elijah for vainly imagining that he could serve both God and mammon. Although Elijah continued to preach, his later years were marked by irritability, faultfinding, and conflicts within the local Baptist association.

Elijah Craig

Application: I teach church history at a Baptist seminary, and when two of my students heard the story of Elijah Craig, they decided that I needed a bottle of "Baptist Heritage." So they presented me with a good-sized bottle of Elijah Craig Bourbon Whiskey! When I opened the package, I initially greeted the gift with internal dismay because I despise alcohol, having grown up with an alcoholic, abusive father. But I immediately decided to receive the gift in the spirit in which it was intended—with affection and humor.

But what do I do with a bottle of whiskey on a Baptist seminary campus? Someone suggested that I empty it out and put the bottle on display. Well, I decided that a full, *sealed* bottle of whiskey is better than an empty one!

So I tackled the problem head-on. I took the bottle to faculty prayer meeting, told the whole story of Elijah Craig and my students, and made a devotional application. Elijah Craig lived most of his life preaching the gospel and planting churches, but today his name is attached to bourbon whiskey. The gospel is a life-giving force, but alcohol can be a force that destroys individuals and wounds families. When my life ends, I will leave behind a legacy. My name will be attached to my children and grandchildren, to my students' transcripts, and to any scholarship that I produce (or, in the case of this article, my initials). I pray that my legacy is positive and uplifting to individuals, to families, to churches, and to the kingdom of God.

Postscript: When I delivered this devotional message to the faculty, one of my colleagues snapped a picture of me holding the bottle of whiskey, probably hoping to blackmail me later! In the background, however, is the president of my seminary, and fortunately, he is laughing. My job is secure—at least, for now!

R.B.

Joseph Smith Jr.

Dates: 1805–1844

Synopsis: Joe Junior was a creative, charismatic, and controversial character. Early on, Mr. Smith determined that all existing denominations erred, so he created a new one. He also "discovered" that the Bible contained errors, so he corrected it. He claimed to restore the saints to apostolic authenticity in these latter days, and his followers assert they are Christians, but addition, subtraction, and multiplication led to division.

Biography: Shortly before his death, Joseph Smith Jr. said, "No man knows my history." I imagine he wished that were so. He grew up in the Finger Lakes region of western New York. Due to the profusion of revivals preached there during the Second Great Awakening, people called it the "burned-over district." Pentecostals, Millerites, Quakers, Utopians, and spiritualists abounded. No question the Smith boy was spiritual: among other forms of folk magic, Joe had a white stovepipe hat in which he placed "seer stones," by which he claimed to discover buried treasure. In 1823, after the angel Moroni showed him where some golden plates were hidden, he used similar stones to translate them from "reformed Egyptian" into King James English. And who can argue the sacredness of King James?!

At first, Joseph continued with the treasure hunting while he introduced others to his visions—including one Emma Hale from Pennsylvania who became his (first) wife. Then, after being charged with "glass-looking" in Chenango County, Smith and a couple of his followers baptized each other and started a church. As the church grew, they were harried from New York to Ohio, then to Missouri, and finally to Nauvoo, Illinois. There they founded a communal theocracy in which Mr. Smith was basically "theo" and arguably "cracy." He cobbled together a religion from pieces of Methodism, the Masons, and Melchizedek.

Joseph Smith Jr.

Too bad he couldn't really discover buried treasure. He could have hocked those golden plates in his Ohio period, when he was issuing bank notes to fund his ambitions. He dreamed of restoring Zion in Independence, Missouri, and later he wanted to build a magnificent temple in Nauvoo, Illinois. But his bank went bust.

He eventually included "Jesus Christ" in the name of his church, but rather than turning the other cheek, this founder fought back against anti-Mormon sentiment, with unfortunate upshots. He fled an angry mob in New York. He was tarred and feathered in Ohio. He sparked the Mormon War of 1838 in Missouri. In each of those three states, the locals were satisfied to shuffle him off across state lines. However, when he interfered with the Fourth Estate in Indiana, he crossed the line. When the opposition published a polemic, Smith pulverized their printing press. Illini bear a lot, but don't brook censors. The Mormon militia was numerous and boisterous, but no match for the maddened masses. On June 27, 1844, his fledgling flock acquired a martyr, and the rest is history.

churchfail: Smith espoused plural marriage; "sealings" sustained the glass ceiling. He backed baptism for the dead, proposing you could permute your profane patriarch to piety posthumously. And he adapted the mysterious rites of the Freemasons into secret sacramental ceremonies—Gnosticism redivivus—by which inductees become kings/queens, priests/priestesses, and even gods in the afterlife. (Adam and Babylon already tried that, with unmixed results.) He said his restored rituals were the only genuine form of apostolic Christianity; all other rites were wrong. (Red flag! Red flag!)

He added to the Bible, he subtracted anybody who disagreed with him, and he multiplied wives. After his martyrdom, his flock divided. The majority followed Brigham Young, some (including Mrs. Smith and Joseph III) formed splinter groups, and others just went home. Some of Junior's heresies persist, in other cases various branches backtracked from his beliefs.

Application: The Bible is perfect the way it is, thank you. While there are examples of plural marriage in the Bible, in all cases there were negative repercussions. And there are no special secrets whereby some congregants can gain an edge. There is one gospel; it is perspicuously presented in the Bible. Take it or leave it.

The Old Testament blames the downfall of the northern kingdom of Israel on Jeroboam, who replaced authentic worship of God with a made-up religion. Some of the faithful defected to Judah, where a few priests still faithfully honored Yahweh; those who didn't flee south had only themselves to blame when they were carried away.

Don't get carried away. Eschew Smith's sect.

D.S.

Hong Xiuquan

Dates: 1814–1864

Synopsis: Hong Xiuquan—whose nineteenth-century proclamations that he was the brother of Jesus, a Heavenly King, and also God's Chinese Son, are hard to swallow, just as the syllables of his tongue-numbing moniker are hard for westerners to swallow—was a Southern Chinese quasi-Christian mystic and militaristic revolutionary. In 1851, during China's Opium Wars, ostensibly basing his beliefs and his battles on the King James Bible instead of Confucius, Xiuquan established what he and his followers called a Heavenly Kingdom of Transcendent Peace. What followed—the largest pre-Mao Civil War in world history—might make hell seem preferable.

Biography: Hong Xiuquan (hereafter, Hong, for short) was born on New Year's Day in 1814 in a China ruled by the Manchu Dynasty (imagine a blend of the administrations of U. S. Grant and Warren Harding with equal pinches of Genghis Khan and G. Gordon Liddy). He came from a poor family who had names we westerners find as difficult to pronounce as his—which may be the reason he changed his name from Hong Huoxiu, rather than the popular pretext that he simply abhorred alliterations. A considerably more probable explanation is that a dream about his older brother, i.e., Jesus, led him to think that the Messiah Himself had remonikered him. This would not be the last of his delusions.

In 1836 Hong first heard the gospel from a missionary named Edwin Stevens. By 1837 he had converted and began seeing visions and dreams. Faraway Freud would have convulsed on his couch. In addition to the name change, Hong felt he had a mandate from heaven to rid not only China but also the whole world of demons. He began by burning statues and books of Buddha and Confucius, and then sought swords with which to slay demons—presumably

Hong Xiuquan

corporeal ones. He also opposed tobacco and alcohol (as would Hitler later). In his initial tangential fundamentals, Hong was wrong—a rhyme that would have made a far more mnemonic and accurate second name. But he got worse.

By 1847 Hong began to study the Bible with a Southern Baptist missionary named Issachar Roberts, and he had already begun to create a small cult. Roberts was so suspicious of Hong that he refused to baptize him. Hong's cult comprised the poor and disenfranchised from the Manchu government, and, before long, this "brother of Jesus" led what has come to be known as the Taiping Rebellion, in which casualty estimates range from twenty to fifty million. He preached utopia, but his template differed a bit from the method poor Christians in Acts chose to address social issues.

In the end, the Taiping Rebellion and Hong's Heavenly Kingdom failed after a decade or so of combat, not with a dream-induced Devil himself but with a superhuman American mercenary named Frederick Townsend Ward, whose fascinating biography is ironically entitled *The Devil Soldier*. Though killed in battle with the Taipings, Ward was succeeded by Charles George Gordon, aka "Chinese Gordon," an evangelical Christian, who trumped the Taipings and then moved on to Palestine. (There he lent his name to an alternative site for the crucifixion called Gordon's Golgotha and Gordon's Garden Tomb—all before he went to work for genocidal Leopold II in the Belgian Congo.) Some say that Hong himself died from eating manna, perhaps the kind cooked up by a knucklehead named Nels Ferré, featured elsewhere in this compendium (p. 170).

churchfail: Hong's heresies were self-authenticating. But to belabor just one of them, Hong seems to have misunderstood his mandate from heaven. He opted for the destruction of demons instead of the far more important mandate to make disciples of all nations.

Application: Far from destroying demons, it could easily be argued that Hong's heresies turned them loose with a vengeance. Mao Zedong, who both rhymed with and reasoned like Hong, worshiped Hong as a revolutionary. Ironically, the Manchus whom Hong opposed would later let a Methodist named Charlie Soong—a Duke and Vanderbilt student—into China to sell Bibles. Soong then became the father-in-law of Sun Yat-sen and Chiang Kai-shek, who both mauled the Manchus. Chiang later lost China—and Southern Baptist-rooted missionary/spy, John Birch—to Mao. Hong's misplaced priorities prove the old adage that "once you are riding a tiger's back, it is difficult to dismount." His bizarre doctrines took him further than he intended to go.

J.L.

Mary Baker Glover Patterson Eddy

Mary Baker Eddy

Dates: 1821–1910

Synopsis: Mary ... Eddy (hereafter MBGPE) was a chronically ill and intermittently ingenious woman who became an author and lecturer, the founder of a sizable and influential denomination known as Christian Science (which some have observed is neither Christian nor scientific), and a publisher. While her second of three husbands played fast and free with other women, MBGPE played fast and free with words like "healing," which in her employ had almost infinite elasticity.

Biography: MBGPE was born in Bow, New Hampshire, where as a young girl she became disenchanted with Congregationalism and Calvinism, and near where as an older girl she became enchanted with Spiritualism and séances. Which of these had the worse effect is difficult to divine, but the latter is far more entertaining—if her resume is accurate that she channeled up folks from the apostles to Abraham Lincoln.

The primary product and export of New England in the days of MBGPE were ideas. These were the days of Ralph Waldo Emerson, Henry David Thoreau, William James, and Margaret Fuller for good measure. But they were the days not only of transcendentalism and pragmatism but also of mesmerism, hypnotism, British Israelism, Shakerism, Hinduism, Buddhism, Eastern Mysticism, and something called Quimbyism, concerning the last of which some have charged prophetess MBGPE with plagiarism. At the very least, MBGPE drank deeply from all these isms and a whole lot more.

Just how deeply she drank from biblical wells rather than bizarre wells like these is an open and disturbing question. She read Jonathan Edwards's *Treatise on Religious Affections* and no doubt other such works. In her reaction against the theology of her childhood, however, she wrote in her autobiography that circa 1866 she had withdrawn from society for three years in order to search the Scriptures and meditate. Her worthy but questionable goal was the attainment of the primitive purity of the church, something virginal. Commenting on the success of her aspiration, H. L. Mencken opined,

The peculiar mixture of vapors and sagacities which marked Mrs. Eddy's sayings and doings from end to end of her long life showed few of the characters of the virginal mind. Rather it would be more plausible (without throwing the slightest doubt upon her virtue) to compare her peculiar wisdom to that of an ancient bordello-keeper, for in it a sharp sense of reality and a weakness for the occult were curiously mingled. She was seldom if ever taken in by concrete human beings, but there was never a time when she did not believe quite incredible things about the powers and the principalities of the air.[14]

MBGPE's special focus was on healing. Notwithstanding mountainous evidence to the contrary, she came to believe that she had the power to heal à la Jesus. Bewilderingly, others came to the same conclusion, which eventually resulted in the publication of her book, *Science and Health*, in 1875, and in the building of First Church of Christ, Scientist, in Boston 20 years later. To these material entities, she and her deluded disciples—who rejected the reality of matter (and presumably mortar)—added real reading rooms around the world. Perhaps MBGPE's greatest distinction, however, was subtly but clearly disproving Darwin and his doctrine of the survival of the fittest, she being anything but fit.

In addition to Mencken, several other notable Americans weighed in on MBGPE. Among them were Willa Cather, who launched her stellar career with a biography of MBGPE that she later disowned, and Mark Twain, who died the same year as this feminine founder of a faux faith. Twain called her "the most interesting woman that ever lived, and the most extraordinary."[15]

Then, quite correctly addressing the cacophonous concoction of intellectual ingredients that formed her views, Connecticut's comedic "Comet Clemens" called her new religion "a sawdust-mine when she got it, [but] she has turned it into a Klondike."[16]

churchfail: MBGPE had perhaps as many heresies as she had views. Her primary focus on physical health rather than eternal life just might be the father—or mother—of all the rest.

Application: MBGPE's heresies seemed to intensify and magnify when she withdrew from society to find answers on her own without the context of a church that, though having doctrinal difficulties of its own, is still the pillar and ground of the truth. The gathered church and the communion of the saints matter, and it is for very good reason that neither she nor we should forsake assembling together.

J.L.

---

[14] *H. L. Mencken on Religion* (Amherst, NY: Prometheus, 2002), 150.
[15] The Writings of Mark Twain, vol. 25 (New York: Harper & Bros., 1907), 102.
[16] Ibid., 78.

Julius Wellhausen

Dates: 1844–1918

Synopsis: Julius Wellhausen arguably should not be credited for convincing a generation of religious scholars that the worship of Yahweh, the God of Israel, did not have its genesis in Genesis, or for his legacy of undermining belief in the inspiration of the Old Testament. It was, after all, the trustees and faculty at Göttingen and Greifswald who hired a secular scholar to a sacred station.

Biography: Wellhausen was born May 17, 1844, in Hamelin, Germany, 560 years after the Pied Piper rid that hamlet of rats and rug rats. The son of a Protestant pastor, Julius studied theology at Göttingen under Georg Ewald and then taught Old Testament history there. In 1872 he began teaching theology at Greifswald but resigned after ten years due to his conscience. He said he was interested in the scientific treatment of the Bible, and he gradually realized that such an approach left his students unsuited for spiritual service.

churchfail: Hey, Julius, don't get me wrong. I praise you for packing it in when your principles pricked you. I just wonder how you—and the seminary's stewards—could have missed for ten years the obvious observation that a teacher of theology should believe in God and that a Protestant pedagogue of the sacred Scripture should esteem it solemnly rather than scientifically.

Wellhausen didn't invent the documentary hypothesis; ironically, he cobbled it together from a number of earlier sources. His legacy was to express it in a form that, for a century, critical scholars accepted as gospel.

The hypothesis starts with skepticism about authorship. For years Christians accepted Jesus's implication (Matt 8:4) that Moses wrote the Pentateuch (Genesis through Deuteronomy). There are admittedly a few phrases that must be excepted, such as the notice of Moses's death (Deut 34:5-12). Rather than seeing these as additions to what Moses had written—incorporated by a compiler who was inspired by the Holy Spirit—Julius used them as an excuse to dismiss Mosaic authorship outright.

Instead, he contended that initially there were two documents that allowed willy-nilly worship, one that referred to God as Yahweh (*Jahweh* in German: J) and the other that called God *Elohim* (E). In Josiah's day an editor who promoted centralized worship added the book of Deuteronomy (D) and wrote a revisionist history of

Julius Wellhausen

Israel to make it look like that had always been God's intention. Likewise, during the exile some priests (P) went in and made it look like God had always meant for priests to be in power and well paid. The four sources, JEDP, became shorthand for the hypothesis.

Devised in Darwin's milieu, Wellhausen's hypothesis assumed an evolutionary view of religion. Nineteenth-century German theologians contended that just as men evolved from apes, Jewish worship evolved from lower forms: from superstition to pantheism to polytheism to monotheism, and from free family worship to centralized civil worship to superintended sacerdotal worship. Wellhausen's school rejected the idea that one God created all humanity and revealed His will to mankind. Rather, people created God and worked out how to worship Him. As beliefs changed, the Bible evolved too; accretions and amendments reflected new ideas.

It can't be denied that biblical authors made use of existing works. Second Samuel quotes from the Book of Jashar (1:18), and Luke said that he organized what had been handed down from eyewitnesses (1:1-3). Couldn't editorial selection be part of the process of the inspiration of Scripture? But proponents of the documentary hypothesis can see only the secular aspect of employing source material. They claim that the Pentateuch is a mash-up of multifarious material; the sources were misused and the editors were incompetent. For some reason, they reject the possibility that the Holy Spirit could lead an author to incorporate previous oral and written sources into a coherent report of actual, factual history.

For ten years Julius Wellhausen taught this scriptural skepticism and doctrinal Darwinism at a Christian seminary.

Application: The Bible is the revealed Word of God. It accurately reports how the portal to paradise was shut and how God opened it again through Abraham and Moses and Israel and, ultimately, through Jesus. This is the spiritual substance of Scripture.

Anyone merely interested in the scientific study of the Bible should not be employed in the sacred trust of preparing men for ministry. While good scholarship is commendable, adherence to fundamentals is fundamental. Trustees are entrusted to see to it, and congregations are compelled to oversee the trustees.

D.S.

Samuel Porter Jones

Dates: 1847–1906

Synopsis: Samuel Porter Jones was and still is far better known as simply Sam Jones. He was a Southern Methodist revivalist and author of several books full of his sizzling sermons. One of them is entitled *Hot Shots* and another is *Thunderbolts*. If he had been a pagan, he would have given Zeus or some other angry Greek god a run for his drachmas. Though very much unlike Dwight L. Moody, Jones has been called "the Moody of the South" because of the widespread success of his evangelistic endeavors and his influence on Billy Sunday, Billy Graham, Bob Jones (no relation), and James B. Duke. For his part, Duke built a university as a tribute to any Methodist revivalists like Sam Jones who revivaled Durham, North Carolina, on their sawdust trails.

Biography: Sam Jones was born into an Alabama home full of preaching relatives. Before becoming a preacher himself, Sam worked at several odd jobs and then settled down into the legal profession. He also settled down into hard liquor, which besides the Lord would be one of the two "L" words that would characterize the rest of his life. His sermons were largely 200 proof—or higher.

Sam had no formal ministerial training to equip him for the vocation to which he felt called. His qualification for ministry was based primarily on his simple testimony that the God of his fathers had saved him. Dramatically. At his father's deathbed, where he promised to abandon alcohol for the rest of his life. And on the basis of that promise (which he appeared to keep) he built a preaching ministry that covered the South and the Southwest. Sam became Billy Graham before Billy Graham became Billy Graham, even preaching in Charlotte a quarter of a century BB (Before Billy).

Like the later Graham, Sam drew large crowds wherever he went on the gospel warpath, from Wilmington to Waco. In Nashville, Tennessee, he was so well received that a riverboat captain named Tom Ryman built a magnificent auditorium for him to preach in. Originally named the Union Gospel Tabernacle, it was eventually renamed in honor of its donor, though its appealing historic stones still preach the gospel to those curious enough to explore the origins of what became the home of the Grand Ole Opry.

Sam's reception in Waco was not as warm. There he met with a counterattack in *The Iconoclast*, a publication edited by William Cowper Brann, who was even more sensational as a journalist than Jones was for Jesus. Brann, who was H. L. Mencken before

H. L. Mencken was H. L. Mencken, is still read today, while Jones is virtually forgotten. Both men boasted that their mission was to expose hypocrisy, and Brann found the perfect foil in the famed preacher. Brann called Jones "a peripatetic blatherskite whose preaching was eleven-sevenths slang."[17] So far no record has been found of Sam verbally boxing Brann back.

Samuel Porter Jones

Sam died in the saddle after preaching in Oklahoma. His funeral was conducted in Atlanta, Georgia, in its then-famous Baptist Tabernacle. Among his eulogists was the equally famous and sensational Congressman and Populist presidential candidate, Tom Watson, whose memory C. Vann Woodard has kept alive (though Woodard overlooked Watson's eulogy). Interestingly, Brann had no time for Watson either, calling him an "intolerant and narrow-brained blatherskite" and a "hatchet-faced, splenetic-hearted, narrow-headed little hypocrite" from Gooberdom [i.e., Georgia] whose "editorials are used only to underlay carpets, paper pantries and for purposes less polite."[18] Watson called Sam Jones "the greatest Georgian this generation has known, the greatest, in some respects, that any generation has known." Today Sam is largely absent from Georgia history textbooks.

churchfail: Though orthodox enough to be licensed by the North Georgia Methodist Episcopal Church South, Sam's sermons sometimes gave an uncertain sound. Taken by themselves, without any additional context, it is sometimes difficult to tell if Sam preached that personal reformation was the way to heaven or whether it was by way of the cross. While Sam no doubt loved the Lord, he seemed to preach more about liquor and its evils than about the new birth on which Billy Graham would later dwell. In addition, Jones adopted the racism of his Southern neighbors, frequently using forbidden words to punctuate his politically incorrect points.

Application: It is a good and useful rhetorical device to allow salt to savor your gospel language, but it is not a good practice to let the salt trump the clarity of the fundamental message of grace through faith.

J.L.

---

[17] *The Complete Works of Brann: The Iconoclast* (New York: Brann Publishers, 1896), 4:298.

[18] Ibid., 10:195–98.

John Alexander Dowie

Dates: 1847–1907

Synopsis: John Alexander Dowie was a Congregational pastor, an itinerant free-lance evangelist who focused on divine healing and the restoration of Christianity to its original condition, a world traveler, an author, a publisher of an influential periodical titled *Leaves of Healing*, a savvy real estate developer of Zion, Illinois, and a certifiable quack. He was equal parts Mary Baker Eddy, Joseph Smith, and Father Divine with proleptic pinches of Jim Bakker, Oral Roberts, Benny Hinn, and Pat Robertson thrown in for precise measurement.

Biography: Dowie was born in Edinburgh, Scotland. At the age of seven he experienced what appears to have been an evangelical conversion. At 14 he moved to Australia with his parents and, at 21, returned to Scotland for three years of college. He then traveled back to Australia where he was ordained and called to a prestigious pulpit in a suburb of Sydney. At 31 he left the formal ministry and began to focus on divine healing as the centerpiece of his vocation. Encouraged by some success, he began to think globally. He embarked for England in 1888 by way of the United States, which he never left.

Landing first in San Francisco, Dowie peddled his dubious doctrines up and down the Pacific coast and then moved to Chicago in 1890. Capitalizing on the 1893 World's Fair in that fair city, with his tabernacle strategically placed at the entrance to it, Dowie's efforts began to pay dividends in terms of people and profits.

In 1899, dressed as a tramp, Dowie bought 6,500 acres on Lake Michigan halfway between Milwaukee and Chicago. While author Erik Larson has fingered Dr. H. H. Holmes as "The Devil in the White City" of Chicago in 1893, the damsel-dissecting "doctor" was no match for Dowie, who eventually ruined far more lives with a Ponzi scheme designed to build his

John Alexander Dowie

utopian city called Zion, Illinois—from 8,000 initial suckers to 200,000. The city eventually went bankrupt in proceedings before a Teddy Roosevelt-appointed Northern Illinois federal judge named Kenesaw Mountain Landis, who a few short years later would oversee the far cleaner Black Sox scandal. Dowie's alleged earlier visit with Roosevelt apparently proffered no perks.

In 1896, prior to the building of his Mormon-inspired city of Zion, Dowie singlehandedly transformed his followers (he would claim a half million of them worldwide by 1904) into what he called the Christian Catholic Apostolic Church. He appointed himself as its General Overseer, unabashedly declaring himself to be its dictator before being tossed out of it by the end of his astounding and fraud-filled life. By 1899 he declared himself to be the fulfillment of biblical prophecy, in particular Malachi's "Messenger of the Covenant." Not much later he claimed to be Elijah the Prophet redivivus, who would restore all things as they were in New Testament times (presumably without the impurity practiced by some Corinthians during apostolic days). Had he lived longer, he probably would have gotten around to claiming to be Jesus the Christ. Dowie, a borderline polygamist whose disciples were sometimes clad in nothing more than "Edenic righteousness," turned out to be neither Elijah nor Christ, of course. Journalists, preachers, and bartenders—all of whom he offended from his pyrotechnic pulpit—came to that conclusion long before his "Full Gospel" followers (and one recent scholar) did.

churchfail: Unlike some heretics, Dowie did not hide his absurdities with veiled language. Though pleasant in private, he boldly brayed his bunkum in public. While he claimed to preach a "Full Gospel," whatever that meant, in reality his gospel was heavily biased toward healing, hardly the primary accent of the Bible that he claimed to believe was inerrant and inspired. While he would on occasion invoke the time-honored expression, "the Kingdom of God," the ideal domain in Dowie's dreams was really Zion, Illinois, to which he applied Old Testament prophecies. Most Bible scholars would say those prophecies had their application 5,000 miles east of Lake Michigan, nearer the Sea of Galilee.

Application: As with rattlesnakes, people like Dowie often emit danger signals. Many observers critically noticed his lavish Pullmanesque lifestyle, funded by the entire savings of his devotees, and also his portly frame, fueled by the copious consumption of comestibles other than the pork and oysters that he determined were ungodly. In spite of Jesus's precaution to "Let no man deceive you," hundreds of thousands drank the Kool-Aid of this clergyman who much resembled a bearded thundercloud.

J.L.

Charles Taze Russell

Dates: 1852–1916

Synopsis: Charles Taze Russell, aka "Pastor" Russell, was a Pennsylvania peddler of apparel, pupil of Bible prophecy, and prolific pamphleteer and publisher who denounced the proliferation of Christian denominations—and then used his prosperity to produce a new denomination known today as Jehovah's Witnesses. Compounding the irony, Russell's new sect spawned several subdivisions under his successors.

Biography: As a boy growing up under the inspiration of Pittsburgh's Presbyterians and faraway London's famous Baptist boy preacher, Charles Haddon Spurgeon, Russell warned others in his town of the terrors of hell, as if he had been born and raised there instead of in the city whose blast furnaces were a distant second. By the end of his life he had hosed hell and gutted *gehenna*, to say nothing of other cardinal doctrines of Protestant Christianity like the Trinity and immortality. He wanted to restore first-century Christianity, which he idealized while overlooking the carnality of some Corinthian confessors with their close kin (1 Cor 5:1).

To spread his new doctrines, Russell conducted Bible studies in homes, taught in lecture halls, and sold his propaganda through writing and self-publishing. Like his Pennsylvanian-turned-Californian countrymen, oilmen Lyman and Milton Stewart (who later bankrolled 300,000 copies of *The Fundamentals* encapsulating the very orthodox doctrines Russell opposed), Russell spent part of his comparatively compact fortune peddling his personally-developed beliefs by freely sending millions of them in pamphlet form throughout the world, thus giving his movement international status. By some standards he became one of the most widely read authors on earth, both during and after his lifetime.

One of Russell's readers and a committed communicant of his movement was the

Charles Russell

144

mourning mother of a dead infant in Abilene, Kansas. She would later give birth to Dwight David Eisenhower. Given that the Bible Students with whom she fellowshipped opposed war, the irony of Ida E's son becoming what he became needs no belaboring. Like her millennially myopic mentor, her perplexing plunge into pacifism also paralleled her absorption in the Apocalypse, certainly the central theme of Russell's theology. Playing the prophetess, she identified the post-WWII period as the "one hour mentioned in Revelations [sic] 17 and 18," thus betraying by her use of the plural that she may not have been any more reliable as an interpreter than she was as a reader.

Like almost anyone involved in religious controversy, Russell was often the object of personal attacks—the accusations ranging from business irregularities to marital infidelity. The latter brought into courtroom proceedings the almost exponentially improbable juxtaposition of Jesus, Jehovah, and jellyfish. Russell had allegedly compared his sensuous touches for a tender young lass to that last-mentioned creature, a comparison creating a whale of a sensation. His legal counsel, eventual successor, and doctrinal revisionist, Judge J. F. Rutherford, prevented the tentacles from stinging and the charges from sticking.

churchfail: Not altogether surprisingly, Russell's new denomination was initially known as Russellism à la Lutheranism. The religious recipe for Russellism was one part Presbyterian, one part Congregational, one part Adventist, one part Baptist, and plenty parts of hermeneutical gymnastics. Though the denial of a traditional hell became a cardinal concern of Russell and his followers, his real preoccupation was with the second coming of Jesus and its attendant kingdom of God. For that emphasis Russell deserves a big bouquet. For his claim that both arrived in 1914, he showed that his head was more bone than brain. This—like his even earlier view that a strain of grain he called "Miracle Wheat" was a harbinger of the heavenly kingdom—was not only heretical but hilarious, comparable to the claim of a prominent evangelical prophetess that "an outbreak of cobras in Borneo" presaged the Parousia! If Russell's version of the kingdom of God has indeed already come, and this is what it looks like, the world might be tempted to see if Sheol is more suitable—if Russell hadn't already eliminated that option.

Application: "Pastor" and publisher Russell once boasted that his *Watchtower* magazine was "the only publication on earth that has ever announced the presence of our Lord." Finding himself in a chorus of one should have prompted him to pause and ponder. Perhaps it did, but apparently that's all it did. On the other hand the fact that the Plymouth Brethren sect and other evangelicals also profess to have reimposed the "primitive church's purity" shows that Russell was not alone in all things.

J.L.

Crawford Toy

Dates: 1836–1919

Synopsis: As an American author and academic, Crawford Toy taught a number of subjects including Old Testament, Hebrew, Greek, and other Oriental languages. He began his career at the Albemarle Female Institute in Charlottesville, Virginia, where he met and almost married one of his students, Lottie Moon—later an icon in Southern Baptist life. Then, after being incarcerated during the Civil War in Baltimore's Ft. McHenry, where the grandson of Francis Scott Key of "The Star Spangled Banner" fame had also been incarcerated for Southern sympathies, Toy taught at the University of Alabama. He then left Alabama to teach at his and Edgar Allan Poe's alma mater, the University of Virginia. Later he taught at The Southern Baptist Theological Seminary where he himself had once been in the first class ever to graduate. He left Southern Seminary in a celebrated controversy and finished his teaching career at Harvard (1880–1909), segueing in Boston from his Southern Baptist roots to Unitarianism.

Biography: Crawford Howell Toy was born in Norfolk, Virginia, on March 23, 1836, right after the faraway Texas Revolutionary Battle for the Alamo, a battle that poignantly presaged his own coming last stand in Southern Baptist life. Toy's mother being the granddaughter of a Revolutionary War officer, tiny Toy was no stranger to revolutionary ideas that in his particular case still ripple in Southern Baptist life. Ironically, Toy's final teaching position at Harvard was Hancock Professor of Hebrew and Other Oriental Languages, a professorship endowed by the family of Boston Revolutionary John Hancock.

While Hancock wrote large on Boston's landscape, Toy wrote large on the Baptist equivalent. After graduating from the University of Virginia, he studied at the conservative Southern Baptist Seminary and at the liberal University of Berlin. At Berlin he ingested not only Darwinian evolution but also an approach to the Bible known as "higher criticism"—shorthand for "The Bible is an interesting but largely untrustworthy hodgepodge" (see p. 138). After swallowing these liberal ideas, Toy never spewed them out. When he returned to teach at the Baptist seminary, he found his views in violation of tenets he had agreed to teach there. As a result, he resigned and moved on to Harvard.

146

Not only did Toy resign his professorship, but his prospective wife, Lottie Moon, resigned him. While Toy moved on to Harvard, Moon had already moved to China where she spent a career promoting an authoritative Bible and where she chose not to compromise her fundamental beliefs, as Toy had his, for the sake of desirable companionship. She labored long and alone in that distant land—and also in Japan where she spent time in the home of another Southern Baptist missionary whose young son, Arthur McCollum, was learning Japanese. Arthur would later use his native tongue to translate for America WWII intercepts of Tokyo's cables; and he would employ his English language to write an eight-action memorandum that FDR used to lure the Japanese—some of them converts of McCollum's father and of Lottie—to fire the first shot of the Pacific conflict.

Crawford Toy

What is perhaps just as interesting as Toy's lost wife, Lottie, is the wife he eventually did marry. Though far lesser known in this story, there is good reason to get to know her. She and President Woodrow Wilson became pen pals. Their letters still survive, though Crawford Toy's own papers have not yet surfaced. In one of those letters to the President, she expressed the opinion that it was he, yes, Woodrow Wilson, who was in a position to usher in the kingdom of God. As anyone knows who understands the Treaty of Versailles, Woodrow Wilson is far better known for ushering in WWII.

churchfail: Toy's heresy from a Baptist standpoint was his simple abandonment of the Bible as his rule for faith and practice. If he ever thereafter wrote out a confession of whatever faith he did have left at Harvard, it has not survived, while the Abstracts of Principles he had to confess and sign at The Southern Baptist Seminary are still extant. That his wife believed Woodrow Wilson could bring in the kingdom of God suggests a whole host of heresies yet untapped.

Application: When one abandons the authority of the Bible, he or she can end up anywhere. Nature abhors a vacuum. So does a noggin.

J.L.

Harry Emerson Fosdick

Dates: 1878–1969

Synopsis: Harry Emerson Fosdick, the Jerry Falwell of theological liberalism, rose to national fame as a pugilistic pastor of one Presbyterian church, two Baptist churches, and one interdenominational New York City megachurch (near Grant's tomb—in more ways than one, according to some). He became a professor of homiletics at Union Seminary in New York City, authored at least 40 books, and hosted a radio program. As a racial progressive and occasional pacifist, Fosdick also wrote hymns, including "God of Grace and God of Glory," which is often sung by fundamentalists.

Biography: Harry Emerson Fosdick was born on May 24, 1878, in Buffalo, New York. In 1885 he was born again into a traditional Christian home. In 1900, after studying under William Newton Clarke at Colgate University, he was born again again, this time into the world of liberal theology, from which he never emerged until his death on October 5, 1969—and possibly not even then.

During Fosdick's 91 years on this planet, though occasionally on Pluto, he interacted with some of the twentieth century's most notable men: John D. Rockefeller, Billy Sunday, William Jennings Bryan, John Foster Dulles, and Martin Luther King, the last of whom called Fosdick "the greatest preacher of the century." Indeed, it was Fosdick's preaching that created this ecumenical cocktail.

Sandwiched between Jonathan Edwards's famous 1741 sermon, "Sinners in the Hands of an Angry God," and W. A. Criswell's infamous 1980 "Wheelbarrow Sermon," was Fosdick's 1922 flaming fatwa entitled "Shall the Fundamentalists Win?" It was a stem-winder that helped make the 1920s roar. In his sermon, whose warp was sweetness and whose woof was light—but whose sweetness was bitter and whose light was darkness—Fosdick flailed on fundamentalists as if they were borrowed mules. It is an assortment of denials rather than definitions, of innuendoes rather than identifications, all in the name of toleration and liberalism. Yet God is to be thanked that Fosdick taught only a generation of preachers rather than air traffic controllers.

Fundamentalists fought back. William Jennings Bryan—a fundamentalist Presbyterian and Woodrow Wilson's former Secretary of State—led the charge. Bryan later participated in the comparatively insignificant Scopes Trial (1925, p. 204), which garnered more publicity than his conscientious resignation from Wilson's cabinet over

Harry Emerson Fosdick

America's entry into a withering World War. Fosdick supported that calamitous conflict; Bryan supported Fosdick's defrocking.

To Fosdick's defense, before a Presbyterian church body, came John Foster Dulles, the son of a Presbyterian minister. He later became President Eisenhower's Secretary of State who helped initiate the Cold War and who fostered the CIA's overthrow of the Iranian government in 1953. Though Dulles saved Fosdick's Presbyterian pedigree, he did not save his pulpit.

To Fosdick's rescue came John D. Rockefeller, Jr., who built a megachurch for Fosdick: Manhattan's Riverside Church, in Morningside Heights on the Hudson River. Rockefeller, somewhat spiritually schizophrenic, also supported the fundamentalist barnstormer Billy Sunday, having bankrolled Billy's 1917 New York City revival. Like liberal Fosdick, Sunday also supported America's entry into WWI, using his revival to recruit young men to fetch faraway France's feet from the fire. It is difficult to know which caused more young men to be lost—Fosdick's militancy or his heterodoxy. Later, to remedy his part in the destruction of men's bodies, Fosdick became a pacifist, but he failed to repair the damage to men's souls promulgated by his heresy.

Two men answered Fosdick's sermonic question, "Shall the Fundamentalists Win?" J. Gresham Machen—once a Princeton Seminary professor and then a founding father of Philadelphia's fundamentalist Westminster Seminary—answered the cleric's question with a penetrating inquiry of his own: "The question is not whether Mr. Fosdick is winning men, but whether the thing to which he is winning them is Christianity."

Perhaps even more penetrating was a question posed by a trustee concerning the prospective merger of Fosdick's financially failing Union Theological Seminary and his own sister seminary in Manhattan: "Why should we tie our lifeboat to the Titanic?"

churchfail: While an apostle of ambiguity concerning his own beliefs, in his famous sermon Fosdick unambiguously denied at least four cardinal doctrines of historic fundamentalism, better known then as orthodox Protestantism. In short, Jesus said He was coming again; Fosdick said He was not.

Application: When one abandons the cardinal doctrines of Christianity, there are other religions available to consumers of faith or the lack thereof. Fosdick would have made a far better Buddhist than a Baptist.

J.L.

Russell Herman Conwell

Dates: 1843–1925

Synopsis: Russell H. Conwell—soldier, lawyer, journalist, author, and lecturer—is primarily known today as the longtime pastor of the first evangelical megachurch in America, and perhaps in the world. He is the Conwell in Gordon-Conwell Theological Seminary.

Biography: Russell H. Conwell was first and foremost a Baptist clergyman in Philadelphia from 1882 until his death in 1925. His church was called The Baptist Temple, and it is alleged by some to have been the largest Protestant church in America at the time. The historic building that once seated more than 3,000 congregants is still standing on the campus of Temple University, which Conwell also founded; but his congregation has long since ceased.

Also still standing on the campus, much to the embarrassment of Temple's administration, is a statue of a Civil War Union soldier named Johnny Ring. With one arm the statue holds a sword and with the other a large Bible. The statue is embarrassing because it was erected in memory of an event that almost certainly did not occur, at least not as Conwell told it to his authorized biographer Agnes Burr.

This non-event in question is particularly important because Conwell referred to it as pivotal in his conversion and call to the ministry as well as in the explanation of how he was able to accomplish so much in his quite colorful career. According to the fascinating but false account by Dr. Conwell, whose doctorate remains a mystery, Johnny Ring was not only devoted to Christ but to Captain Conwell. In the Battle of New Bern, Ring ran across a flaming bridge to retrieve Conwell's sword that he had left behind in his tent. Ring raced back across that bridge, sword in hand and clothes aflame, and died just a few days later after dramatically detailing to his nurses his love for Conwell and why he rescued the sword.

Russell Herman Conwell

150

One of the disturbing holes in this story is that Civil War records show that Ring died several months after the alleged gallantry in a tuberculosis ward far from that battlefield. But those records did not keep clergyman Conwell from explaining—a bit reluctantly, according to his biographer—that because of Ring's sacrifice on his behalf, he would live two lives: one for himself and one for Christian Ring.

In one of those two lives Conwell traveled across America, delivering a captivating lecture—"Acres of Diamonds"—6,000 times on the Chautauqua circuit. The discourse was as durable as Lincoln's Gettysburg Address, if its invocation by Paul Harvey, Zig Ziglar, Norman Vincent Peale, Napoleon Hill, and other motivational speakers is any indication. However, because his personal conversion story is demonstrably dishonest, it is risky to rely on every portion of his peroration—some tales tall and some even taller—without additional documentation. Docents and directors at the Drake Museum in Titusville, Pennsylvania—where Conwell's Quaker State contemporary Edwin Drake discovered oil in 1859—were totally unfamiliar with the most sensational story about their town with which the Reverend regaled spellbound spectators.

Thus, it is difficult to verify many details of his life of far lesser importance than his conversion account, an account he may simply have embellished a bit to help God use it for His glory. For example, did he really attend or graduate from Yale? Did he really meet Lincoln, Gladstone, Charles Dickens, Garibaldi, etc.? Was he really the attorney for Mary Baker Glover Patterson Eddy of Christian Science fame? In short, the scholarly biography of this Baptist clergyman remains to be written.

But one detail of Conwell's life that that we do know, though absent from his biography, is his court martial for desertion in the same battle in which Johnny Ring allegedly died. Was Conwell, then, really in the battle of Kennesaw Mountain two years later?

churchfail: Though doctrinally and functionally a Baptist, some of Conwell's writings raise questions. His "Acres of Diamonds" prosperity gospel would have made Ken Hagin tip his hat. In 1865, at Albany Law School, Conwell called himself a Universalist, which might explain why he did not seem to worry about the whoppers he cooked up, many years before Burger King trademarked the idea.

Application: God is magnified by precise details of His saving grace; and though He is not diminished by the embellishment of one's personal testimony (or diminished by anything for that matter), the net result of such storytelling can be the neutralization of the good that one does.

J.L.

J. Frank Norris:
The Pistol-Packing Preacher

Date: 1877–1952

Synopsis: Known as the most famous "Fighting Fundamentalist" in the South, J. Frank Norris's pugnacious passions made him one of the most epic churchfails of his day—worthy of two articles in this book (see p. 160).

Biography: John Franklyn Norris's sharecropper dad was an alcoholic, and once, when his son emptied out his liquor bottles, he beat him severely. Nonetheless, when horse thieves threatened his dad, Frank came to his defense and was shot three times. So he grew up fighting and never got over it.

Norris preached at two churches *simultaneously*: First Baptist, Fort Worth, and Temple Baptist, Detroit. He often doffed his coat and rolled up his sleeves, looking like a bare-fisted fighter in the pulpit.

While Norris was the most infamous Texas Baptist, the most respected was George W. Truett, pastor of First Baptist, Dallas. These pastors were rivals just like their cities. Truett had the misfortune of accidentally shooting a friend on a hunting trip. Thereafter one of Norris's cronies would accost Truett, "How can a man like you presume to occupy a Baptist pulpit?" Later, Norris's prank would backfire on him when he himself ended up on the trigger end of a shooting.

With his church only a block away from "Hell's Half Acre," Norris had plenty of chances to fight enemies that weren't Baptists—like gambling, prostitution, and liquor. The head of the Retail Liquor Dealers' Association, Bill Blevins, tried to hire a gang to "take out" Norris, but when his plan failed, he went to the church and got saved! "Since I could not put him out of business, I decided to join him."

Other liquor retailers continued to harass Norris. During the winter of 1912, fires destroyed his church and his house. A grand jury of his enemies tried to pin arson on him, but he was ultimately acquitted. The district attorney, "the tool of the liquor interests," however, suffered a horrible death in a head-on collision while his Cadillac was full of liquor. The following Sunday, Norris carried a broken bottle filled with liquor and fragments of brains into the pulpit. Norris preached on the text "Thou art weighed in the balances, and art found wanting."

J. Frank Norris

Even more than he attacked fellow Baptists, Norris attacked Catholics, and the mayor of Fort Worth was H. C. Meacham, who was not only Catholic but also the owner of a department store chain. During the summer of 1926, Norris accused Meacham of using his office to benefit his downtown store and a Catholic school. This offended Meacham—after all, what's the point in being a city official if you can't use your position for personal gain? So in retaliation, Meacham fired six employees who were members of Norris's church. Again, what's the point in being the boss if you can't fire people to get even with your enemies?

On July 11, Norris preached that Meacham wasn't "fit to be mayor of a hog pen." The following Saturday, a Meacham supporter, D. E. Chipps, phoned a threat to Norris and followed up with a visit. It was obvious that Chipps wasn't coming to confess his sins. Reports said he kicked the door open and shouted, "You blankety, blankety blank, I'm going to kill you!" (I think we're expected to fill in the blanks.) During the ensuing confrontation, Norris pulled a gun and shot the unarmed Chipps, killing him. His gun, apparently, was not filled with blankety blanks! As a result, people began calling Norris the Pistol-Packing Preacher, Two-Gun Norris, and the Shooting Salvationist.

Again Norris had his day in court, but not in Fort Worth. The judge could not find an impartial jury—everybody in Tarrant County either exalted Norris or wanted to hang him high! In Austin, he was acquitted once more.

churchfail: J. Frank Norris grew up fighting and carried his pugilistic ways into the pulpit. In spite of—or because of—his notoriety, he filled up both his churches. For many of the common folk, he seemed to be fighting against the political elites. But Norris fought friends as well as enemies. His fellow Baptist clergymen thought up this ditty, which could serve as his epitaph:

And what to do with Norris was a question broad and deep.
He was too big to banish, and he smelled too bad to keep!

Application: Jesus said peacemakers will be blessed and called sons of God, and Paul said we should try to live at peace with everyone.

R.B.

George White McDaniel

Dates: 1875–1927

Synopsis: Baylor alumnus George White McDaniel was a Southern Baptist pastor, an author, and, in 1924, president of the Southern Baptist Convention. A reputed "champion of Baptist principles" and also a fundamentalist who successfully fought the Virginia legislature against compulsory Bible reading in that state's public schools, he was nevertheless vitally involved in one of the most sensational episodes in Texas history—an episode that might have sent the premier apostle of religious liberty and America's first Baptist, Roger Williams, even deeper into cardiac arrest. McDaniel was also a member of the Virginia Baptist Historical Society, though his hagiographer makes no mention of the episode in question.

Biography: McDaniel was born in Navasota, Texas, and was born again and baptized there at the age of 17 in the Navasota Baptist Church. His ancestors were Methodists— so Methodist, in fact, that his father's name was Francis Asbury McDaniel. In spite of those roots he ended up at Baylor, where he boarded in the home of Texas Baptist icon, Dr. B. H. Carroll, pastor of the First Baptist Church of Waco, chairman of Baylor's trustees, and a participant in the episode cryptically hinted at above.

As a college senior, McDaniel married a faculty member and daughter of Judge John B. Scarborough, a Baylor trustee. Judge Scarborough was the uncle of Lee Scarborough, later the successor of president B. H. Carroll at Southwestern Baptist Seminary, and also the father of another daughter named Dorothy. Dorothy, a consort of Edna Ferber and Vachel Lindsay, studied English at the University of Chicago and Oxford, and then taught at both Baylor and Columbia University. All this to say, McDaniel was walking in very tall cotton—a subject Dorothy wrote about after cutting her English eye teeth on Waco's "Wizard of Words," that is, William Cowper Brann, in whose eventual assassination on April Fool's Day 1898 all of the above were complicit in varying degrees.

Perhaps it was that tall cotton of coattail relatives in which McDaniel strutted (the Baylor president called him "aristocratic") that made him feel he, a prize-winning Baylor debater (whose debate partner and Baylor faculty member, R. H. Hamilton, would eventually kill his own son-in-law), could participate in the events leading to Brann's murder. Brann was a local journalist who boasted 100,000 worldwide readers of the broadside he entitled *The Iconoclast*. Brann was an H. L. Mencken before H. L. Mencken was H. L. Mencken. In a series of essays, Brann blasted Baylor's Baptists because they had imported a youthful Brazilian lass to study there with the intention that she return to her own country to convert Catholics. While in Waco, she became pregnant, probably in the home of Baylor president Rufus Burleson and by a brother of Burleson's son-in-law. Quite naturally, the Baptists attempted to keep this skeleton in the closet, but to no avail. Brann revealed it beneath all the stars deep in the heart of Texas, in one essay calling the tiny, premature innocent her "two-pound Baylor diploma." All Baylorites broke loose and poured their wrath and fists upon Brann.

George White McDaniel

One of the many indignities meted out to iconoclast Brann was to kidnap him and drag him, hog-tied, around the campus of Baylor. Some witnesses say he was stripped naked first. In one dramatic episode, Brann was forced to retract what he had written. The student who forced the pen into his fingers was the future president of the Southern Baptist Convention: George White McDaniel. Later McDaniel would purge his past by proclaiming religious liberty throughout the land and also, more importantly for his resume, by omitting his participation in this sorry affair from the ample literature that flowed from his own pen.

churchfail: McDaniel, whom his hagiographer said was not much into academics at Baylor, made the simple mistake of misreading the text, "For we wrestle not against flesh and blood but against principalities and powers." By any standard, William Cowper Brann had one of the sharpest minds in America; and when neither McDaniel, the ostensibly skilled debater, nor his tutors could outdebate and wrestle intellectually with Waco's Brann—while they lobbed harmless verbal shots against the long since dead and far away Frenchman, Voltaire—they resorted to means not prescribed by St. Paul.

Application: Fisticuffs are not appropriate against the fiery darts of Satan; how much less are they suitable against the legitimate sting of critic and conscience.

J.L.

William Louis Poteat

Dates: 1856–1938

Synopsis: William Louis Poteat was a prominent Baptist educator, author, lecturer, long time (1905–1927) president of Wake Forest College (now University), and a strident Darwinian evolutionist. He evolved not simply from assorted asexual amoeba and monkeys, but from a distinguished family that through his mother included in its tribal tree James McNeill Whistler and sea-captain Thomas Graves; the latter brought the second ship of settlers to Virginia in 1608. William's brother Edwin married the daughter of famed fundamentalist A. J. Gordon, and Edwin eventually became the president of Furman University. William's nephew, Edwin Jr., became the pastor of John D. Rockefeller's Euclid Avenue Baptist Church in Cleveland, Ohio, and later the pastor of Pullen Memorial Baptist Church in Raleigh, North Carolina, which in 1992 became the first Baptist church in the state to perform a wedding for gays.

Poteat's students at Wake Forest College included

- Gerald W. Johnson, the close friend and colleague of H. L. Mencken, who praised Poteat as one of "a few hard-boiled and heroic men" having "veins filled with manganese" in an otherwise southern Sahara devoid of scholarship;
- Wilbur J. Cash, a Pulitzer nominee who wrote *The Mind of the South* and was hanged by himself or by Nazi spies in Mexico;
- Josiah W. Bailey, a United States Senator;
- Rev. Thomas Dixon Jr., the rabid racist author of *The Clansman*, which inspired D. W. Griffith's 1915 film, *The Birth of a Nation* (Woodrow Wilson and the US Supreme Court watched this flick in a private showing at the White House);
- and John Charles McNeill, North Carolina's first poet laureate and a favorite of Governor/Senator/Duke University President Terry Sanford.

Biography: William Poteat was born in 1856 on a large slave-owning plantation in North Carolina. He began to attend Wake Forest College in 1872 and returned there in 1878 to teach science, even though he had no training in that field and never would earn a degree in it. By 1881 he had begun a closet flirtation from afar with Charles Darwin. In 1882 he had a near-fatal vocational wreck at Wake Forest when the trustees offered the presidency of the school to Amzi C. Dixon, who was the brother of Thomas Dixon and, later in 1910, was the creator of *The Fundamentals*, which generally eviscerated evolution.

156

William Louis Poteat

But Dixon declined—and according to some per-ceivers of Poteat's potions, so did Wake Forest University, if the recent testimonial of one of its Divinity School students that marriage between man and beast is permissible is any indication.

It does not require a rocket surgeon to under-stand Poteat's influence among North Carolina Baptists with the relationships and connections cited above. In the early 1920s, Poteat's participa-tion in North Carolina's proleptic equivalent of Tennessee's Scopes trial began to trump the time he spent presiding at Wake Forest. In 1919 Rev. T. T. Martin, a Mississippi revivalist, had begun lob-bing negative editorials Poteat's way in the pages of Kentucky's *Western Recorder*. Poteat argued in his lectures that people like Martin simply did not understand him, but Martin and others (like the "Texas Tornado," J. Frank Norris, and William B. Riley of Minnesota's Northwestern College) did indeed understand him, which is why they went after him. Sam Ervin Jr., the future Watergate prosecutor but then just a lowly North Carolina leg-islator and racist, sided with the scientist.

Thus, Nell Battle Lewis, an editorialist for the *Raleigh News and Observer*, has argued that T. T. Martin's attacks on Poteat represent "the beginning of the anti-evolutionary agitation in the South." George N. Coad, researching this subject for the New York *World*, believed that "the attempts to bar evolution from the schools by law . . . was actually caused by the agitation of certain Baptist evangelists and editors against Poteat."[19] Or, in short, the Scopes trial can be traced to William Louis Poteat. Touted as a vocal Progressive, Poteat the scientist was strangely silent about racial equality, preferring to pick on his Baptist brethren's historic doctrines rather than the entrenched racial dogmas of his Tar Heel peers.

churchfail: If Poteat's doctrine of evolution was not heresy, his doctrine of the cruci-fixion was. As a lad he saw it as an act of substitution, but his view evolved, and when he was an adult he considered it a simple example. Evolution happens.

Application: Ideas have consequences. Before adopting ideas like Poteat's, it is a good idea to listen to his critics as well as to one's own.

J.L.

---

[19] Quoted in Suzanne Cameron Linder, "William Louis Poteat and the Evolution Controversy," *The North Carolina Historical Review* 40 (1963): 138. Accessed January 11, 2016. https://archive.org/details/northcarolinahis1963nort.

Bertie Bridges Crimm

Dates: 1886–1950

Synopsis: Bertie Bridges Crimm—better known as B. B. Crimm, or even as "Cowboy Crimm" for alternately wearing a large black or white Stetson when he preached—was a sensational Southern Baptist Texas revivalist in the first half of the twentieth century. Any way one looks at him, Crimm is even better known at the beginning of the twenty-first century for his most famous convert and late pastor of the enormous First Baptist Church of Hammond, Indiana, Jack Hyles. Hyles himself is now even far better known as the father-in-law of his successor shepherd and son-in-law, Jack Schaap. In 2013 Schaap began serving a twelve-year sentence in federal prison for [21 words removed to protect those under 21].

Biography: B. B. Crimm was born poor on March 1, 1886, in New York, Texas. As soon as he was old enough to learn his given name, he dropped it in favor of his initials. As a young man he ran with a wild crowd of cattle rustlers, later leading some of them to the same Christian faith that he eventually adopted.

It is with respect to his sensational sermonizing that this Texan troubadour some-times had a full-blown knucklehead stuffed under his ten-gallon hat. Many people who heard Crimm in their childhood have testified how he began some of his sermons in an unusual way. Say they, "He would first tell the women [here 23 words were removed in order to make this sketch readable for children and in mixed company]."

Whether clergyman Crimm borrowed this unbiblical bite from Billy Sunday or whether Sunday borrowed it from him is a revelation that awaits the Last Judgment. Either way, both of their characterizations of [here another seven words have been removed] runs completely counter to descriptions found in a very Scriptural Song by an inspired King Solomon who certainly was [here another 15 flew the coop]. Crimm also had a sermon enti-tled "Highway to Heaven," a path which even pagan country western singers have found to be a more Scriptural synecdoche than this minister's

Ten-gallon Hat

"Gates of Hell" metaphor. In so doing, Crimm fell into the unfortunate and ever-continuing trap of condemning unbiblical sexual behavior by bawdy innuendo rather than praising the biblical variety in no uncertain terms.

Crimm sometimes closed his sermons as sensationally as he began them. According to one memoirist, Cowboy would occasionally give an altar call in which he invited all those who had committed adultery to come forward. After a long and uncomfortable pause during which no one moved or breathed, Crimm would add, "And I want all those whom God has spared from that horrible sin to come forward with them"—after which the aisles filled up. According to another memoirist, this Baylor football player-turned-tent-revivalist should have responded to his own call with the first group.

churchfail: Not all heresy involves a denial of the traditional cardinal doctrines like the resurrection, the deity of Jesus, the second coming, or the inspiration of Scripture. Sometimes it can be the mere perversion of language in the pulpit on some topic that is still very, very serious, such as how we all got here and how many more will yet join us.

Most congregations are never counseled about conception. Well, Evangelicals, how's that working for you? The prevalence of promiscuity among the faithful mirrors that of the general population. At the other extreme, some preachers seem preoccupied with procreation; the result is more titillation than pastoral guidance, and again, the people perish. In the twentieth century, Crimm packed out his revival tents because of his indiscretion and innuendo. As I write, a minister who shall remain unnamed is mushrooming his megachurch by mentioning unmentionables. He has interpreted Song of Solomon 2:3 to refer to [only two words killed here] and has encouraged wives to [a whole bunch of words elided here]. He also said that, as part of the rhythm method of birth control, [23 words, including one hyphenated word, expunged here]. Preachers like this guy and Crimm revel in their randiness.

Application: Leaders face the danger of focusing on fornication to such an extent, that it turns into an unhealthy obsession. Pastors need to speak clearly yet respectfully about God's marvelous design for marriage and to speak ruefully of how it has been perverted—and to tread carefully, prayerfully, and humbly.

J.L.

J. Frank Norris:
The Texas Tornado

Date: 1877–1952

Synopsis: This churchfail was so sensational—that's the key word—that he deserves a double drubbing (see p. 152).

Biography: John Franklyn Norris was born in Alabama, but he became famous—or infamous—in Texas. Converted at a Baptist revival meeting, Norris took on his first pastorate in Mount Calm, Texas—probably the only time in his life that he was associated with anything "calm"! He hit his stride at First Baptist Church, Fort Worth.

His call in 1909 to this affluent church was not unanimous. J. T. Pemberton warned, "If he comes, there will be the all-firedest explosion ever witnessed in any church. We are at peace with the world, the flesh, and the devil, and with one another. And this fellow carries a broad axe and not a pearl handle pen knife." [20]

Contradicting the apt warning, the first two years of Norris's pastorate were perfunctory, and Norris was in a spiritual funk. He told his wife, "I am going to quit the ministry."

She said, "When did you ever begin?" OUCH! Not exactly a role model for the submissive wife!

But when Norris went to Kentucky to preach a revival, the preacher was the one revived! When he returned to Fort Worth, he decided to get out John the Baptist's axe, as Pemberton had prophesied, and apply it to the "root of dancing, gambling, saloons, houses of ill fame, ungodly conduct, high and low, far and near." Soon afterward, there was an exodus of capitalists, cattle kings, bank presidents, and "diamond bedecked sisters of the Ladies Aid." Six hundred of Fort Worth's finest left the church, but Norris wasn't worried. He went down to the highways and hedges of Hell's Half Acre, only a block away, and filled the church again. The membership grew from 1,200 in 1909 to over 12,000 in 1928.

He not only filled FBC, Fort Worth, but also Temple Baptist Church, Detroit. In 1934, he took on this second pastorate, preaching in one city one Sunday and flying to

---

[20] Michael E. Schepis, *J. Frank Norris: The Fascinating, Controversial Life of a Forgotten Figure of the Twentieth Century* (Bloomington, IN: WestBow, 2012), 40.

Norris and J. Roach Straton

the other the next. He began with 800 members in Detroit and counted nearly 8,600 ten years later. In 1946, Norris boasted that he pastored 25,000 persons in two churches, "the largest combined membership under one minister in the world." Multisite church when multisite wasn't cool!

churchfail: How did Norris fill up two mega-churches? Sensationalism! He would publish the titles of his sermons, and—when local newspapers refused to accept his advertising—he flooded the streets with handbills. One handbill advertised, "The Ten Biggest Devils in Fort Worth, Names Given." All ten men were notified, but only one came to contest the charges. He was hooted off the stage when Norris got him to admit that liquor interests controlled a large share in the local newspapers.

After the Fort Worth baseball team lost to their Dallas rivals, Norris preached on "Why Dallas Beat Fort Worth in Baseball." In his sermon, he devoted only one sentence to the answer—"because Dallas was prepared for the game." Then he made his evangelistic points: "Boys, you had better get prepared for the game of life" and "Knock a home run for Jesus!"

Once a banner at the church asked "Should a Prominent Fort Worth Banker Buy High-Priced Silk Hose for Another Man's Wife?" The next Sunday night, a church member testified that she sold silk stockings to a banker and another man's wife returned them. Norris, however, instead of revealing the man's name, explained that the offender had confessed, repented before God, and begged Norris to withhold his name. Norris did so but used the opportunity to launch into a sermon on repentance that was followed by many converts.

When he preached against evolution, he brought monkeys into the sanctuary to introduce the ancestors of the Darwinists. After Prohibition was passed, he conducted a funeral for John Barleycorn, complete with a pine casket filled with liquor bottles. One Sunday, Norris baptized a famous cowboy champion and brought his trick horse into the auditorium.

Application: J. Frank Norris was one of the most colorful and sensational preachers of all time. He attracted a sizable following at both his churches. Many of these were converts to Christian faith. But what cannot be determined is how many he pushed away from the gathering of the saints because of his sensationalism. The departure of 600 in 1911 might be only representative of the number of those who were turned off to Christianity because of Norris's one-man show.

R.B.

William Marrion Branham

Dates: 1909–1965

Synopsis: William Marrion Branham was a Midwestern mystic, a peripatetic Pentecostal tent revivalist, a mass evangelist, an alleged faith-healer, and an author who will be found at the roots of far better known charismatics like Oral Roberts, A. A. Allen, Gordon Lindsay, F. F. Bosworth, T. L. Osborn, Jimmy Swaggart, Kathryn Kuhlman, Kenneth Hagin, Kenneth Copeland, and Benny Hinn. He will also be found in the roots of just about anybody else on earth on whom angelic voices and visions in childhood magically bestowed Mayo Clinic-like medicinal powers but could not remedy redneck rhetoric and coarse King's English—notwithstanding that Branham once claimed he had healed King Edward VI of Great Britain, and that William Upshaw (a Georgia Congressman, a trustee of Bob Jones University, and the 1932 Prohibition Party presidential candidate against FDR) claimed that Branham supernaturally healed him at age 84 after he had been crippled for 66 years. Branham is still posthumously poisoning people's perspectives.

Biography: Branham, a clerical clown whose name really should have been Barnum, as in P. T., was born poor and multi-siblinged in Burkesville, Kentucky, but was raised near Jeffersonville, Indiana. Jeffersonville was a mere stone's throw from Louisville and The Southern Baptist Theological Seminary that was presided over at the time by E. Y. Mullins, a contributor to *The Fundamentals*. How Branham managed to doctrinally drift as far down the religious river, as he physically wandered worldwide from the Ohio River in which he—very much to his otherwise dubious credit—baptized his converts, is a mystery that is easily solved. He simply never went to seminary. What is worse, he never studied formally anywhere. This lack of social and intellectual intercourse did nothing

William Marrion Branham

to help him in what was almost certainly a sincere desire to understand the Bible—and, no doubt, to feel the speaker's high.

The one author we do know of whom Branham studied was Clarence Larkin, the Philadelphia Baptist and creator of marvelous, if not altogether accurate, charts of how the world's future was going to flesh out. Larkin majored on two specific books of the Bible: Daniel and Revelation. So did Branham. By the time Branham was through, however, his theological recipe for understanding reality was a mix of Gnosticism, Islam, Talmudism, Scofieldian dispensationalism, Mormonism, Dowieism, anti-Trinitarianism, and Pyramidism along with an unhealthy dose of ad hoc improvisation thrown in for bad measure.

Branham's followers were not much better off. They were never quite sure if their leader was the second coming of Elijah, the second coming of John the Baptist, or the second coming of Jesus Hisself. Like the last, Branham claimed to have raised the dead—specifically, a young lad in faraway Finland where verification of facts is a bit more difficult for American skeptics. And like Jesus, Branham left the impression with his followers that he would self-resurrect upon his eventual demise. That demise took place in a Texas car wreck in December 1965, and he died on Christmas Eve. He was buried four months later after the impassioned prayers and hopes of his deluded disciples failed, like him, to materialize.

In spite of Branham's humble upbringing, his self-esteem appears not to have suffered unduly. His tombstone in Jeffersonville is shaped like the Egyptian pyramids in whose abstruse and elastic symbolism he believed. In large letters along the sides of the pyramid are the names St. Paul, Martin Luther, John Wesley, and Branham. Apparently without the help of that monument, no ordinary person would have involuntarily made that free-association in spite of his oft-haloed head.

churchfail: Though ordained in a Missionary Baptist Church in Jeffersonville, Branham's beliefs were perhaps only 10 percent Baptistic and 90 percent eclectic. His primary focus was not on the coming kingdom of God, à la the message of Jesus whom he professed to follow, but on present physical miraculous healing, some of which appears to have convinced newspaper editors in need of a boost in circulation of its authenticity, but none of which made it into the medical journals. That he believed that Eve had sex with the Satanic serpent and gave birth to Cain as a result is a harmless throwaway compared to his pitiful false prophesying that St. John's long-awaited millennium would arrive in 1977.

Application: One of Branham's strong suits of appeal was his down-home, humble, common-man-sort-of-person persona. But he perfectly illustrates that though God doesn't need PhDs, rocket surgeons, or the educated in general to do His work, He doesn't need incurable and infectious ignorance either.

J.L.

George Baker[?], aka "Father Divine," aka "God Almighty"

Dates: 1873 or 1880 or 1882–1965

Synopsis: George Baker, or possibly Frederick Edwards, a cultic clergyman whose origins he cared more about obscuring than clarifying, eventually settled on "Father Divine" as his main ministerial moniker, though he had no objection to his disciples calling him "God Almighty" or "Father Eternal." Born black and poor in a shanty, quite likely on a Hutchinson Island rice plantation in the Savannah River, Baker climbed to the pinnacle of power in major metropolises like New York City and Philadelphia, where he preached incredibly bizarre doctrines designed to bring into existence a universal interracial utopian democracy. He also published a periodical captioned *The New Day,* and he claimed twenty million followers. Cult leader Jim Jones professed to be Divine's reincarnation.

Biography: Father Divine is easily one of the most fascinating and fraudulent figures in twentieth-century America. Though his ultimate origins are shrouded in mystery, he began to emerge from Southern shadows in a black Baptist church in Baltimore, where he first taught Sunday School and then fell under the spell of a itinerant evangelist named Samuel Morris. Morris had proclaimed himself the "Father Eternal," and Baker became his assistant and "Son," prompting him later to testify like Jesus, "Before Abraham was, I am"—and once in Valdosta, Georgia, "I be God." Both bi-vocational, the Father Eternal drove a junk wagon while the Son mowed lawns.

Baker then began to preach in various places throughout the Southeast. He would later claim that he was lynched 32 times but brought himself back to life just as many times. Eventually he ended up in the North, more specifically in Sayville, Long Island, where he managed to acquire a house in a white neighborhood. He began to practice prodigious hospitality toward the poor by bringing them to his house for banquets of free food with cakes the size of automobile tires, and where he reportedly poured 200 cups of coffee from a pot that would hold no more than twelve.

Eventually and understandably, the house became quite crowded, and neighbors began to complain. An attempt was made to evict Father Divine and his followers from the town. Less than a week after a judge issued this ruling against

164

Divine Lorraine Hotel, Philadelphia

God, the judge died. Divine propagandized this death as the result of his own personal retribution, the first of many such proclamations against anyone who ever said anything negative about him. Will Rogers, Huey Long, Adolph Ochs (publisher of the *New York Times*), and Hirohito (who ignored a letter of warning from Divine) all met similar fates because of the clergyman's curses—though in Hirohito's case it was Nagasaki and Hiroshima that took the hit. Conversely, Eisenhower owed his election to Divine.

Divine's devoted disciples really swallowed this baloney, as they also swallowed his plentiful free food and relied on his employment agency for work in Depression-era Harlem. Undeniably he rendered remarkable social services to some of the most pitiful and unwanted people imaginable. Though some of the sources of his funding were the followers who gave all of their earnings to him in exchange for bed and board, it is almost inconceivable that he was able to build the empire that he did just from that. Critics claimed that Rockefeller or the Russians were underwriting him. Whether they did or not, the fact remains that given his business savvy, Divine had the practical equivalent of a Harvard MBA.

churchfail: Father Divine's amorphous and blasphemous theology could also have come from Harvard. Claiming to be an evangelical, he espoused doctrines so counter to that system of belief that it boggles the ordinary brain. His self-identification as God was, of course, self-authenticating balderdash. More subtle was the substance of his sweet-sounding Utopian expressions. One might agree with them to some degree, but a true evangelical should wonder what Divine had against preaching the simple kingdom of God that Jesus proclaimed. Divine's view that it was sinful for married people to engage in sex is as astounding in theory as it is in practice—or non-practice.

Application: Father Divine rightfully drew people's attention to the injustice suffered by African Americans and successfully made improvements to lift them up. But his attempts to create utopia by force failed, as will the attempts of anyone who labors to construct paradise or to build the spiritual kingdom of God in concrete.

J.L.

Paul Johannes Tillich

Paul Tillich

Dates: 1886–1965

Synopsis: Paul Johannes Tillich was a Prussian preacher's progeny gone bad. Born in Germany, he there attained the highest academic credentials and taught in its finest universities. Fired by the Nazis in 1933, Tillich immigrated to America where he continued and then finished his teaching and writing career at Union Theological Seminary, Columbia, Harvard, and the University of Chicago. He simply couldn't hold down a job. In spite of that, many consider him one of the most influential theologians of the twentieth century. No one, however, considers him the most understood.

Biography: Tillich was born in Brandenburg when American fundamentalists had already long labored their concern about the cancer of German rationalistic theology. It was Tillich that they were seeing through a glass darkly, even though rationality was not this professor's strong suit. They were more prophetic than they knew, Tillich eventually reciprocating their flaming forecast by suggesting in his *Systematic Theology* that "fundamentalism has demonic traits."

As a lad Tillich took an interest in Holy Writ and humanism, which developed into a lifelong interest in the overlapping of theology and philosophy. He became an existentialist even though no one, including the existentialists, quite seems to know what an existentialist is.

In Tillich's case it was probably something between a philosopher and a philanderer. While the sainted Jimmy Carter only lusted in his heart, the adult and adulterous Tillich took action, on one occasion even seducing the wife of a Lutheran pastor in the bushes by a lake on the campus of Duke University. She was neither his first nor his last conjugal conquest. The press, obsessed with "demonic" fundamentalists like Jimmies Swaggart and Bakker, gave Tillich a free pass, probably in the expectation that this kind of conduct is simply a Harvard professor's perk. Philandering to the very end, Tillich was buried in New Harmony, Indiana, near one of his nymphs instead of near his tortured spouse, Hannah.

Tillich not only messed with women but also with words. He impregnated standard vocabulary with totally new but adulterated meanings, what one might call gospel gobbledygook. A clear example of this appears in a baccalaureate sermon entitled "Salvation" that the profligate professor preached in June 1963 at the First Presbyterian Church of Princeton, New Jersey. This was once the home church of Presidents Grover Cleveland and Woodrow Wilson, and also of fundamentalist scholars, presumably demons, like Princeton's Charles R. Erdman, J. Gresham Machen, and Robert Dick Wilson.

Though often a lawyer's nightmare with his anti-definitional language, on this occasion Tillich spoke clearly enough to be understood by the common man. Lifting some of the words held most sacred in the entire New Testament to the minds of his hearers, he proclaimed,

> [Eternal life] is not what popular imagination has made of it, escaping from hell and being received in heaven, in what is badly called "the life hereafter." The New Testament speaks of eternal life and [it] is not the continuation of life after death.[21]

Proving negatives is generally difficult work, and the pompous professor failed here. But then came the impregnation, i.e., Tillich's dilated definition of what *eternal life* really is:

> Eternal life is beyond past, present, and future: we came from it, we live in its presence, we return to it. It is never absent—it is the divine life in which we are rooted and in which we are destined to participate in freedom—for God is the eternal.[22]

Well, that overrides the definition given by Jesus, who is apparently another "demonic" fundamentalist. When a student of Tillich once asked his biographer, Wilhelm Pauck, some disturbing questions about Tillich's ideas, Pauck replied, "For you, theology is a matter of great seriousness. For Tillich it is all just a word game."

churchfail: Tillich failed by taking time-honored phrases like "life everlasting" and restructuring them to his own liking. Of all ostensible theologians, he may have had a monopoly on doctrinal deviance yet unfathomed—but not worth fathoming further.

Application: Paul Tillich appeals to ostensible intellectuals but not to the hoi polloi who can barely digest Hot Pockets, let alone existentialism. Beware of any theologian who cannot make himself understood to the trombone section in a swing band.

J.L.

---

[21] Paul Tillich, *The Eternal Now* (New York: Scribner's, 1948), 114.
[22] Ibid.

Karl Barth

Dates: 1886–1968

Synopsis: Many consider Karl Barth to be the most influential theologian of the twentieth century. This is certainly debatable, though there is no doubt that he was influential, if not always understood and, much to his discredit, not always misunderstood. The jury is still out—but not for long—on whether Karl Barth's picture on *Time* magazine or Hal Lindsey's royalties from *Late Great Planet Earth*—reaching fifteen million book sales—qualifies one for first place in the Gospel Book of Records. One of those two men certainly had a far greater impact on American foreign policy with his theology than the other, and American foreign policy is no mean yardstick.

Biography: Karl Barth was a Swiss PPK (professor's and pastor's kid) who followed in his father's flocking and philosophical footsteps. He first practiced his professions in Switzerland and then in Germany. After refusing to heil Hitler in 1935, he returned to Switzerland, from which he would travel abroad to lecture to listeners who often doubled as literary lemmings.

One of Barth's listeners, but no lemming, at a University of Chicago lecture in 1962 was Carl F. H. Henry, then editor of *Christianity Today*. Barth, who did not have his WWJD or WWJS (Whom Would Jesus Scald?) bracelets on that day (or ever), scornfully referred to Henry's magazine as *"Christianity Yesterday,"* for which oratorical offense Barth was bright enough to apologize later. Henry had merely asked the supposed Swiss saint to clarify his view on the resurrection of Jesus, which according to St. Paul qualifies as a legitimate theological question.

Henry's question was rooted in the inscrutable writings of Br'er Barth, who often made James Joyce's prose seem to flow like pulp fiction. He had written a commentary on the book of Romans that some say exploded like a bombshell on Europe when it first came out, but which was actually more like an eggshell from which he hatched his view of history called *Heilsgeschichte* ("salvation history"). No one quite seems to know just what "salvation history" is, but it certainly sounds holy. In reality and practice, however, it is an escape from the canons of normal history, which is what prompted people like Henry to wonder if people like Barth were coming from Switzerland or Freedonia.

For a sequel to his commentary on Romans, Barth wrote a massive compilation of his theological views entitled *Church Dogmatics*. No one is quite sure what he said in these volumes that had never been said by someone else before; nor because of his two dimensions of history—salvation history and the real kind, a "Jesus of history" and a "Jesus of faith"—is anyone quite sure exactly what he meant by what can be deciphered from his dogmatism. When tempted to consult it for exegetical or practical wisdom, remember the old proverb, "Though a castle totter upon its foundations, it is still a castle; and though a dung hill be piled to the sky, it is still a dung hill." Digesting a few pages of this work will help readers determine if it is more like Westminster or waste matter, like Fortress Marienberg or a filthy manure bucket. His *Dogmatics* should have been subtitled *Dragon's Teeth* and hidden under a pillow to see if some truth fairy would have left any cold cash for it.

Karl Barth

Like other liberal theologians, Barth's personal philandering has never been held against him, as it has been held against evangelical Jimmies Bakker and Swaggart. However, Barth did have redeeming qualities. For example, he loved Mozart. Yet one wonders what Mozart would look like—and sound like—had Barth interpreted him as he did Jesus. Was there perhaps a "Mozart of faith" and also a "Mozart of history"?

churchfail: Theologians are divided today on whether or not Barth really believed in the bodily resurrection of Jesus. Those same theologians are rarely divided over whether or not St. Paul believed in the bodily resurrection. For one to profess the vocation of Christian theologian and be ambiguous on this fundamental theme is heresy, even if it is only heresy of the *Heilsgeschichte* variety. Space forbids an excoriation of his socialism, which again seems to run counter to the credo of the Carpenter of Canaanland, whom he professed to admire.

Application: If you believe in the resurrection of Jesus, proclaim it gladly and don't get angry and sarcastic if someone quizzes you about it.

J.L.

Nels Fredrick Solomon Ferré

Dates: 1908–1971

Synopsis: Nels Ferré was an educator, author, and lecturer who—in the 1940s through the 1960s—exerted a profound influence on American Christianity. He exacerbated existing liberalism into the approximate equivalent of an amorphous Asianity by his syncretistic visits to India and Japan.

Biography: Nels Ferré was born in the far north of Sweden into the paternal home of what two of his adoring children have characterized as "a conservative Baptist clergyman, a leading figure in that fiercely evangelical denomination." If indeed his father, Frans, was what they say, it can no longer be said that the acorn does not fall far from the tree, as offspring Ferré fell further than perhaps any acorn in history—if universalism spells any great difference from fierce evangelicalism. At the same time, knucklehead Nels, like many other liberals, retained a love for conservative Christian hymns, especially "Faith Is the Victory," after which he named a daughter and mini-memoirist, Faith Victoria Ferré.

At the age of 12, Ferré experienced a traditional conversion experience, as fundamental as Billy Sunday's, complete with "fire-breathing evangelists," the mark of the beast, and a literal hell "with souls bubbling in a flaming cauldron." This experience later aroused within him "a determination to rid Christian theology of the blight of an exaggerated literalism." In the end, however, he rid Christianity of everything else as well.

Ferré came to America in 1921, shortly after his conversion and after he had exhausted the free educational opportunities in Sweden. He won an all-expenses-paid fellowship in the fall of 1927 for study at Boston University, where he came under the influence of the liberal Methodist philosopher, Edgar Brightman. Brightman viewed the first six books of the Bible—and, therefore, all the rest—as essentially unreliable, a textual hodgepodge. By 1938 Ferré had earned a doctorate at Harvard, where he served as the graduate assistant for philosopher Alfred North Whitehead, whom Charles Hartshorne has called "the greatest speculative mind of the twentieth century." At first Ferré did not fall far from these two trees. Yet one might argue that by the time of his death in Wooster, Ohio, the final Ferré fell even further from these professors than he fell from his father. His liberalism and abstruse language knew no bounds.

Nels Ferré

Upon completing his education, Ferré taught at several institutions around America. He began teaching at Andover Newton Seminary, holding there the Abbott Professorship of Systematic Theology, allegedly the oldest chair in theology in the United States. He later taught at Vanderbilt, Parsons College, and the College of Wooster in Ohio. Among his many students were two of his five children, who published a memoir of their professor–parent in a 1996 essay. Common themes they found in his teaching were "average actual," "selective actual," "reflexive superspective" (later morphed to "reflexive superperspective"), "unimunity," "coinherence," and "contrapletal logic," all of which he no doubt extracted by alchemy from either the Sermon on the Mount or from his thumb.

Fundamentalists, not fathered by Ferré, saw something quite different in his teaching and decided to burn him in effigy, especially when he made light in far more clear language of the historical evidence for the virgin birth. His suggestion that Jesus was probably conceived out of wedlock through the agency of a blonde German soldier did nothing to quench the flames. One fundamentalist recalled that in Ferré's diatribes against biblical literalism, he even referred to the manna eaten by the children of Israel as technically quail dung, though there is difficulty documenting dated dung.

And it came to pass in those days that Ferré's fables began making inroads among Southern Baptists. Fed up with Ferré, church members in Rocky Mount, North Carolina, spewed him out of their mouths like the Laodiceans and pulled out of the SBC. This separation served as a wake-up call to others within the Convention who decided to stay and reform from within, resulting in the historic Conservative Resurgence (aka the Fundamentalist Takeover) that began in 1979.

churchfail: Ferré failed by substituting his own personal views of eternity and even simple grammar in place of Jesus's. Not content with the exclusivity and nature of Christ's kingdom of God, Ferré invented his own "end time" and manufactured a vocabulary to match it with words like "unimunity," an elliptical compound of "unity" and "community."

Application: When people do not like the basic biblical message, they must be careful not to invent their own futures by vacuous proclamations about worlds they have no way of producing.

J.L.

Charles Edward Coughlin

Dates: 1891–1979

Synopsis: Charles Edward Coughlin (rhymes with boondogglin'), better known as "Father Coughlin," was a Canadian-born closet politician clothed in the clerical costume of the Catholic clergy. Some would say he was a wolf in sheep's clothing or a sheep in wolf's clothing, while other mixers of menageristic metaphors would argue that he was an apocalyptic dragon in anaconda duds. He may have been these and even more. He was among the first religious figures in America to use the then newly-invented radio to broadcast his views, supplementing that medium with a publication entitled *Social Justice* and a pulpit in a parish named the National Shrine of the Little Flower near Detroit. He has been called one of the most influential Americans of the 1930s, reaching over thirty million listeners with his bombastic broadcasts.

Biography: Born in Hamilton, Ontario, of Irish Catholic parents, Charles Coughlin became a seminary-trained priest. His Irish roots would eventually bring him into conflict with the Prohibition-fighting paterfamilias of the Kennedys over negative remarks Coughlin made about FDR. Coughlin had once been FDR's biggest fan, shamelessly hawking the Savior's endorsement of Hyde Park's native president with the slogan, "The New Deal is Christ's Deal." Later, fickle Father C. would equate FDR with the Devil's Deal.

As Coughlin's career began to expand exponentially, so did the controversies. He may have become more political than pulpital, though no one has actually compiled a comparative count of his invocations of Christ versus communism or the Savior versus socialism. People know him more today for his secular battles against

Charles Coughlin

172

communism and socialism than for his ministerial meditations on the Messiah and the kingdom of God.

Coughlin's attacks on communism, though certainly welcome in America, made him bedfellow to a bevy of combatants who had not carefully thought through the worthiness of one of their weapons. The names of Henry Ford, Adolph Hitler, Gerald Winrod, Mordecai Ham, and William Bell Riley come readily to mind (the last two being instrumental in the development of Billy Graham: Ham by converting Graham in 1934, and Riley by promoting the young preacher at age 30 to the presidency of Northwestern College in 1947). These five, and many more, hawked as authentic a document entitled *The Protocols of the Learned Elders of Zion*, which, in short, claimed to be composed by a cabal of Jews outlining their plan to take over the world.

Though the ultimate origin of the *Protocols* is still enshrouded in mystery, it is certain that the alleged authors didn't write them. By hyping their veracity, Coughlin and the others eventually undermined their own credibility in what was otherwise a commendable quest to quash the Commies. The Bolshevik Revolution still hung fresh in their 1930s frontal lobes, as did the creation in war-torn Germany of the Bavarian Soviet Republic on April 12, 1919 by a Jew named Eugen Leviné (who inspired Richard Nixon's nemesis, Whittaker Chambers, to become a Soviet spy). In such an atmosphere, those threatened by what they had recently observed in Russia, and then in Germany, were not always careful textual critics.

As Coughlin's power expanded, so did his opposition, from the Vatican to his immediate superiors. The US government antagonized him the most. Unhappy with the freedom of speech granted to Coughlin in the Constitution and reemphasized by FDR in friendly fireside chats, the government began to block his radio programs. When Coughlin resorted to printing his preachments, the US Attorney General threatened to deny mail service to him. Just exactly who was more dangerous in the end, Coughlin or Congress, is an open question. After being threatened with an indictment for sedition and the prospect of defrocking, the Father finally took a hint and went back to simple parish work.

churchfail: Anyone who would call FDR's New Deal "Christ's Deal" is patently a heretic, though not a bad enough example to be burned at the stake *à la* Servetus (p. 198) but maybe grilled a bit by one's peers. Perhaps this priest's greatest heresy was the overuse of his pulpit for political rather than preaching purposes, though he might argue that they were one and the same.

Application: History has shown that one of the finest tools for fighting error, whether communism or Congress, is precision. For lack of that, especially with respect to the *Protocols*, Father Coughlin was unable to silence his more powerful opponents in the best tradition of good prophets.

J.L.

Uldine Utley

Dates: 1912–1995

Synopsis: Uldine Utley, a convert of the far better known Aimee Semple McPherson (p. 206), was a nationally-known Pentecostal child evangelist who helped to make the 1920s roar. As a child with the appeal of a then future Shirley Temple, Utley grew to be a girl alternately called the "Garbo of the Pulpit," a "Terror of the Tabernacle," and even "Joan of Arc of the modern religious world" by the famed fundamentalist Baptist, John Roach Straton. He should have known better. A rumor that the attractive Utley once preached in her swimming suit at Straton's Calvary Baptist Church in New York City (where Billy Sunday and Billy Graham also preached, where Van Cliburn played the piano, and where the brother of Kathy Gifford is the pastor at this writing) is almost certainly 150 percent false. Nevertheless, that rumor has served to draw contemporary attention to this now largely forgotten female who spent her waning years in an insane asylum.

Biography: Uldine Utley, whose full name on her San Bernardino epitaph is Uldine Mabelle Utley Langkop, was born in Durant, Oklahoma. In her 1931 biography entitled *Why I Am a Preacher,* she testified of what has all the appearance of a genuine Christian conversion in Fresno, California, in 1921 under the miraculous and multi-tongued ministrations of McPherson. Uldine's miracle was being healed from the desire of a career in the theater. But her simple testimony to a personal worker that day—to wit, "I'm only a little girl, I know, but I am going to be a little David and fight old Goliath"—is not only orthodox but touching enough to help explain her comet-like career.

The 1920s into which the young lass began literally leaping has been called a heyday for

Uldine Utley

child evangelists. Her own pulpiteering began in California by giving simple testimonies of her conversion in her own church and other local churches and private homes. Those testimonies grew longer and longer, eventually morphing into full-blown Foursquare Gospel sermons and her first major revival in Oakland, California. By the mid-1920s this pint-sized pulchritudinous preacher had come to the attention of New York's Gospel Goliath, Straton, who became a bit of a patron. He promoted her from Philadelphia to Savannah, Georgia, where some allege she left the First Assembly of God Church there in her wake. To some degree she left Straton's prestigious central Manhattan Baptist Church a bit divided over her doctrines after spending 19 weeks in the Big Apple.

Perhaps the peak of Uldine's career came on October 31, 1925, when she addressed 14,000 people in Madison Square Garden. As one result, she began to receive more and more notice from the media including short but sensational feature stories in the pages of *Time,* the *New York Times*, the *Boston Sunday Post*, and the *Christian Century* in Chicago, where she joined a Methodist church and was given a license to preach. To cover her charismatic crusades, she and/or her handlers published a newsletter captioned *Petals from the Rose of Sharon*, and she also had her own custom-made hymnbook—published by Billy Sunday's song leader, Homer Rodeheaver—for use in her revivals.

By 1932 Rev. Utley preached in smaller venues, like the Butler Methodist Episcopal Church in Butler, New Jersey, and locations around the Chicago's World's Fair of 1933. In 1938 she married a salesman, Wilbur Langkop, after which her stardom began to dim. Shortly after marriage, her new husband committed her to a mental hospital, in and out of which she resided for the rest of her life. Though largely forgotten today, playwright Robert Riskin never forgot Uldine. He wrote a Broadway play, *Bless You, Sister,* about her after attending one of her tent revivals. The play evolved into the movie *The Miracle Woman* (1931), directed by Frank Capra.

And though disremembered except by scriptwriters and specialists, one contemporary admirer recalls this "Gospel Golden" girl as having evangelized one Dr. John Sung in December 1926, after which Sung evangelized 200,000 Chinese who have now grown to 200,000,000, though specific details are wanting.

churchfail: Uldine Utley committed the heresies typical of the fishy faith healers of her era.

Application: The big question about Uldine Utley—and the many other young girl preachers like her—is whether people were drawn to them because of the New Testament or simply by the novelty of it all. If the novelty and carnival atmosphere are acceptable, their superiority over the New Testament is not, and they are likely to be forgotten.

J.L.

Momentary churchfails

These are good people doing bad things—decent Christians with skeletons in their cloisters. It's hard to go three-score and ten years without enacting at least one inane endeavor.

Tertullian and Montanism

Date: 212

Synopsis: Tertullian was brilliant . . . and just a bit gullible.

Biography: Tertullian's early life was marked by paganism not piety. Hailing from Carthage in North Africa, he was one of those sophisticated lawyer types. He acted the part of any normal, red-blooded Roman and took advantage of all enjoyments the empire had to offer. That is until he witnessed the execution of Christians. He watched amazed as Christians stared Roman officials and death in the face and maintained fervent devotion to their Savior. So, like any good lawyer, he investigated this amazing Way and discovered that what they believed wasn't so far-fetched after all. Tertullian converted to Christianity in his forties and never looked back . . . well . . . at least until he felt that Christians were no longer acting like Christians.

When Tertullian joined the rank-and-file Christian community, he applied his intellect and skillful writing abilities to passionately defending and explaining the Christian faith. He was the first Christian to write in Latin and is widely known as one of the most lucid thinkers in the early church, and his theological treatises remain some of the seminal works of early Christianity. But Tertullian's illustrious career fizzled out in the end when he capitulated to a heresy called Montanism (pp. 28, 210).

churchfail: That Tertullian accepted heresy is one of the great enigmas of early Christianity. How could a brilliant Christian theologian who composed many highly measured and reasoned works against the famous heretics of his day—including Praxeus and Marcion—fall into heresy? It's just head-scratching! But whatever the true reason, Tertullian fell for the Montanists, a heresy known for its charismatic leanings and rigid moralism.

It was probably the emphasis on ethics that sparked his change of heart, because sometime around 212 Tertullian became fed up with hypocrisy in the church. The moral rigor of the Montanists reflected more of the Christian ethic that attracted him in the first place. Like an old curmudgeon, Tertullian felt that Christians had lost their passion for the Lord. He longed for the good ol' days, when they were willing to be burned for their beliefs. Always the idealist, Tertullian criticized the church and called out blatant hypocrisy. Tertullian argued that while the Montanists didn't have their doctrinal ducks in a chorus line, at least they were living good moral lives. But in his

178

rejection of hypocrisy, he fell into heresy. It shouldn't be surprising, though, that some of the Montanists were acting more like Christians than the Christians themselves. This was certainly not the last time the church would fail to live up to the high calling of the Christian life.

Application: Tertullian's spiral into heresy reminds us that, from the early days of the church, the people of God have struggled to live out the gospel faithfully. There are some who go willingly to the fires of martyrdom and pay the ultimate sacrifice, while others struggle to give up even an hour on Sunday morning (especially during football season!). It's no wonder even the best and brightest church leaders can become so fed up with the church that they want to chuck the whole lot of them. It is easy to fall back into thinking that we need to give up on one group and go find real Christians who are living the right way. Certainly those within the Montanist movement displayed some admirable holiness, but simple saintliness is a deficient defense for submitting to off-target tenets. And it is important to remember that Scripture has no shortage of examples of Christians not acting like Christians (just read 1 Cor 5:1-2!).

Tertullian

We shouldn't give up on the church when people in the church sin; we should learn to minister in the midst of the messiness. The Lord said the church would always be filled with a mixture of wheat and tares (Matt 13:24-30) or sheep and goats (Matt 25:31-33), and it is not always easy to perceive the difference. When fellow believers are caught in sin, we don't abandon them; we bring it to their attention (Matt 18:15-17) and pray that they will be restored (Gal 6:1). We cannot find the one true and perfect church where everyone acts like Jesus all the time. Instead, the church is where the Spirit is at work sanctifying those who follow Christ.

S.P.

Origen

Origen

Dates: 185–254

Synopsis: Origen was a good egg, but he had some cracked ideas, like the preexistence of souls and *apokatastasis*, an ancient version of universalism that included the redemption of Satan.

Biography: Origen was born in Alexandria, Egypt, around 185 and was raised in a Christian home. In fact, his father Leonidas was the teacher of the local Christian school. Roman Emperor Septimius Severus built his reign on traditional values, but unfortunately for Leo, "traditional" for Severus meant paganism. So he passed a law against converting to Christianity and persecuted proselytes and their pedagogues. When Roman soldiers came to arrest Leonidas, Origen wanted to go with his father to prison and even to death. But Origen's mother prevented him from going by hiding his clothes. (I wonder how she managed to get his clothes away from him? I imagine her saying, "No, son, you can't volunteer for martyrdom until you take a bath!" Then, when Origen got out of the bathtub, NO CLOTHES! What to do? He was willing to die for his faith, but he was not willing to streak through town!)

His father's death left the teaching post empty, and Origen filled it. He became a rock star among Christian teachers and attracted students from all over—including some students of the female persuasion. Maybe because he wanted to avoid criticism about teaching members of the fair sex or maybe because he took Matthew 19:12 too literally, the story goes that he castrated himself—OUCH! For an exegete who usually interpreted Scriptures allegorically, he picked an unusual passage to interpret literally.

Demetrius, the bishop of Alexandria, eventually became jealous of Origen's popularity and extended the right foot of disfellowship to him. So Origen relocated to Caesarea of Palestine, where he became just as famous and popular. He was one of the most prolific writers of the early Christian church, cranking out more books than V. C. Andrews—without using a ghostwriter! He did this through dictation. The story goes he would dictate seven different works to seven different secretaries simultaneously! Perhaps this explains why his theology is so controversial—he and his secretaries put his trains of thought on different tracks.

When Decius became emperor, he started another persecution against Christians, and Origen had another shot at martyrdom. This time Origen succeeded: he was imprisoned and tortured. Although he was released before he died a martyr's death, he survived only a few more years and is honored as a confessor.

churchfail: As long as Origen stuck to the Bible and the apostles' teaching, he was good as gold. He taught that there is only one God, almighty, Creator of the universe; Jesus Christ is the co-eternal Son of God—if God is eternally Father, then Jesus is eternally the Son; the Holy Spirit's glory is no less than that of the Father and the Son; there are rewards and punishments in the afterlife; and there will be a final resurrection of the body. So far, so good.

But on this firm foundation of biblical, apostolic doctrines, Origen built some speculative structures that Frank Gehry would be proud of. First, one creation was not enough for Origen—he believed that there were two creations. Now, a lot of biblical scholars believe that Genesis 1 and 2 contain two different accounts of creation. Origen, however, taught that God first created spirits without bodies and without genders—after all, the Bible says, "male AND female." When some of the spirits fell into sin, God released Creation 2.0, this time the material world. God formed our bodies from the earth, made some of them male and others female, and employed them as vessels to hold human souls, which are actually fallen, preexistent spirits. Those who know both the Bible and Greek philosophy recognize that these ideas do not come from Moses but from Plato.

But Origen did not stop there; he went on to reincarnation. He taught that our spirits—or "intellects"—recycle until we get it right. Even the Devil, who also is a spirit, gets another chance, gets redeemed, and everyone lives happily ever after in Origen's version of Platonic Universalism.

Application: We should stick to the clear teachings of Scripture. Origen was an influential and world-famous Bible scholar, traveling to Rome, Arabia, Palestine, and Athens. He wrote sermons and commentaries on nearly the whole Bible. But when he got away from the Word of God and slid down the slippery slope of speculation, he fell into a pile of philosophical feces.

R.B.

Nicholas of Myra

Dates: 270–343

Synopsis: Nicholas of Myra was a faithful, generous, orthodox bishop, but you didn't want to get on his naughty list! Saint Nicholas is the legendary figure behind Santa Claus—*far* behind! Very little is known about his actual history, but there are many legends.

Biography: Nicholas was born in Myra, a town on the southern coast of what is now Turkey, to wealthy parents who died when he was young. So he grew up as an orphan, raised by the church, taking the term PK (preacher's kid) to a new level—he was a CK (church's kid).

Many stories are associated with Nicholas—most about his charitable, even miraculous, acts of kindness. Understandably interested in orphan care, he often threw gold coins through their windows into their shoes at night. If the windows were closed and locked, he would throw money down the chimney.

One story tells about a poor man with three daughters who could not get married because their father had no dowry to pay. Marrying off daughters has always been an expensive affair! But if they did not marry, they would end up as slaves or prostitutes—sadly, the sex-trafficking industry was active even then. On the night before each daughter became eligible for marriage, Nicholas snuck into their house and put a bag of gold into her stocking hung by the chimney to dry. The three bags of gold led to the three gold balls that hang outside of pawnshops. Nicholas was the original Pawn Star!

Being sound in Christian doctrine and generous with his money, Nicholas was appointed bishop of Myra. Soon, however, the Roman emperors Diocletian and Galerius inflicted the Great Persecution on the church. The prisons were so full of Christians there was no room for real criminals. The jailers beat Nicholas and burned him with hot irons until his skin was as red as Santa's coat! But Nicholas was a good jailhouse preacher who maintained his confession of faith in the Lord Jesus Christ. When Emperor Constantine saw the light (literally—he saw a vision in the sky!), he freed all the Christians imprisoned for their faith. When Nicholas walked out of prison, the people saw his bloody, burned, scarred arms, and they shouted, "Nicholas! Confessor!"

(The early church honored martyrs and confessors. A martyr—from the Greek word *martus*, meaning "witness"—witnessed to faith in Jesus even unto death. A confessor confessed faith in Jesus through imprisonment and torture but did not die. Those who gave in to persecution were called *traditors*, traitors. See Donatism, p. 44.)

No sooner did persecution end than another crisis began in Christendom. A priest in Alexandria, Egypt, named Arius (p. 46), began to teach heresy: that Jesus is a lesser being than God but greater than man; that there was a time when Jesus did not exist; that Jesus is the first of God's creation. Well, that put Arius on Nicholas's *naughty list*! At the Council of Nicaea, many bishops gathered to discuss the doctrine of Christ's nature—with Nicholas in attendance.

Nicholas of Myra

churchfail: When Arius began to sing a song that Jesus was a created being and not fully God, Nicholas got so mad that he slapped him! The other bishops were rather taken aback by Nicholas's failure of anger management, but they agreed with him in principle, and Arius was kicked out of the ecclesial club. Before he left Nicaea, Nicholas made a list of bishops and checked it twice to find out who was naughty or nice!

Because of Nicholas's miracles, generosity, and orthodoxy, the church canonized him after his death. Of course, God calls all of us to be saints—set apart to serve Him and to strive for holiness. Everyone who is a Christian is a saint. But today, people know this man as *Saint* Nicholas, and he is remembered in many countries. In Holland, for example, he is known as Sinterklaas, and on December 6 children set out their shoes at night and find gifts and candies in them in the morning. In America, children hang up stockings, unknowingly in imitation of Nicholas's gift-giving to the three daughters. And they pronounce his name "Santa Claus"!

Application: So, when you think of Santa Claus, think of good old Saint Nicholas—a confessor, who endured suffering for the sake of Christ; a bishop, who took a stand for Christian doctrine; and a pastor, who cared for members of his flock.

But when you disagree with people's theology, don't slap them!

HO, HO, HOMOOUSIOS!

R.B.

Augustine of Hippo

Dates: 354–430

Synopsis: Augustine's ideas influenced the church for centuries. In dealing with a split in the church, he built an entire theological practice on a parable. In the process, he rationalized using force to facilitate faith.

Biography: Augustine of Hippo had a long and winding road to faith. His mother was a Christian, his father not. At age 17, he left his small rural town for the big city of Carthage. Away from his mother's influence, he was soon living with a woman with whom he would stay for some 15 years. They had a son, but sadly, he died at age 17. Augustine struggled with sexual temptation for years, famously praying, "God, grant me chastity, but not yet." At least he was honest.

The world of ideas attracted the young scholar, and he joined the Manichaeans, who believed in a world where good and evil (light and darkness) are equal forces at war with each other. But the force was strong in young Augustine, and he jettisoned their dualistic philosophy.

Augustine and his family eventually moved across the Mediterranean to Milan, where he encountered the celebrated cleric, Ambrose (p. 62). Convicted by God's Spirit and lured by Ambrose's logic, Augustine embraced Christianity at the age of 31. Over the following decade, Augustine would return to North Africa, suffer the loss of his mother and son, leave his lover, be ordained a priest, and be chosen as bishop of Hippo, in present-day Algeria.

Augustine was a pivotal figure in church history. His ministry bridges the Early and Medieval periods. Both Protestants and Catholics embrace his theology. As a former Manichaean, he ably shed light on the dark errors of their ways. Augustine defined the Just War Theory, which describes the circumstances and means by which war may ethically be waged. In his

Augustine

Confessions, Augustine honestly presented his autobiography with both failings and triumphs in life and faith. In his *City of God* he explored how God can still be sovereign while the nation declines.

But Augustine got into trouble over the Donatist controversy. The Donatists grew out of persecution, during which some bishops surrendered Scripture to the authorities (p. 44). This earned them the moniker of "traitor" and called into question the validity of the religious rites performed by these priests. In particular, were priests that they ordained, really ordained? Were their baptisms legitimate? The Donatists declared them null and void, stating that anyone sprinkled by a priest ordained by the *traditors* must be rebaptized by the OK clergy. Augustine saw this as an attack on the unity of the church.

What to do with these obstinate objectors to official teaching? Why, they must be brought back into the church. If reason and persuasion don't do the trick, then *make* them see the light. In Luke 14 Jesus tells a parable of a bridegroom inviting guests to his wedding. When the guest list was still insufficient, he tells the servants to go to all the highways and byways and "compel them to come in." With this parable, Augustine defended the use of force to bring heretics back into the church. In "A Treatise concerning the Correction of the Donatists," he argued that strong-armed salvation was permissible because the church "persecutes her enemies and arrests them . . . to secure their eternal salvation." What is more loving: to let someone die and go to hell or be "saved from it by the employment of compulsion"? This thinking later became the basis for the Inquisition. Force heretics to recant in order to save their souls. An additional step was to execute them so they can't lapse again. Not a good example of tough love.

churchfail: Augustine may have understood Christian faith, but his application was an epic, albeit momentary, fail. Any faith not freely expressed is not freely embraced. Putting a gun to his head may get him to say religious words, but it will have no effect on his heart and soul. Only the Holy Spirit convicts people of sin.

Augustine failed by building a thesis of his theology on one line from a parable. Parables are illustrations—stories told to make a point. Principles should not be procured from a piece of a parable; doctrine should only be derived from clear teaching in Scripture.

Application: Religious liberty has been a touchstone tenet of Baptist belief from the beginning. We must never forget that when the religious liberty of one group is suppressed, all liberty is at risk.

L.H.

Patrick of Ireland

Dates: ca. 389–461

Synopsis: The Trinity—try to explain it and you'll lose your mind, but try to deny it and you'll lose your soul. Patrick of Ireland tried to use a shamrock as an analogy, but the analogy fails!

Biography: St. Pat's Day is acknowledged on nearly every calendar with a shamrock symbol on March 17. Too often it is celebrated with green beer and gay parades, with no recognition of the patron saint of Ireland and the true founder of the Irish church.

Patty was born in Britain to a Christian family. His father served as a deacon and his grandfather as priest, but Pat the teenager was not particularly pious. However, God used adversity to bring Patrick to Himself.

When Patrick was 16, pirates captured him and sold him into slavery in Ireland, where he tended sheep. Nothing like hard times to bring a fellow to his senses—especially the sense of smell around sheep! Patrick's faith in and love for God grew as he said a hundred prayers each day and each night. When the bowl was full of prayer-incense, God answered Patrick by showing him a way of escape to the coast. There he boarded a ship to Britain—he left home a lukewarm Christian and came back on fire for Jesus!

He did not linger long at home. Just as Paul saw a vision of a Macedonian, appealing to him to come and preach the gospel, so Patrick saw a vision of an Irishman, begging him to return to the place of his captivity. In spite of all he had suf-

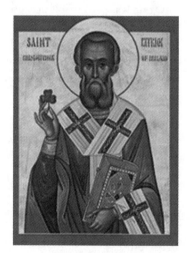

Saint Patrick

fered there, he returned to evangelize Ireland in 431—again as a shepherd, but this time to found a flock of converts, acquainting the land of Eire with life eternal. Erin go bragh!

Legends surround Patrick's ministry. Soon after he arrived, he encountered a pagan chieftain Dichu, who tried to kill him. However, Dichu was unable to move his arm until he was willing to extend Patrick the right hand of fellowship. Dichu became Patrick's first convert. The absence of snakes in Ireland gave rise to the idea that Patrick banished them. According to the legend, snakes attacked him, so he chased them into the sea, brandishing his shillelagh in Ireland just like Aaron slung his staff to swallow the sorcerers' serpents in Egypt.

Think how hard it is to make the Trinity intelligible to Christians who grew up with this baffling belief. Then picture Patrick's pedagogical problem to teach the pagan Irish that God is Three-in-One. Needing an analogy, he looked over a three-leaf clover that he'd overlooked before. Patrick's shamrock seminary must have been effective because he baptized thousands of converts and planted hundreds of churches.

churchfail: Although his teaching won converts, if he used a shamrock to illustrate the Trinity, his analogy was a heresy known as partialism. The shamrock is formed by three leaves, but it is not an effective analogy because it pictures the Father, Son, and Holy Spirit as components of the one God. Therefore, each person of the Trinity is only one third of God until the three come together to become fully God.

Fortunately for Patrick and his Irish flock, a fully developed Trinitarian theology is not necessary to become a Christian. Good thing, or the soul harvest would be seriously small!

Application: Although the term *Trinity* is not in the Bible, the teaching clearly is: God is three persons; each person is fully God; there is one God. But be careful when using analogies to explain this doctrine. Besides the shamrock, here are some other bad analogies:

- The Trinity is like water because it can assume three forms: liquid, ice, and steam. But this analogy manifests modalism—the idea that God is one substance that appears in three modes (p. 40).
- The Trinity is like an egg: yolk, white, and shell. But this analogy teaches tritheism because the egg is made of three distinct parts and, therefore, is not a unity.
- The Trinity is like the sun: star, light, and heat. But this analogy articulates Arianism—that Christ and the Holy Spirit are subordinate creations of God the Father.

So we are better off confessing the Trinity as true biblical teaching but also a mystery—avoiding bad analogies. Otherwise, like Patrick, we could be insulted by Donall and Conall on YouTube: "Come on, Patrick! Get it together, Patrick! That's a bad analogy, Patrick!"

R.B.

Francis of Assisi

Date: 1224

Synopsis: Francis of Assisi, founder of the twelfth-century Order of the Friars Minor, aka the Franciscans, led a local gang of rich rowdies until he became a prisoner of war, streaked naked out of the church to follow Lady Poverty, preached to birds, and invented the nativity crèche. He was also the first recipient of the stigmata.

Biography: Francesco Bernardone (1181–1226) was the son of a wealthy cloth merchant whom he assisted in Assisi until he reached the age of 20. In a border dispute in 1202, Francis was taken prisoner and held captive for a year. After his return he backslid into his old ways of dining, drinking, and debauching until a long illness interrupted his frolic. Climbing on his warhorse again in 1204, he galloped along until a vision reversed his direction and diluted his desire for the lifestyle of the rich and silly. Calculating to assuage his aching soul with a pilgrimage to Rome, Bernardone was so moved by the beggars outside St. Peter's that he exchanged his Armani attire for an army blanket serape and spent the day nagging Vatican tourists for alms. Back in Assisi, he said cheerio to his old chaps, managed to get disowned by Mr. Bernardone, and resolved to repair old churches and sin no more.

St. Francis

During a Sunday mass, Francis heard the "sell all and follow Me" text of Matthew 10:7-19 as his personal marching orders, so he discarded his walking stick and top hat to don dilapidated duds and set out to save Assisi souls. As soon as he had gathered eleven like-minded men, he drew up a short and primitive Rule, and on a visit to Rome in 1209, kissed Pope Innocent III's ring to get verbal approval for the infant Order. Eager to walk and talk like Jesus, Francis began dispatching his friars two by two to preach and serve as day-workers for farmers and merchants to earn fruit and bread, no lira and no leftovers allowed. The ladies wanted in on it too, so in 1212 Francis recruited Lady Clare to found a similar society centered in the sanctuary of San Damiano.

In 1217, because his small Order of friars had been supersized, the barefoot minister general divided it into provinces with ministers appointed to supervise each one. With that bit of good housekeeping, in 1219, this traveling troubadour determined to put a stop to the Crusades by sailing to Egypt to share the four spiritual laws with the Sultan al-Kamil, the nephew of Saladin. This sheik was so taken with the sweet nature of the man from Assisi that, after the Arab army kicked the Crusaders out of Palestine, the Franciscan Order alone was granted permission to remain as guardians of the holy sites.

Upon return from the land of the Pyramids—and despite being diseased with malaria and trachoma—Francis recruited his friend Cardinal Ugolino, the future Pope Gregory IX, to stop all the friar fussing by codifying his cool sayings and practices into a regular Rule, which was approved in 1223 by Pope Honorius III. Francis then resigned as minister general and handed over daily operations to his successor. Also in 1223, married people began joining in the Third Order of the Franciscans, and Francis created the first Christmas crèche with live animals and with the manger doubling as the altar. In September 1224, while on a forty-day fast, Francis received the gruesome gift of the five wounds of Christ on the cross, the stigmata. He died in 1226 at age 45 in the little hut next to the Portiuncula church.

churchfail: More than anyone since Jesus, Francis knew the spiritual value of poverty and that life was much more than the accumulation of things. He also knew how to love and value creation without worshipping it. Finally, he had an unstoppable heart to share the gospel no matter the difficulties or distance involved—Francis of Assisi was not a sissy.

However, above all else, the barefoot monk adored the Eucharist as practiced by medieval Catholic theology. For him, partaking of the body and the blood was the way of mystical union with God. His conservative Catholicism caused him to substitute this ritual for the righteousness that comes by faith. More properly, the Lord's Supper is a celebration of blood-bought righteousness, not the apprehension of righteousness by participation.

Application: Better to follow Francis's model of generous, unaffected faith than his model of shoelessness and stigmata.

R.D.

Pope Gregory X

Dates: 1210–1276

Synopsis: This story is not so much about heresy per se. Instead, it mourns what could'a' should'a' would'a' been—middle knowledge in the middle of Mongolia.

Biography: Upon the death of Clement IV in 1268, the College of Cardinals convened about 50 miles north of Rome in Viterbo, where Clement had died, to elect a new pope. At that time, Charles d'Anjou of France was on a military campaign in Sicily. Approximately half of the 19 cardinals supported his ambitions and put forward French candidates. The other half presented Italian candidates. After nearly two years—during which two of the electors expired—they still had not agreed on a nominee. So the burg's burgesses removed the roof of the palazzo where they were meeting, locked them in, and fed them only bread and water until they completed their task.

The Viterbesi misunderestimated the cardinals' capacity to embrace asceticism. A diet of bread and water is almost indulgent if it's good Italian bread. And any decent churchman would rather remain recalcitrant in the cold rain and hot sun than give an inch of ground on his convictions. They persisted for more than a year. Eventually, in September 1271, they ceded authority to an internal (not infernal) committee of six. Finally, two-and-a-half months after that, the committee selected Teobaldo Visconti, an Italian who had spent most of his career north of the Alps, away from the political fray. When Teo received Catholicism's ultimate call, he was in the Holy Land with England's Prince Edward, as papal plenipotentiary to the Ninth Crusade.

You might say that when Peter's vicars picked a pope they bickered ever. Then again, you might not—at least not five times real fast. Incidentally, it was this three-year electoral fiasco that prompted a reformation, if you'll pardon the term, in the procedure for picking the pontiff. Among the rules employed were cloistering the College of Cardinals, progressively pruning their provisions, and suspending their salary for the time span. Such stipulations propelled the process appreciably.

churchfail: In 1271, soon after Visconti became Gregory X, Niccolo and Matteo Polo popped in at St. Peter's to convey a message from Kublai Khan: Send a hundred missionaries and some oil from the lamp of the Holy Sepulcher. But the Holy See had blown all its resources trying to defend Acre, their foothold—nay toehold—in Palestine, against the Mamluks. Indeed, Gregory was using his sacerdotal soapbox to raise capital, matériel, and personnel for the next assault on the Levant. As a result, there weren't any subjects or soldi left to save souls in the uttermost part of the earth, Jesus's command notwithstanding. The Roman church had conscripted soldiers for Crusades but hadn't kept up their quota of ambassadors for Christ. So Greg grabbed two friars and some lamp oil and sent them with the peripatetic Polos, who had now been joined by 17-year-old Marco. The friars turned out to be chickens, and they turned back—I guess all the brave Christians were in Acre slaughtering souls. But the Polos were not *pollos*, they were not Polo shirks: they delivered the lamp oil. K. Khan had requested the Popeye-powerful Word of God, but all he got was olive oil.

Gregory X

Looking back, it's really too bad that the Catholic Church was not on task at the time. Assuredly the sovereign God had everything under control, but from a mundane point of view it seems that if 100 sincere missionaries could have spread out across central Asia in 50 pairs, many yurts might have been won to Christ. In the ensuing years, the long-term consequences of those initial steps on the steppes could'a' been stupendous in Mongolia, China, and Russia. Papa Greg should'a' sent a *centum* of stouthearted men. Who knows how the Two-Thirds World would'a' been different . . . if only.

Application: Jesus commissioned the church to make disciples. He didn't say anything about violently driving the infidels out of Palestine, away from the "traditional location of the garden tomb." Nor did He sanction huge sanctuaries, command crystal cathedrals, or authorize theme parks, for heaven's sake. If all our consecrated cash is tied up in adding a macchiato machine to the coffee shop in the money-changer annex of our narthex, and if our pious parishioners are busy competing in the ecumenical battle of the bell choirs, what will we do when a door opens to evangelize the Supreme Sultan of Outer Kumar and his white-ripe fields?

D.S.

Brutal Betrayal of Ulrich Zwingli

Dates: 1484–1531

Synopsis: Ulrich Zwingli depended on the Zurich City Council to establish and maintain his reformation. He sided with the frightful councilmen and betrayed his fantastic students over the issue of believer's baptism.

Biography: In 1484 Ulrich Zwingli was born in Switzerland, the son and grandson of civil magistrates and the nephew of a parish priest. With these connections, Zwingli was destined for great things, and eventually he landed the most important job in the Swiss church: priest of Grossmünster, the Great Church of Zurich. Zwingli launched the Swiss Reformation in 1523, just a few years after Luther started his Reformation in Germany, and ever since, Zwingli has been #2 in the history of Reformers—but he tried harder!

Zwingli had a number of disputes with the Roman Catholic Church. Buying salvation from the pope was a bad deal (p. 108). He didn't want to give up eating sausage just because it was Lent. But mostly, clerical celibacy cramped his sex life. He had tried abstinence—according to his own testimony—and managed for six months or a year at a time. When accused of seducing the daughter of an influential citizen, he denied that the father was *that* influential—and then he claimed that the daughter seduced *him*. Finally, in Zurich, he settled down with a rich widow and lived with her as his clerical concubine. He couldn't reform himself, so after he reformed the Swiss church, he married and legalized his sex life.

When Zwingli convinced the City Council to support his Reformation ideals, he was supported by the "Swiss Brethren," comprising several Bible students, including Conrad Grebel, the son of a city councilman; Felix Manz, the illegitimate son of a priest; and George Blaurock, a former priest. As Zwingli and his students studied the New Testament, they all became convinced that biblical baptism was intended only for believers, not infants. Maybe Zwingli should be considered the first teacher of Baptist heritage? If so, he would flunk his own final!

The City Council refused to cease the centuries-old practice of infant baptism, which was the foundation of the church-state union. And Zwingli—just like Luther before and Calvin after—depended on the state to establish and maintain his reform.

Ulrich Zwingli

So he betrayed his students. He had taught them that the Bible was the sole authority, but he yielded to the magistrates' authority. His students, however, followed their consciences instead. When they refused to allow their children to be baptized, Zwingli challenged them to a public debate. Since he couldn't use Scripture to defend infant baptism, he resorted to name-calling. He called them "Anabaptists," or re-baptizers.

But to these so-called Anabaptists, this was not a second baptism, but a first true baptism. They had decided that if they rejected infant baptism, they had rejected their own baptisms. So in a secret meeting at Manz's house—right behind Zwingli's church!—Blaurock asked Grebel to baptize him. After Blaurock was baptized, he baptized the rest of the congregation. In a way, this event on January 21, 1525, was as important to church history as Luther's nailing up the 95 Theses on October 31, 1517—even if the day is not commemorated by children going trick-or-treating!

churchfail: In this case, Zwingli was the one doing the tricking. He sided with the City Council when they outlawed the Anabaptists, hunted them down, imprisoned them, and then executed them. They oftentimes drowned them as if to say, "You want to be re-baptized? We'll baptize you a *third* time!"

In less than five years, all three of the original Anabaptists were dead along with many others. During the sixteenth century, more Anabaptists were martyred by Christians—both Catholics and Protestants—than those Christians who died at the hands of pagan Romans during three centuries of persecution.

Illustration: As a long-time fan of Marvel comics, I often compare Zwingli's treachery toward his former students to a favorite *Fantastic Four* story: "The Brutal Betrayal of Ben Grimm." The Thing, who is super strong but whose body is grotesquely covered by rock-like, nearly impervious skin, blames his friend, Mr. Fantastic, for an accident that turned him into a monster instead of the handsome Benjamin J. Grimm. In this story, he betrays his team, including the Invisible Girl and the Human Torch, and joins up with their enemies, the Frightful Four. In the end, he comes to his senses and aids his friends—unlike Ulrich Zwingli, whose brutal betrayal culminated in the Anabaptists' martyrdom.

R.B.

Martin and Katie:
The Protestant Parsonage

Date: June 13, 1525

Synopsis: By taking a wife, this monk created the concept of home life for evangelical clergy. All married pastors (at least the happily married ones) owe Luther a debt of thanks!

The love story: Martin Luther was not the first of the Reformers to marry. For example, Ulrich Zwingli, the Reformer in Zurich, had lived with a widow for years (p. 192). When the bishop of Constance turned down his petition to marry, Zwingli led the City Council to instigate reformation and to repeal clerical celibacy.

Several years earlier, Luther had already become convinced that clerical celibacy was not only unbiblical, but also unnatural. God created man for marriage, and those who opposed it were ashamed of their own manhood. Nonetheless, Luther did not plan to marry: "At present I feel that I shall never take a wife. Not that I am insensible to my flesh or sex (for I am neither wood nor stone); but my mind is opposed to wedlock, because I daily expect the death of a heretic." At the same time, Luther lived as a pathetic bachelor. He didn't make his bed for months, so the sheets were mildewed from his perspiration. His frequent fasting may have been due to his lack of culinary skill as much as to his spiritual discipline.

Enter Katharine von Bora! She was one of several nuns who came under Luther's influence and sought release from their vows. In 1523 the nuns escaped in fish barrels and came to Wittenberg. One observer wrote, "A wagon load of vestal virgins has just come to town all the more eager for marriage than life. May God give them husbands lest worse befall!" Luther

Katherine von Bora

did his best to secure a husband for each runaway nun, but Katharine was picky! She had her heart set on Luther himself. When Luther went home, he joked with his dad about the situation. But the punch line fell flat as the elder Luther took it very seriously—after all, he was thinking about grandchildren! So Luther began to look at marriage differently and thought up reasons to get married: "to please his father, to spite the pope, and to vex the Devil."

At first, Luther had few romantic notions about marriage. Early on, he said, "I am not infatuated, though I cherish my wife." Later on, he warmed up a bit: "I would not exchange Katie for France or for Venice, because God has given her to me and other women have worse faults." No one would invite Luther to speak on the Love Languages!

On June 13, 1525, in a small ceremony, Martin and Katharine became man and wife, no longer monk and nun. If Martin was an old groom at 41, Katie was not a young bride either, although she was 15 years younger. Frederick the Wise, Elector of Saxony and Luther's longtime benefactor, gave the newlyweds the Augustinian Monastery, where Luther had lived as a monk and which Katie now turned into a hostel for income. In fact, Katie epitomized the Proverbs 31 woman, excelling in housekeeping and in business.

Luther's wit and wisdom could well be included in modern marriage manuals: "There's a lot to get used to in the first year of marriage. One wakes up in the morning and finds a pair of pigtails on the pillow that were not there before." "If I should ever marry again, I would carve myself an obedient wife out of stone." "In domestic affairs I defer to Katie. Otherwise, I am led by the Holy Spirit."

husbandfail: Martin and Katie had six children—although, sadly, two daughters died young. Luther had to deal with a house full of noisy children and a nagging wife. Many pastors today can sympathize with Luther, who locked himself into his study for three days. Many pastors' wives also can sympathize with Katie, who finally took the hinges off the door and demanded that her husband come out and help!

Application: Life with Martin and Katie sometimes seems like a TV sit-com. But, as with all good marriages, there were times of laughter, tears, and love. In Luther's words, "There is no bond on earth so sweet nor any separation so bitter as that which occurs in a good marriage. . . . A wife is easily taken, but to have abiding love, that is the challenge. One who finds it in his marriage should thank the Lord God for it." Amen!

R.B.

Martin Luther

Date: 1543

Synopsis: Luther was arguably the torchbearer of the Reformation, but in an airhead moment he called for the banning of all Jews from Saxony and the burning or confiscating of their property.

Biography: As an Augustinian monk, Luther confessed he found no inner peace from constant Catholic confessions. Finding justification behind his reforming efforts, he posted his 95 Theses to the Internet of his day—the Castle Church doors in Wittenberg, Germany. His leadership in the Protestant Reformation led to his excommunication from the Catholic Church via a papal bull—no kidding! His followers were known as Lutherans—what a coincidence!

churchfail: Jesus was a Jew; His mom was too, so were His family, disciples, and a slew of His first followers. Yet, after Rome destroyed the temple in Jerusalem in AD 70, Christians began to pull up their Jewish roots and generally adopted an anti-Semitic attitude toward the wandering sheep of Israel. By the time Luther came on the scene, Jews had been uprooted from most countries or herded into ghettos. Although they were allowed to loan money as bankers, liberal government bailouts left them high and dry. Often their property was seized, or they were given six months to have a clearance sale—everything must go or be donated! European Gentiles falsely accused Jews of some rather ridiculous murders and even alleged that they caused the Black Plague by poisoning the wells—though it was the Gentiles' hearts and minds that seem poisoned.

In 1523 Luther wrote an essay: *Jesus Was a Jew.* Early in his preaching and writing, he

"Judensau" Carving, St. Mary's Church, Wittenberg

blamed the Roman Catholic Church for making it so difficult for the Jews to see the truth about Yeshua their Messiah. He argued that if they just had the chance to hear the good news, they would convert. He even said that Roman Catholics "have dealt with the Jews as if they were dogs rather than human beings; they have done little else than deride them and seize their property." Oh how Luther's views would change as he became a grumpy old man!

By 1536 it seems that Luther had given up on Jewish evangelism and was pleased when Jews were run out of his region. In 1543 he wrote *On the Jews and Their Lies*. Not only did this treatise call for the burning of synagogues and Jewish schools and the banning of Jewish free speech, it also referred to Jews as whores and full of the Devil's poo-poo—pardon my French. Four centuries later, another German, Adolph Hitler, quoted from Luther's anti-Semitic writings to bolster Germany's popular support for Hitler's final solution to the "Jewish problem"—the Holocaust. The Nazis republished Luther's *On the Jews and Their Lies* and used it as Nazi propaganda throughout World War II. Though countless millions of Protestant Christians found eternal life, in part, because of the teachings of Luther the Reformer, many millions of Jews lost their lives, in part, because of his anti-Semitic animosity.

Application: Had it not been for Jewish Christian missionaries carrying out the Great Commission of the King of the Jews (Matt 28:19-20), the good news of salvation would never have spread to all the nations. While Luther's Reformation was a breath of fresh air to those seeking forgiveness for their sin by grace alone through faith alone in Christ alone, it is not news that Luther's views on the Jews rightly meet with deplorable reviews. We might be induced to excuse this dark side of Luther because he was only a man of his time, as we would also allow for many of the churchfails in this book, but we should be careful to remember that Jesus came to His own first, and He still loves His own very much. We should too.

The Jews were the ones who shouted, "Crucify Him!" but they were not the only ones to blame. We who are sinners are as much at fault. As Stuart Townend wrote about the cross, "It was my sin that held Him there."[23] He who willingly died on our behalf is to be worshipped for His love for people from every tribe and language and people and nation.

K.C.

---

[23] "How Deep the Father's Love for Us," Kingsway's Thankyou Music, 1995.

John Calvin and the "Servetus Affair"

Michael Servetus

Date: 1553

Synopsis: This redoubtable reformer had an epic churchfail when he burned a heretic at the stake in Geneva.

Biography: From an early age, the French law student John Calvin fell under the spell of Martin Luther's Reformation ideas. Calvin began to write his own theology textbook, the *Institutes of the Christian Religion,* which went through five major editions in Latin (and three in French) and became the first standard Protestant theological textbook in Switzerland. Though he was more of a scholar than an activist, he was talked into leading the Reformation in Geneva, which became Europe's main city of refuge for persecuted Protestants from Catholic countries throughout Europe. These refugees learned Calvin's theological and moral ideas, and those who spread the Genevan good news were thereafter known as "Calvinists," planters of Reformed churches around the world.

churchfail: In Switzerland, the major cities led a magisterial form of the Reformation, insisting that all theology and morality be agreed upon and enforced by local magistrates. Calvin's *theology* comprised eighty chapters in his final edition of the *Institutes.* His ideas on Reformation *morality* were also systematic and extensive—inevitably giving rise to opponents. Some found the rules against church non-attendance, dancing, laughing during a sermon, gambling, and public disrespect for Calvin to go a bit too far. Perhaps these rules were put into place because the Berthelier brothers were belching, sneezing, and breaking wind so loudly during Calvin's Sunday sermons that no one could hear his eloquent elocution.

Enter Michael Servetus, a doctor from Spain who dabbled early and often in theology. One time Servetus called out Calvin for a theological cock fight in Paris. Calvin showed up, but Servetus chickened out. When he was just twenty years old, Servetus wrote a theological book arguing against the Trinity, the eternal existence of Jesus Christ, original sin, and infant baptism. He even suggested that the end of the world was near and the Archangel Michael was about to wage a worldwide war in which Servetus would become a casualty. His prediction was prescient, but the agent of his annihilation would be no angel.

Calvin would later write a letter to a co-worker indicating that if Servetus ever came to Geneva, his life would not be spared. Apparently Servetus didn't get the memo, and in a mindless moment of his own in August 1553 he chose to spend a month in Geneva. French refugees recognized Servetus attending Calvin's own church one Sunday. They knew he had recently escaped from prison in France, where he had been convicted of heresy by Catholic authorities and sentenced to burn at the stake there. Calvin, himself a fugitive from factious French factions, had Servetus arrested and a two-month trial ensued. Calvin wrote up 38 accusations against Servetus as a witness for the prosecution. Servetus's and Calvin's discourse degenerated from biblically and historically based rejoinders to name calling and trash talking. In October, Servetus was convicted of heresy and burned at the stake slowly and painfully by the leaders of this city of refuge from religious persecution. With refuges like this, who needs persecutors? Catholic and Protestant leaders alike around Europe were pleased with Calvin and the council for quenching the conflagration of heresy via Servetus's scorched skeleton.

Application: We might be tempted to excuse Calvin as being a man of his time. Heretics were routinely drowned, drawn and quartered, burned at the stake, beheaded, or tortured and killed in other ways that evoke memories of the early church martyrs under Roman persecution. In the modern era of religious toleration, acts of intolerance are quickly condemned, but sixteenth-century Europeans had no concept of local religious pluralism. Each European country or territory had to be formally either Catholic or Protestant.

While we might prefer their passion for theological purity to our theological pluralism and their high morals to our moral relativism, many verses from the New Testament urge us to patiently seek and help the lost, not to burn them alive. In 1903 a group of Calvinists erected a plaque just south of Geneva at the site where Servetus was burned, which reads, "We, devout and grateful sons of Calvin, our great reformer, yet condemning an error which was the error of his century, and firmly devoted to the freedom of conscience according to the true principles of the Reformation and the gospel, have erected this monument of atonement on October 27th 1903." Let us not throw out the theological baby with the bathwater of religious intolerance.

K.C.

John Knox

Date: ca. 1513–1572

Synopsis: An old children's song encourages the little tongue to "be careful what you say." Too bad it was written after John Knox delivered his diatribe against matriarchal monarchs. He fired his salvo just as the target moved. As a result, he lost a potential ally.

Biography: John Knox was born sometime between 1505 and 1515 to a farm family in Haddington, Scotland. He chose to be ordained, or perhaps foreordained, as a priest. He studied under the famous philosopher John Major (not to be confused with the later Prime Minister of England) and ministered at St. Andrews, Scotland.

The king of Scotland, James V, married Mary de Guise of France in 1538, securing close relations between Scotland and France. The de Guise family were staunch Catholics who would later play an influential role in the St. Bartholomew's Day Massacre of French Protestants in 1572. In 1542, James V died shortly after the birth of his only surviving child, a daughter, named after her mother, Mary. This left his wife as ruler. Henry VIII tried unsuccessfully to arrange a marriage between his five-year-old son, Edward, and the infant Mary. Talk about robbing the cradle! The French-favoring Cardinal Beaton—who had earlier excommunicated Henry for divorcing his first wife, Catherine of Aragon—nipped these nuptials of nascent royalty in the bud.

When rejected, Henry put a bounty on Beaton's bean. He also tried to invade Scotland. Henry's death in 1547, the successful relocation of young Queen Mary to France in 1548, and the active French support for Scotland ended the conflict.

Knox had already had a run-in with the elder Mary. Crafty Cardinal Beaton convicted the Calvinist supporter, George Wishart, of being Henry's henchman, and the fiery preacher was hanged and burnt in 1546. The plan backfired, and the Cardinal was killed three months later. Knox joined the conspirators in St. Andrews as their chaplain, but the French captured the castle and took Knox captive as a galley slave for over a year. This difficult learning experience was truly the school of hard Knox. After his release, he lived in exile in England where he played a part in reforming the English church. Knox participated in revising the *Book of Common Prayer*. This meant he helped shape worship and theology for the whole country. He eventually became a royal chaplain to King Edward. Who knew the Scots and English could actually get along?

Hopes of continuing reformation of
the English church died in 1553 with a new
15-year-old monarch. Faced with the almost
impossible choice between accepting a Scot
as the next king or a woman as their first
queen, Parliament preferred the princess.
Ironically enough, she was named Mary. The
formerly banished daughter of Catherine
of Aragon, Mary ascended the throne and
sought to return the country to Catholicism.
Her ardent persecution of Protestants earned
her the sober sobriquet "Bloody Mary." With
Mary on the throne, Knox traveled to Geneva
where he lived in exile, drinking deeply from
Calvin's cup.

John Knox

There was now Queen Mary of England,
Dowager Queen Mary as Regent of Scotland,
and infant Mary, Queen of Scots. It was into
this estuary of estrogen that Knox essayed
to enter by producing his most recognized
work. He wrote his *First Blast of the Trumpet Against the Monstrous Regiment of Women*
in 1558, aiming his fiery barbs at the three ruling Marys. He thundered that female
rule is "repugnant to nature" and an affront to God and creation.

His timing was atrocious. The work was barely in print when Bloody Mary died,
replaced by her Protestant-leaning half-sister, Elizabeth. Knox found it difficult to
explain that he meant to excoriate those *other* monstrous women, not her. As a result,
Elizabeth chose to shun Presbyterian principles in favor of her moderate middle way
and banished Knox from England thereafter.

churchfail: There is a thin line between righteous indignation and self-righteous
anger. In using such inflammatory language in denouncing the queens he did not
like, Knox left no room for one he could accept. The powerful Presbyterian preacher
would have benefitted from less bombastic banter.

Application: It is easy to vent our wrath by letting loose with both barrels. There is
a lot of noise and a scatter pattern of destruction. What is often overlooked is the collateral damage of the unexpected target hiding behind the intended one. Our words
are to be seasoned with grace. O be careful little tongue what you say.

L.H.

Salem Witch Trials

Date: 1692

Synopsis: Fear of spiritual warfare led to a frenzy of accusations that people in Salem were involved in witchcraft.

Biography: The Puritans were a pious group of Christians initially within the Church of England who believed that their leaders were too slow in moving the church away from its Roman Catholic roots and toward its Reformed Protestant future. Some of them, the "Separatists," decided to turn tail and set sail for the new Massachusetts Bay Colony to build a church as a "city upon a hill," so the rest of the people in the Church of England could look across the pond and see what a nice, shiny church would look like. Some of the colonists thought that God blessed the righteous with peace, health, and prosperity, so when the effects of war, disease, and hunger devastated the settlement, they assumed God was still angry at them for being spiritual slackers. As they set their standards higher, they began to see their proverbial glass as half evil.

churchfail: Since the fourteenth century, witches had been actively hunted down and persecuted by European Catholics. Between 1450 and 1750 there may have been as many as 100,000 witch trials across Europe resulting in tens of thousands of executions, most of them women. These fears of witchcraft continued in New England but reached a notable boiling, toiling, and troubling point in the Puritan village of Salem, Massachusetts.

In February 1692 two girls in Salem began to have physical fits that seemed to exceed what was normal for epileptic seizures. Their symptoms included shrieking, bodily contortions, and hiding under furniture (much like a modern teenager reacting to the confiscation of a cell phone). A Puritan minister claimed a witch must have cast a spell on the girls. Soon other girls began to display similar symptoms. Not long after, these accused "witches" were rounded up and put on trial. Some inter-family and inter-town rivalries contributed to the fervor of accusations flying around freely in the next few fortnights. Some of those who admitted to practicing witchcraft accused others of doing the same, and before long, the local witch jail exceeded its inmate capacity.

During the summer, the governor ordered witch trials in three counties. Nineteen suspects were found guilty and hanged, seven died in prison, and one man was pressed to death during a torture session. Many joined in the frenzy of accusations, and many feared those who seemed intoxicated by the thrill of accusations. Finally, the voice of reason set in. Calm, authoritative Puritan leaders like Increase Mather called for an end to the hysteria, and it abated. Years later Samuel Sewall, one of the witch trial judges, confessed before his congregation that he and others had fallen prey to the frenzy of accusations and asked for forgiveness.

However, the legacy of the witch trials continued long after things cooled off in Salem. Even though the hunting down, torture, trials, and executions of the accused "witches" was much greater and more widespread in Europe than in Massachusetts, little ol' Salem inherited the shame throughout American history as the icon of misplaced religious fervor. Puritans have been more associated with the Salem page in the book of American history than with any of many causes and events that are worthy of our admiration. To this day, anyone who is being accused of anything can use the term "witch hunt" to try to reverse the accusation. Ironically, the same non-critical thinking that went into the Salem accusations in the first place echoes in these deflections of accusations by glibly accusing the accuser of being on a witch hunt.

Trial of Mary Walcott

Application: Perhaps the symptoms the girls displayed in Salem in 1692 were of satanic origin; perhaps they are better explained by other spiritual or physical causes. That said, spiritual, emotional, and even political causes fueled the passionate accusations. Jesus called Satan a liar and the father of lies (John 8:44). Even the name "Satan" means accuser. It stands to reason that if Satan is going to affect the minds of humans, one prominent tendency would be an extraordinary passion to accuse people of villainy, whether the accusations are true or not. Although God perfectly recognizes and deals with sin, in love He also provides mercy and grace. Those who would follow God faithfully in their lives should examine suspected sin or satanic activity primarily from God's perspective rather than falling prey to passionate accusations whose sole purpose is to destroy rather than to understand, love, forgive, and restore.

K.C.

Scopes Monkey Trial

Date: July 10–21, 1925

Synopsis: The trial of *The State of Tennessee v. John Thomas Scopes* was more about Fundamentalism v. Modernism. The fundamentalist prosecutor, William Jennings Bryan, made a monkey of himself as a witness for the defense.

History: When evolutionary theory and liberal biblical criticism invaded America, fundamentalism rose up to oppose modernism. Fundamentalists subscribed to the five fundamentals of the Christian faith: the inspiration of Scripture, the deity of Christ, His substitutionary death, His resurrection, and His second coming. So vigorously did these Christians defend these doctrines they became known as "Fighting Fundamentalists." In the early twentieth century, fundamentalists constituted a political force to reckon with. In Tennessee, they had influenced the Butler Act (no relation to this author!) that prohibited teaching in public schools any theory that denies biblical creation or affirms man's descent from animals. Students already act like animals without encouraging them to follow family tradition! Modernists, of course, were no pushovers and fought back through the American Civil Liberties Union. The ACLU convinced John Scopes of Dayton, Tennessee, to school the fundamentalists and test the law. The publicity-hungry leaders of Dayton agreed to this arrangement—and their hunger was plenty satisfied!

The local prosecutor was a man named Sue Hicks, the inspiration for Johnny Cash's "A Boy Named Sue"! But someone much more famous was tagged to be on Hicks's team— William Jennings Bryan. Bryan was a former presidential candidate and secretary of state as well as a lay preacher and devout defender of fundamentalism. Scopes's ACLU-paid defense attorney was the equally infamous Clarence Darrow, who once said, "I am an agnostic; I do not pretend to know what many ignorant men are sure of."

Clarence Darrow and
William Jennings Bryan

With these two powerhouses squaring off against each other, this "trial of the century" was guaranteed to become a spectacle. It was the first trial to be broadcast on national radio and was promoted as the "Monkey Trial."

When the trial began, Dayton had turned into a carnival, with lemonade stands, performing chimpanzees, and banners proclaiming "Read Your Bible." At least a thousand people congested the courtroom while thousands more congregated outside. The trial opened with prayer, although Darrow objected. Judge Raulston overruled him: the trial needed all the prayer it could get!

The prosecution stated its case in only two hours, then it was Darrow's turn. He brought in his line-up: eight scientists and four religionists. But the judge ruled their testimony inadmissible. Deprived of his expert witnesses, Darrow looked around. In a surprise move, he called as witness *for* the defense William Jennings Bryan, special prosecutor *against* the defendant! Equally surprising, Bryan agreed: "I am simply trying to protect the Word of God against the greatest atheist or agnostic in the US."

Darrow countered, "We have the purpose of preventing bigots and ignoramuses from controlling the education of the US."

churchfail: Unfortunately, Bryan had not practiced law for 30 years, while Darrow was a crafty criminal lawyer. At one point, Darrow pressed Bryan on the date of the Flood: "What do you think that the Bible says?"

Bryan answered: "I never made a calculation."

Darrow: "What do you think?"

Bryan: "I do not think about things I don't think about."

Darrow moved in for the kill: "Do you think about things you do think about?"

Bryan fell on his sword: "Well, sometimes!" Realizing that he was not helping his cause, Bryan spoke to the judge: "Your Honor, I think I can shorten this testimony. The only purpose Mr. Darrow has is to slur at the Bible!"

Darrow snapped: "I object to that! I am examining you on your fool ideas that no intelligent Christian on earth believes!"

After eleven days of drama, the jury took only eight minutes to find Scopes guilty of violating state law. The judge fined him $100. The epic fail, however, was not Scopes or Darrow, but fundamentalism, which was pilloried in public opinion and dismissed by modernists as rural, narrow-minded, backward, and anti-intellectual.

Bryan died five days later.

Application: William Jennings Bryan should be remembered as a leading layman of his day, not as the clumsy custodian of Christian fundamentalism at the Scopes Monkey Trial. Peter admonishes Christians, "Honor the Messiah as Lord in your hearts. Always be ready to give a defense to anyone who asks you for a reason for the hope that is in you. . . . with gentleness and respect" (1 Pet 3:15-16).

R.B.

Aimee Semple McPherson

Date: 1926

Synopsis: This female evangelist with a quirky personality led a successful ministry but mysterious personal life.

Biography: Aimee Elizabeth Kennedy was born in Ontario, Canada, in 1890. At 17 years of age she put her faith in Jesus Christ as the result of the revival preaching of an Irish Pentecostal evangelist by the name of Robert Semple. Within a year they married and a few years later headed to China as missionaries. When Robert died within months from malaria, Aimee returned to America to pursue her calling as an evangelist. She eventually settled down in Los Angeles and made the Angelus Temple her ministry headquarters. The Foursquare Gospel Church arose from her ministry there. She supplemented her enthusiastic preaching, speaking in tongues, and healing ministries with a radio ministry and theatrical shows to communicate the gospel.

In an era in which women's roles were limited in the church, home, and society, "Sister Aimee" succeeded as a popular evangelist and preacher. It is not uncommon for evangelistic rock stars to face human and angelic persecution. Aimee's bold preaching and dazzling Hollywood-style tendencies clashed with her conservative theological views and the expected quiet behavior of good Christian women. America became infatuated with her success and her reported scandals.

Scandals: In 1926 Aimee went with her secretary to Venice Beach for a swim. Suddenly, Aimee disappeared. After much searching, people presumed she had drowned, so many mourners made their way to Los Angeles to pay their respects. Soon rumors arose that she had actually been kidnapped and her captors had demanded a ransom. A few weeks later she made her way back from Mexico to Los Angeles much to the delight of her followers (and thus laying to rest rumors of her drowning).

Over the years she had made her share of enemies. Her support for fellow traveling evangelist, William Jennings Bryan, and his campaign against the theory of evolution drew the ire of many modernists. Her being a bold female evangelist frustrated others. Some of her detractors were simply those opposed to her preaching about Jesus. Nonetheless, under much press coverage the matter of her alleged kidnapping came before a grand jury. The results of the hearings were that no identifying suspects could

Aimee Semple McPherson

be pursued in conjunction with her kidnapping, nor was she guilty of fabricating the whole thing just for a rendezvous with an alleged boyfriend.

Her relationships with men also fell under public scrutiny. Her second and third marriages ended in divorce, which was unacceptable for Christian leaders—much less female leaders. Rumors spread of romantic affairs, and certainly the public could understand men being attracted to her. Instead of the dowdy, very conservatively dressed, quiet women who led other Christian groups in that era, Aimee slimmed down, bobbed her hair, dressed like the glamorous Hollywood starlets, and had a magnetic, charismatic personality. Her enthusiastic preaching kept people on the edge of their seats, so who could blame a man for pursuing her as his bae? And we should not be surprised if some unscrupulous men claimed success where there was none.

Application: Those whom God uses most mightily are those whom Satan and the world attack most vigorously. The zeal, charisma, and persuasiveness of popular speakers make them effective but also hated. Did Aimee's fiery personality and insatiable enthusiasm cause her to make bad decisions? Probably. Did those same traits attract the attention of her detractors? Certainly.

Whether she was to blame for anything related to her reported kidnapping or troubled relationships with men, Aimee consistently asked her followers to forgive those who had persecuted her. She sought to exploit even her bad press and gain momentum from those controversies to spread the gospel further. Toward the end of her life she traveled widely, drawing huge crowds and using every opportunity to preach God's love and forgiveness for sinners. Imitating Jesus's tandem ministry of healing and preaching, Aimee's burden to share God's love for lost souls was rarely in question from anyone who met her or heard her preach. We can learn a lesson from Aimee in this: when we are persecuted (whether we deserve it or not) we should never lose sight of the course God has set for our lives, and we should ask Him to empower and lead us along the path of loving God and loving people.

K.C.

Apocalyptic churchfails

Here are the prophets Moses warned us about in Deuteronomy 18:22. They announce, "Jesus is coming again! And again! And . . . oh, never mind." For some reason, none have been stoned—at least not in the literal sense, though mind-altering chemicals might explain a lot.

Montanus of Phrygia

Date: ca. 170

Synopsis: Montanus's concerns for spiritual zeal in the church led him to claims of extra special direct revelations from the Holy Spirit, including incorrect details for the second coming of Jesus.

Biography: Little is known of Montanus's early life, but we assume he was born and not hatched. We first find him in Phrygia in central Asia Minor. Phrygia was notorious for its worship of the goddess Cybele, aka the "Mountain Mother" (she was especially worshipped in the local mountains). Montanus soon took to the mountains himself and formed a "rock" band called "The Montanists," with two prophetesses, Prisca (aka Priscilla) and Maximilla, singing backup (p. 28).

Many in the Catholic Church admired Montanus and his followers for their calls for moral revival but found some of their dogma a little unsettling. The church bishops in Montanus's day were dressing ostentatiously and eating scrumptiously rather than living simply and humbly like Jesus and His disciples. In first-century churches, the Holy Spirit had been sending friend requests, IMs, and Snaps to average Christians. However, the second-century bishops, in order to protect the church against heresies like Gnosticism, claimed that if the Holy Spirit was going to communicate with anyone directly, it was going to be the bishops themselves.

Montanists, by contrast, lived humble lives, selling their property to give to others in need, and shared with everyone the messages they believed they received directly from the Holy Spirit. The bishops didn't like being left out of the loop. One time, when Montanus was channeling the Holy Spirit, he used the same first person pronouns he heard the Holy Spirit use, and some hearers wrongly thought Montanus was himself claiming to be God. "What we've got here is failure to communicate" (*Cool Hand Luke*, 1967).

churchfail: While it was inspiring to see a popular spiritual revival break out in the late-second-century church, at one point an apocalyptic line was crossed. Jesus told His disciples that no one knows the day or the hour when He will return to the earth for His second coming (Matt 24:36). However, Montanus, Priscilla, and Maximilla began to claim that they received revelations that the New Jerusalem would descend from heaven and land smack dab in the middle of a mountain next door in the town of

Cybele

Pepuza—a rock concert to end all rock concerts! How convenient for them! That's better than pizza delivery! So many Montanist followers left their homes to see this event that some nearby towns emptied. Imagine them looking up in the sky, waiting for a city to descend from heaven, which, sorry to ruin the story, never ended up happening. That's it! The ruling bishops had enough of this monkey business and decided to shut down the circus by formally pronouncing that the Montanists were just a bunch of heretical clowns.

Montanus left quite an impact on the church. His calls for a return to personal holiness were well received and echoed for many centuries right up into the present day (p. 178). His, Priscilla's, and Maximilla's claims of receiving messages directly from the Holy Spirit would also see similar counterparts in a variety of piety parties, including the modern Pentecostal and Charismatic movements of the twentieth century. His condemnation of the bishops' prancing around in their fancy dresses—like Cinderella's stepsisters—would be one of the main concerns of medieval monks and leaders of the Reformation. Montanus's emphasis on the Holy Spirit was exactly what Christian theologians needed as they sought to explain the importance of the Holy Spirit in their councils and books about the Trinity. Other heretics throughout church history would predict the second coming of Christ just like Montanus did and with identical results: onlookers' laughing at Christians looking up at the sky and waiting for the immediate return of Jesus before it was time for Him to return.

Application: The Bible clearly teaches that Jesus Christ will return. Jesus (Matt 25), the angels (Acts 1:11), and the apostles (Titus 2:11-13) all told Jesus's followers to be prepared morally and to look expectantly for Jesus's literal return that would come "soon" (Rev 22:20) on the day God the Father chooses (Mark 13:32). While we would not be right to laugh at any Christian who eagerly awaits Jesus's return or calls for personal holiness, we are right to reject any specific prediction of the exact place or time the second coming will occur.

K.C.

William Miller

William Miller

Dates: 1782–1849

Synopsis: Some people never listen, no matter how many times they are told. Jesus clearly stated no one knows the day and time of His coming in power, but there always seems to be at least one person who believes that he is the exception to the rule—that God has given him exceptional insight to the signs of the times so that he can make it known.

Biography: William Miller was the son of a Revolutionary War captain. During the War of 1812, he followed in his father's military footsteps, also reaching the rank of captain. He broke ranks from the Baptists of his youth to wander with the Deists for a time. He did an about face when he emerged from a chaotic battle unscathed. Miller concluded that God was not a distant, disinterested commentator on creation, but a partial participant. He started attending a Baptist congregation, where he was asked to read a sermon while the pastor was away. Convicted by the message, he became a serious, self-taught scholar and servant of the Savior.

Miller read widely. By 1818 he came to believe that Daniel 8:14 referred to Jesus's second coming, each one of the 2,300 days in Daniel's vision representing a year. The countdown began with Artaxerxes's decree in 457 BC allowing the Jews to rebuild the temple in Jerusalem. Simple math—without regard to lunar or solar calendars—led to the conclusion that the end would come by 1843.

Initially, Miller kept his views to himself. He did not write about them until 1822. A decade later a local newspaper ran a series on his views, resulting in an avalanche of anxious inquirers. Unable to respond to each individually, Miller published in 1836 *Evidence from Scripture and History of the Second Coming of Christ, about the Year 1843*. He could have titled it, *44 Reasons Jesus Will Return by 1844*. To his credit, Miller himself did not set an exact date, preferring a general period from March 21, 1843 to March 21, 1844.

However, this was announced during a perplexing period of sideways spirituality. Beginning in 1800, the Second Great Awakening spread across the frontier. As seems generally to be the case, any revival creates new movements of questionable orthodoxy in its wake. The 1830s and '40s saw many such movements. The Shakers, who believed in the impurity of all sex, enjoyed the height of their popularity. Joseph Smith found (then lost) golden tablets from the angel Moroni that only he could read with stone glasses (or was it when he was stoned?). Henry David Thoreau championed the innate goodness of humanity and malevolence of religion in Transcendentalism. The Oneida Community believed in sharing all things, including wives. People were willing to have their ears tickled with any new teaching.

Miller's cautious approach did not stop his followers from incautious action. As the Day of Destiny drew closer, his disciples didn't tend their crops or pay their debts. Why bother, with the world ending so soon? Some people donned white robes and gathered on hilltops to be the first to greet the returning Savior.

The year 1843 came and went. No second coming. Then March 21, 1844, came and went. The second chance for the second coming also came and went. The date moved to April, and finally October 22, 1844. When Jesus did not return by any of these dates, Miller acknowledged his error. This became known as the Great Disappointment. Whether people directed their disappointment at Miller's accuracy or Jesus's failure to return depended on the individual. The movement collapsed. Many of the dearly disappointed left Christianity altogether. Miller died in his disappointment in 1849.

churchfail: Whenever people think they have figured out when God's final countdown to the second coming starts and ends, they have set themselves up for epic failure. Miller thought he knew exactly when the countdown began. He also miscalculated his calculus. Remember: always show your work so the Teacher can point out the errors. Fool me once . . .

Application: Living with uncertainty can bring a lot of stress. Having a date with which to work provides confidence, a sense of urgency, and a deadline. Everyone works harder as a deadline looms, and many wait until the deadline before even starting. The countdown began with the resurrection. Time is short, no matter the date of the last day. Get to work!

L.H.

Harold Egbert Camping

Dates: 1988, 1994, 2011

Synopsis: This redoubtable radio pastor had his epic churchfail when he was absolutely positive that he was not wrong . . . not really, not this time, not technically.

Biography: Harold Camping was a Christian radio broadcaster who hosted a call-in program called "Open Forum," where he patiently answered questions about the Bible and theology. His knowledge of the Bible was truly remarkable. But it seems the knowledge went to his head and he went out of it.

churchfail: After studying the Bible closely for many years—somehow overlooking Matthew 24:36 and 25:13 and 1 Thessalonians 5:1-2—Camping purported to have found the key to the numbers and dates. In 1992 he published a book titled *1994?*, which used cryptic numerology and scriptural sleight of hand to conclude that the Church Age ended in 1988, and the return of Christ *might* happen in 1994—hence the question mark in the title of the book. In a debate shortly before P-day (Parousia) 1994, an aspersion-caster challenged him to a rematch two months later. Camping declined, repeatedly insisting it was absurd to schedule anything for that time; there was no point, since he wouldn't be there. Pressed, he still insisted that even the unforeseeable, hypothetical contingency did not exist. Turned out it did.

Judgment Day Billboard

Undeterred, he soldiered on. By the middle of 2010, the gloves were off and the question mark was gone. He was absolutely certain that the rapture would occur on May 21, 2011, and judgment day would follow five months later. With great fanfare and international attention, R-day came and went, but Camping—who *came* to his 15

214

minutes of fame—*went* not. Undeterred, he claimed it had been a spiritual rapture, not visible to the naked eye—which brings to mind the infamous emperor's imperceptible apparel. Tragically, Camping had a stroke a few weeks later. Remarkably, it seemed to have improved his thinking. Shortly before J-day, October 21, 2011, in a private interview, he admitted that nobody could predict the date of the apocalypse.[24]

For Harold Camping, the Day of the Lord came on December 15, 2013. Now his questions have been answered face to face.

Application: Camping was just the latest in a long line of people who didn't hear Jesus when He said that no one knows the day or the hour (Matt 24:36; 25:13) and who didn't hear Paul when he said not to worry about times and seasons because the Day will come "like a thief in the night" (1 Thess 5:1-2). Camping could have saved countless hours of ineffectual investigation and fruitless figuring. Instead of deciphering and declaring the Day, he could have been preaching the clear gospel. To paraphrase the great philosopher Bobby McFerrin, "Don't worry; be ready."

D.S.

This article is nearly 300 words too short! Well, mark that down as merely the latest churchfail.

---

[24] See http://global.christianpost.com/news/harold-camping-exclusive-family-radio-founder-retires-doomsday-prophet-no-longer-able-to-work-59222.

Image credits

Holman Bible Publishers expresses deep gratitude to the following persons and institutions for use of the graphics in *churchfails*. Our aim has been to credit properly every graphic in this volume. If we have failed to do that, contact us at *bhcustomerservice@lifeway.com*. We will make therequired correction at the next printing.

Branham.org: p. 162

Ken Cleaver: p. 196

Fundamental Baptist Sermons (http://fundamentalbaptistsermons.net/ JFRANKNORRIS/jfranknorris.htm): p. 153

Find a Grave (http://www.findagrave.com): pp. 155 (George Seitz); 174 (T. J. Levigne)

Library Thing (librarything.com): p. 171

NCpedia (http://ncpedia.org/biography/poteat-william-louis): p. 157

Paul Tillich Resources, © **1994, Wesley Wildman** (http://people.bu.edu/wwildman/tillich/content_pictures.htm): p. 166

United States Holocaust Memorial Museum, Washington, DC: p. 172

Wikimedia Commons (PD-US): pp. 7 (Pierre Selim); 9 (Jastrow); 10 (Web Gallery of Art); 13 (José Luiz Bernardes Ribeiro); 14 (shakko); 17 (from Nordisk familjebok [1904], vol.1, p. 58); 18; 20; 23 (Mark Sander); 24; 27; 28 (Kimon Berlin); 31 (Jacques Matter); 32 (Icon); 35; 36 (Artaud de Montor); 38; 40; 42; 45 (G.dallorto); 46; 49 (Orf3us); 50 (The Yorck Project: 10.000 Meisterwerke der Malerei. DVD-ROM, 2002. ISBN 3936122202. Distributed by DIRECTMEDIA Publishing GmbH); 52; 55 (Dnalor 01); 57; 58; 60; 63; 64 (Wellcome V0017502); 66; 68; 71; 75; 76; 78; 81; 82; 85 (Pierre-Yves Beaudouin); 86; 88; 90; 92; 95; 96 (Jean-Marc Rosier); 98; 101; 102; 107; 108; 111; 112; 115 (Guusbosman); 117 (Web Gallery of Art); 118; 122 (Berean Bible Heritage); 124 (Hassocks5489); 126; 128; 131; 132; 134; 136; 139; 141; 142; 144; 147; 149; 150; 158 (-oo0(GoldTrader)0oo-); 161; 165 (Joseph Elliott, HABS); 169 (Deutsche Bundespost); 179; 180; 183; 184; 186; 188; 191; 193; 194; 198; 201; 203; 204; 207 (National Photo Company); 211; 212; 214

217

MUFFINS
AND COOKIES

The following Canadian companies were involved in the production
of this Collection: Colour Technologies, Fred Bird & Associates Limited,
Gordon Sibley Design Inc., On-line Graphics, Telemedia Publishing Inc. and
The Madison Book Group Inc.

We acknowledge the contribution of
Drew Warner, Joie Warner and Flavor Publications.

Produced by
The Madison Book Group Inc.
40 Madison Avenue
Toronto, Ontario
Canada
M5R 2S1

MUFFINS AND COOKIES

■ *On our cover:*
Cherry Cheesecake
Muffins (p. 4)

Mmmmm-mmmm, muffins! They're delicious morning, noon and night — and the 22 recipes you'll find here are extra easy to make and good for you, too. Start your day off with *Jumbo Orange-Almond Muffins* or *Carrot and Pineapple Bran Muffins*. Or make a big batch of kid-pleasing *Peanut Butter Oat Muffins* or *Cornmeal Muffins* for after-school snacking.

For a sweet treat with a glass of milk, nothing beats fresh-from-the-oven cookies or easy bars and squares. Whether it's chewy *Chocolate Nut Drops*, crunchy *Orange Coconut Crisps* or easy *Peanutty Crispy Rice Squares*, you'll want to make several batches and freeze them for tasty snacks and lunchbox desserts.

Muffins and Cookies is just one of the eight full-color cookbooks that make up THE CANADIAN LIVING COOKING COLLECTION. Inside each of these colorful cookbooks are the kind of satisfying, easy-to-make dishes you'll want to cook over and over again. Each recipe in the Collection has been carefully selected and tested by *Canadian Living* to make sure it turns out wonderfully every time you make it. When you collect all eight cookbooks, you can choose from over 500 dishes — from marvelous soups to sensational desserts — all guaranteed to make any meal extra special.

Elizabeth Baird

Elizabeth Baird
Food Director, *Canadian Living* Magazine

Cherry Cheesecake Muffins

Vary the flavor by using different jams — blueberry, blackberry, plum — or even marmalade.

1/3 cup	cream cheese	75 mL
2 tbsp	icing sugar	25 mL
1/3 cup	butter, softened	75 mL
2/3 cup	packed brown sugar	150 mL
1	egg	1
1 tsp	grated orange rind	5 mL
2 cups	all-purpose flour	500 mL
2 tsp	baking powder	10 mL
1/4 tsp	salt	1 mL
2/3 cup	milk	150 mL
1/3 cup	whole cherry jam	75 mL
2 tbsp	finely chopped pecans (optional)	25 mL

■ Blend cream cheese with icing sugar; set aside. In bowl, cream together butter and brown sugar; beat in egg and orange rind. Combine flour, baking powder and salt; add to creamed mixture alternately with milk, stirring just until blended but not overmixed.

■ Spoon into large greased muffin tins, filling halfway to top. Add 1 tsp (5 mL) of the cream cheese mixture and 1 tsp (5 mL) of the jam to each; top with remaining batter. Sprinkle with nuts (if using). Bake in 375°F (190°C) oven for 25 to 30 minutes or until firm to the touch. Immediately remove from tins. Makes 12 muffins.

MUFFIN TIPS

• *If desired, replace melted butter with vegetable oil.*

• *Be sure never to overmix muffins. Stir dry and wet ingredients together just until dry ingredients are moistened.*

• *To ensure muffins don't break when you're taking them out of cups, let stand for about 2 minutes to firm up. Then let cool on racks.*

• *Muffins freeze well. Place cooled baked muffins in resealable plastic bags or in airtight containers. Thaw at room temperature or wrapped in paper towel in microwave oven.*

Jumbo Orange-Almond Muffins

To toast the almonds, spread on baking sheet and toast in 350°F (180°C) oven for 8 minutes or until golden.

1-1/4 cups	whole wheat flour	300 mL
1 cup	all-purpose flour	250 mL
1/2 cup	packed brown sugar	125 mL
1 tbsp	baking powder	15 mL
1/2 tsp	baking soda	2 mL
1/4 tsp	salt	1 mL
1/2 cup	milk	125 mL
1 tsp	grated orange rind	5 mL
1/2 cup	orange juice	125 mL
1/4 cup	butter, melted	50 mL
1	egg	1
1 cup	sliced almonds, toasted	250 mL

■ In large bowl, mix together whole wheat and all-purpose flours, sugar, baking powder, baking soda and salt; set aside. Beat together milk, orange rind and juice, butter and egg; add to dry ingredients, mixing with fork just until moistened. Stir in all but 2 tbsp (25 mL) of the almonds.

■ Spoon into 6 greased 3/4-cup (175 mL) custard cups or 9 large muffin cups, filling almost level with top. Sprinkle with reserved almonds. Place custard cups on baking sheet. Bake in 375°F (190°C) oven for 20 to 25 minutes for large muffins, 25 to 30 minutes for custard-cup size, or until tops are firm to the touch. Makes 6 jumbo or 9 large muffins.

(clockwise from top left) Jumbo Orange-Almond Muffins; Giant Peanut Butter Muffins (p. 7); Pumpkin Raisin Muffins (p. 20) ▲

Giant Peanut Butter Muffins

Like a peanut butter and banana sandwich on brown bread — an incredible power start to the day — this muffin eaten with a banana can make you forget it's breakfast.

2 cups	buttermilk or sour milk	500 mL
1-1/2 cups	natural bran	375 mL
2/3 cup	granola	150 mL
3 tbsp	vegetable oil	50 mL
2 tbsp	crunchy peanut butter	25 mL
2	eggs	2
3/4 cup	whole wheat flour	175 mL
3/4 cup	all-purpose flour	175 mL
1/2 cup	packed brown sugar	125 mL
1/4 cup	cornmeal	50 mL
1/4 cup	wheat germ	50 mL
2 tbsp	baking powder	25 mL
1/2 tsp	salt	2 mL

■ Combine buttermilk, bran and 1/2 cup (125 mL) of the granola; set aside. Beat together oil, peanut butter and eggs; set aside.

■ In large bowl, mix together whole wheat and all-purpose flours, sugar, cornmeal, wheat germ, baking powder and salt. Add buttermilk mixture and egg mixture, stirring with fork until completely moistened.

■ Spoon into 6 greased 3/4-cup (175 mL) custard cups or 9 large muffin cups, filling almost level with top. Sprinkle with reserved granola. Place custard cups on baking sheet. Bake in 400°F (200°C) oven for 20 to 25 minutes for regular-size muffins, 30 minutes for custard-cup size, or until tops are firm to the touch. Makes 6 giant or 9 large muffins.

Apple Buttermilk Muffins

Grated apple adds flavor, moisture and nutrition to these muffins.

1 cup	all-purpose flour	250 mL
1 cup	whole wheat flour	250 mL
1/2 cup	packed brown sugar	125 mL
1 tbsp	baking powder	15 mL
1 tsp	salt	5 mL
1 tsp	cinnamon	5 mL
1/2 cup	chopped walnuts	125 mL
2	eggs	2
1 cup	buttermilk	250 mL
1 cup	grated peeled apple	250 mL
1/2 cup	butter, melted	125 mL

■ In large bowl, combine all-purpose and whole wheat flours, sugar, baking powder, salt and cinnamon; stir in walnuts. In separate bowl, beat eggs well; blend in buttermilk, apple and butter. Add to dry ingredients, stirring just until moistened.

■ Spoon into large greased or paper-lined muffin cups, filling three-quarters full. Bake in 400°F (200°C) oven for 20 to 25 minutes or until tops are firm to the touch. Makes about 12 muffins.

Healthy Carrot Muffins

These muffins — an excellent source of vitamin A and a good source of dietary fibre — have just enough sugar, fat and salt to make them taste delicious.

1/2 cup	all-purpose flour	125 mL
1/2 cup	natural wheat bran	125 mL
1/2 cup	oat bran	125 mL
1 tbsp	baking powder	15 mL
1 tsp	cinnamon	5 mL
1/2 tsp	nutmeg	2 mL
1/2 tsp	salt	2 mL
1/2 cup	packed brown sugar	125 mL
1	egg	1
1/2 cup	milk	125 mL
1/4 cup	butter or margarine, melted, or vegetable oil	50 mL
1-1/2 cups	finely grated carrots	375 mL
1/2 cup	raisins	125 mL

■ In large bowl, combine flour, wheat and oat brans, baking powder, cinnamon, nutmeg and salt; blend in sugar until no lumps remain.

■ Beat together egg, milk and butter; stir in carrots. Pour all at once over dry ingredients; sprinkle with raisins and stir just until moistened but not overmixed.

■ Spoon into 8 greased or paper-lined muffin cups. Bake in 375°F (190°C) oven for about 25 minutes or until lightly browned and tops are firm to the touch. Remove from pan to racks to let cool. Makes 8 muffins.

MAKE MUFFINS MORE OFTEN
Store muffins in the freezer for quick breakfasts, lunchbox treats or after-school snacks. After baking, slice muffins in half, then butter them. Put each half back together and wrap individually before freezing.

Blueberry Orange Muffins

Fresh sweet cherries may be used instead of blueberries. Sprinkle tops with rolled oats before baking if desired.

1 cup	lightly packed brown sugar	250 mL
3/4 cup	rolled oats	175 mL
2/3 cup	whole wheat flour	150 mL
1/2 cup	all-purpose flour	125 mL
1 tbsp	baking powder	15 mL
1/2 tsp	salt	2 mL
1/4 tsp	cinnamon	1 mL
	Grated rind of 1 orange	
1 cup	milk	250 mL
1/4 cup	vegetable oil	50 mL
1	egg	1
1 cup	blueberries	250 mL

■ In large bowl, combine sugar, oats, whole wheat and all-purpose flours, baking powder, salt, cinnamon and orange rind. Beat together milk, oil and egg; pour over dry ingredients and mix just until moistened but not over-mixed. Gently fold in blueberries.

■ Spoon into large greased muffin cups, filling three-quarters full. Bake in 400°F (200°C) oven for 15 to 20 minutes or until tops are firm to the touch. Makes 12 muffins.

(clockwise from top)
Blueberry-Orange
Muffins; Cheddar Corn
Muffins (p. 22);
Cherry Cheesecake
Muffins (p. 4) ▼

Carrot and Pineapple Bran Muffins

These tasty little muffins add important fibre to your diet.

1 cup	boiling water	250 mL
1 cup	natural bran	250 mL
1	egg, beaten	1
1/2 cup	finely grated carrot	125 mL
1/2 cup	drained pineapple tidbits, coarsely chopped	125 mL
1/3 cup	packed brown sugar	75 mL
3 tbsp	vegetable oil	50 mL
1 cup	all-purpose flour	250 mL
1/3 cup	skim milk powder	75 mL
1-1/2 tsp	baking powder	7 mL
1-1/2 tsp	baking soda	7 mL
1/2 tsp	salt	2 mL
1/2 tsp	ginger	2 mL
1/4 tsp	nutmeg	1 mL

■ In large bowl, pour boiling water over bran; let stand for 1 hour. Mix in egg, carrot, pineapple, sugar and oil.

■ Mix together flour, skim milk powder, baking powder, baking soda, salt, ginger and nutmeg; add to bran mixture, stirring just until combined but not overmixed.

■ Spoon into greased or paper-lined muffin cups, filling almost to top. Bake in 400°F (200°C) oven for 15 to 18 minutes or until golden and tops are firm to the touch. Makes about 12 muffins.

Cornmeal Muffins

These are as popular with adults as they are with kids. Serve them right out of the oven with soft butter.

1 cup	all-purpose flour	250 mL
3/4 cup	cornmeal	175 mL
3 tbsp	granulated sugar	50 mL
1 tbsp	baking powder	15 mL
1 tsp	salt	5 mL
1	egg	1
2/3 cup	milk	150 mL
1/3 cup	butter, melted	75 mL

■ In bowl, combine flour, cornmeal, sugar, baking powder and salt. Beat together egg, milk and butter; add to dry ingredients all at once, stirring just until moistened.

■ Spoon into greased or paper-lined muffin cups, filling two-thirds full. Bake in 425°F (220°C) oven for about 20 minutes or until golden brown and tops are firm to the touch. Makes about 10 muffins.

Wheat Germ Muffins

These muffins are packed with nutritious ingredients and make perfect lunchbox treats. The recipe can be easily halved.

2 cups	all-purpose flour	500 mL
1-1/2 cups	whole wheat flour	375 mL
1-1/2 cups	wheat germ	375 mL
4 tsp	baking powder	20 mL
2 tsp	cinnamon	10 mL
1 tsp	baking soda	5 mL
1 tsp	nutmeg	5 mL
1 tsp	salt	5 mL
1 cup	butter	250 mL
1 cup	granulated sugar	250 mL
2	eggs	2
1/2 cup	molasses	125 mL
2 cups	milk	500 mL
2 cups	raisins	500 mL

■ In bowl, combine all-purpose and whole wheat flours, wheat germ, baking powder, cinnamon, baking soda, nutmeg and salt. In large mixing bowl, cream butter with sugar; beat in eggs and molasses until smooth. Add dry ingredients alternately with milk, making three additions of dry and two of milk, stirring just until moistened. Stir in raisins.

■ Spoon into large greased or paper-lined muffin cups, filling three-quarters full. Bake in 400°F (200°C) oven for 20 to 25 minutes or until tops are firm to the touch. Makes about 24 muffins.

Apple 'n' Spice Muffins

The traditional combination of apple and cinnamon adds extra flavor but very few calories.

2 cups	all-purpose flour	500 mL
1/3 cup	packed brown sugar	75 mL
1-1/2 tsp	baking powder	7 mL
1-1/2 tsp	baking soda	7 mL
1 tsp	cinnamon	5 mL
1/2 tsp	salt	2 mL
1/4 tsp	nutmeg (optional)	1 mL
1 cup	chopped peeled apple	250 mL
1	egg, lightly beaten	1
1 cup	skim milk	250 mL
3 tbsp	butter, melted	50 mL

■ In large bowl, combine flour, sugar, baking powder, baking soda, cinnamon, salt and nutmeg (if using). Combine apple, egg, milk and butter; add to dry ingredients, stirring just until combined but not overmixed.

■ Spoon into lightly greased or paper-lined muffin cups, filling almost to top. Bake in 400°F (200°C) oven for 15 to 18 minutes or until golden and tops are firm to the touch. Makes 12 muffins.

> MUNCH ON A MUFFIN
> *Muffins are nutritious but they are often high in calories. Our recipes for Apple 'n' Spice Muffins, Carrot and Pineapple Bran Muffins (p. 10) and Banana-Bran Muffins (p. 15) are for slightly smaller versions of some favorites, with reduced sugar and fat and fewer calories.*

Food Processor Orange Date Muffins

These are economical and quick to make and have a delicious old-fashioned flavor.

3/4 cup	pitted dates, loosely separated	175 mL
1-1/4 cups	all-purpose flour	300 mL
1	orange (unpeeled), cut in 8 pieces and seeded	1
1/2 cup	orange juice	125 mL
2	eggs	2
1/2 cup	cold butter, cut in pieces	125 mL
1 cup	whole wheat flour	250 mL
3/4 cup	granulated sugar	175 mL
2 tsp	baking powder	10 mL
1 tsp	baking soda	5 mL
1 tsp	salt	5 mL

■ Toss dates with 1/2 cup (125 mL) of the all-purpose flour. In food processor fitted with metal blade, process date mixture until evenly chopped. Add orange; process until finely chopped. Add orange juice, eggs and butter; process until blended.

■ Stir together whole wheat flour, remaining all-purpose flour, sugar, baking powder, baking soda and salt; add to date mixture and process just until moistened but not overmixed.

■ Spoon into large greased or paper-lined muffin cups, filling three-quarters full. Bake in 400°F (200°C) oven for 15 to 20 minutes or until tops are firm to the touch. Makes 12 muffins.

Banana-Bran Muffins

These muffins have a pleasing mellow flavor.

1 cup	boiling water	250 mL
1 cup	natural bran	250 mL
1/2 cup	mashed ripe banana (1 small)	125 mL
1/3 cup	packed brown sugar	75 mL
1	egg, beaten	1
2 tbsp	vegetable oil	25 mL
1 tsp	vanilla	5 mL
	Grated rind of 1 lemon	
1 cup	all-purpose flour	250 mL
1/3 cup	skim milk powder	75 mL
1-1/2 tsp	baking powder	7 mL
1-1/2 tsp	baking soda	7 mL
1/2 tsp	salt	2 mL

■ In large bowl, pour boiling water over bran; let stand for 1 hour. Mix in banana, sugar, egg, oil, vanilla and lemon rind.

■ Mix together flour, skim milk powder, baking powder, baking soda and salt; add to bran mixture, stirring just until combined but not overmixed.

■ Spoon into lightly greased or paper-lined muffin cups, filling to top. Bake in 400°F (200°C) oven for 15 to 18 minutes or until golden and tops are firm to the touch. Makes about 12 muffins.

JUMBO MUFFINS

To make super-big muffins, you must use large muffin tins that hold at least 1/2 cup (125 mL). Use paper muffin cups and fill them right to the top. The muffins will expand to the size of the muffin tin without overflowing.

• To make even larger muffins, use custard cups, greased or lined with paper muffin cups, then set on a baking sheet. Fill these extra-large ones right to the top of the paper liner. Remember that you'll get slightly fewer of these jumbo muffins, and they may take additional baking time.

Muesli Bran Muffins

These high, moist muesli muffins are made without eggs. Ready-to-eat flake cereal can replace the muesli.

2 cups	all-purpose flour	500 mL
1-1/2 cups	raisins	375 mL
1 cup	muesli	250 mL
1 cup	natural bran	250 mL
1 cup	packed brown sugar	250 mL
2 tsp	baking soda	10 mL
1/2 tsp	salt	2 mL
1 cup	plain yogurt	250 mL
1 cup	milk	250 mL
2/3 cup	vegetable oil	150 mL
1/4 cup	fancy molasses	50 mL
2 tbsp	rolled oats	25 mL

■ In large bowl, mix together flour, raisins, muesli, bran, sugar, baking soda and salt. In separate bowl, whisk together yogurt, milk, oil and molasses. Stir into dry ingredients just until moistened.

■ Spoon batter into large greased or paper-lined muffin cups, filling to top. Sprinkle with rolled oats. Bake in 400°F (200°C) oven for 20 minutes or until tops are firm to the touch. Makes about 15 muffins.

Potato Cheese Muffins

A little leftover potato from suppertime can be used up in tasty muffins for next day's lunch.

2 cups	all-purpose flour	500 mL
1/2 cup	granulated sugar	125 mL
4 tsp	baking powder	20 mL
1 tsp	salt	5 mL
2	eggs	2
1-1/2 cups	milk	375 mL
1/2 cup	cooled mashed potato	125 mL
1/2 cup	shredded Cheddar cheese	125 mL
1/3 cup	shortening, melted	75 mL

■ In large bowl, combine flour, sugar, baking powder and salt. In separate bowl, beat eggs well; blend in milk, potato, cheese and shortening. Add to dry ingredients, stirring just until moistened.

■ Spoon into large greased or paper-lined muffin cups, filling three-quarters full. Bake in 400°F (200°C) oven for 25 minutes or until lightly browned and tops are firm to the touch. Makes 12 muffins.

Spiced Apple Bran Muffins

Adding grated apples to bran muffins bakes in extra moisture and flavor. These can be stored for up to 2 days or frozen until needed.

4	eggs	4
1-1/2 cups	milk	375 mL
1 cup	packed brown sugar	250 mL
1/2 cup	vegetable oil	125 mL
2 tsp	vanilla	10 mL
3 cups	bran cereal	750 mL
2 cups	grated peeled apples	500 mL
1 cup	raisins	250 mL
1 cup	chopped walnuts	250 mL
3 cups	all-purpose flour	750 mL
2 tbsp	baking powder	25 mL
2 tsp	baking soda	10 mL
1-1/2 tsp	cinnamon	7 mL
1/2 tsp	nutmeg	2 mL
1 tsp	salt	5 mL

■ In bowl, beat eggs; blend in milk, sugar, oil and vanilla. Add bran cereal, apples, raisins and nuts; mix well.

■ In large bowl, combine flour, baking powder, baking soda, cinnamon, nutmeg and salt. Stir bran mixture vigorously; add to dry ingredients and stir just until moistened.

■ Spoon into large greased or paper-lined muffin cups, filling to top. Bake in 375°F (190°C) oven for about 20 minutes or until tops are firm to the touch. Makes about 24 muffins.

Spiced Apple Bran Muffins and Pineapple Banana Muffins (p. 18) are perfect for bake sales and bazaars and make great food items for auctioning. Package the goodies in wicker baskets lined with doilies or attractive paper napkins.

Pineapple Banana Muffins

The tropical blend of pineapple and banana bakes into tender, moist and delicious muffins that keep and freeze well.

3 cups	all-purpose flour	750 mL
2 cups	granulated sugar	500 mL
1 cup	chopped nuts or raisins	250 mL
1 tsp	baking soda	5 mL
1 tsp	salt	5 mL
1 tsp	cinnamon	5 mL
3	eggs	3
2 cups	mashed bananas (about 5 medium)	500 mL
1-1/4 cups	crushed undrained pineapple	300 mL
1 cup	vegetable oil	250 mL

■ In large bowl, stir together flour, sugar, nuts, baking soda, salt and cinnamon.

■ In separate bowl, beat eggs; stir in bananas, pineapple and oil until blended. Add all at once to dry ingredients; stir just until moistened. Spoon into large greased muffin cups, filling two-thirds full.

■ Bake in 350°F (180°C) oven for 20 to 30 minutes or until tops are firm to the touch. Makes 30 muffins.

(clockwise from top) Pineapple Banana Muffins; Raspberry Almond Squares (p. 58); Monster Oatmeal Chocolate Chip Cookies (p. 37) ▶

Pumpkin Raisin Muffins

These moist muffins will add spice to everyone's coffee break.

1-1/2 cups	all-purpose flour	375 mL
1-1/2 cups	whole wheat flour	375 mL
2 tbsp	baking powder	25 mL
1 tsp	cinnamon	5 mL
1/2 tsp	nutmeg	2 mL
1/2 tsp	allspice	2 mL
1 tsp	salt	5 mL
1 cup	packed brown sugar	250 mL
1 cup	raisins	250 mL
2	eggs	2
1-1/2 cups	milk	375 mL
1/2 cup	vegetable oil	125 mL
1 cup	canned pumpkin purée	250 mL

■ In large bowl, combine all-purpose and whole wheat flours, baking powder, cinnamon, nutmeg, allspice and salt; mix in sugar until no lumps remain. Stir in raisins.

■ In separate bowl, beat eggs; blend in milk, oil and pumpkin. Add to dry ingredients, stirring just until moistened.

■ Spoon into large greased or paper-lined muffin cups, filling three-quarters full. Bake in 400°F (200°C) oven for 20 to 25 minutes or until tops are firm to the touch. Makes about 16 muffins.

Peanut Butter Oat Muffins

Favorite flavors are combined in these kid-pleasing muffins.

1-1/2 cups	rolled oats	375 mL
1-1/2 cups	whole wheat flour	375 mL
4 tsp	baking powder	20 mL
1 tsp	salt	5 mL
1 tsp	baking soda	5 mL
1/2 cup	raisins	125 mL
1 cup	plain yogurt	250 mL
3/4 cup	liquid honey	175 mL
1/2 cup	peanut butter	125 mL
1/3 cup	vegetable oil	75 mL
3	eggs, lightly beaten	3
1 tsp	vanilla	5 mL

■ In large bowl, combine oats, flour, baking powder, salt and baking soda; stir in raisins. In separate bowl, beat together yogurt, honey, peanut butter, oil, eggs and vanilla until smooth; add to dry ingredients, stirring just until moistened.

■ Spoon into greased or paper-lined muffin cups, filling three-quarters full. Bake in 375°F (190°C) oven for 25 to 30 minutes or until tops are firm to the touch. Makes 15 muffins.

Zucchini Nut Muffins

Zucchini is a popular ingredient for adding moisture and interesting texture to quick breads and muffins.

4	eggs	4
1 cup	granulated sugar	250 mL
1/2 tsp	vanilla	2 mL
1 cup	vegetable oil	250 mL
2 cups	grated (unpeeled) zucchini	500 mL
3 cups	all-purpose flour	750 mL
1-1/2 tsp	baking powder	7 mL
1 tsp	baking soda	5 mL
1 tsp	salt	5 mL
1 tsp	cinnamon	5 mL
1 cup	chopped walnuts	250 mL

■ In bowl, beat eggs, sugar and vanilla for 2 minutes. Gradually beat in oil; beat for 2 minutes longer. Stir in zucchini.

■ In large bowl, combine flour, baking powder, baking soda, salt and cinnamon; stir in nuts. Pour in liquid mixture, stirring just until moistened.

■ Spoon into large greased or paper-lined muffin cups, filling three-quarters full. Bake in 375°F (190°C) oven for 25 to 30 minutes or until tops are firm to the touch. Makes about 16 muffins.

Cheddar Corn Muffins

Make this savory muffin large and serve it for breakfast; make it small and serve it with soup; or split it, stuff with Cheddar and serve as an appetizer.

1-2/3 cups	all-purpose flour	400 mL
1-1/3 cups	cornmeal	325 mL
4 tsp	baking powder	20 mL
1 tsp	baking soda	5 mL
1 tsp	salt	5 mL
2	eggs	2
1-1/2 cups	buttermilk	375 mL
1	can (14 oz/398 mL) creamed corn	1
1/4 cup	butter, melted	50 mL
1-1/2 cups	shredded Cheddar cheese	375 mL
	Paprika or chili powder	

■ In large bowl, stir together flour, cornmeal, baking powder, baking soda and salt. In separate bowl, beat eggs; blend in buttermilk, creamed corn and butter. Pour over flour mixture; sprinkle with 1 cup (250 mL) of the cheese and mix just until moistened.

■ Spoon into large greased or paper-lined muffin cups, filling to top. Sprinkle with remaining cheese. Dust lightly with paprika. Bake in 375°F (190°C) oven for about 25 minutes or until firm to the touch. Makes about 16 muffins.

Cheddar Corn Muffins; Muesli Bran Muffins (p. 16); Figgy Fruit and Oat Bran Muffins (p. 24); Oat Bran Muffins (p. 25) ▶

Figgy Fruit and Oat Bran Muffins

Choose the soft kind of dried figs for these fibre-rich muffins.

1-1/4 cups	all-purpose flour	300 mL
1 cup	whole wheat flour	250 mL
1 cup	oat bran	250 mL
1 tbsp	baking powder	15 mL
2 tsp	cinnamon	10 mL
1-1/2 tsp	baking soda	7 mL
3/4 tsp	salt	4 mL
1	egg	1
1	can (12-1/2 oz/355 mL) frozen apple juice concentrate	1
1/2 cup	milk	125 mL
1/3 cup	vegetable oil	75 mL
1/4 cup	packed brown sugar	50 mL
2 cups	toasted oat cereal, bran flakes or crushed shredded cereal	500 mL
1-1/2 cups	chopped figs	375 mL
1 cup	applesauce	250 mL

■ In large bowl, stir together all-purpose and whole wheat flours, all but 1 tbsp (15 mL) of the oat bran, baking powder, cinnamon, baking soda and salt.

■ In separate bowl, beat together egg, apple juice concentrate, milk, oil and sugar; stir in cereal, figs and applesauce. Stir into dry ingredients just until moistened.

■ Spoon into large greased or paper-lined muffin cups, filling to top. Sprinkle with remaining oat bran. Bake in 375°F (190°C) oven for about 25 minutes or until tops are firm to the touch. Makes about 21 muffins.

Oat Bran Muffin Mix

Here's enough muffin mix for four batches of muffins. Keep a jar handy in the cupboard for when a hankering for muffins hits.

4 cups	oat bran	1 L
4 cups	all-purpose flour	1 L
3 cups	rolled oats	750 mL
3 cups	raisins	750 mL
2 cups	packed brown sugar	500 mL
1 cup	chopped dried apricots	250 mL
1/4 cup	baking powder	50 mL
4 tsp	cinnamon	20 mL
2 tsp	salt	10 mL

ONE BATCH

3-1/2 cups	oat bran muffin mix	875 mL
1	egg	1
1-1/4 cups	milk	300 mL
1/4 cup	butter, melted	50 mL
2 tbsp	coarsely grated orange rind	25 mL

■ In large bowl or airtight container, thoroughly combine oat bran, flour, rolled oats, raisins, sugar, apricots, baking powder, cinnamon and salt. Store in cool dry place for up to 4 weeks. Makes enough for 40 muffins.

■ **To make one batch:** Measure muffin mix into large bowl. In separate bowl, beat egg; stir in milk, butter and orange rind. Stir into muffin mix just until combined. Spoon into large greased or paper-lined muffin cups, filling to top. Bake in 375°F (190°C) oven for about 25 minutes or until tops are firm to the touch. Makes about 10 muffins.

OAT BRAN

The type of soluble fibre in oats — the one that makes oatmeal sticky — seems to help in the lowering of blood cholesterol. And there's more of this beneficial fibre in oat bran than in oatmeal.

• Use oat bran as a breakfast cereal and for pancakes, in meat loaf instead of cracker crumbs, and in muffins and quick breads in place of one-quarter of the all-purpose flour called for in the recipe. If your store does not carry oat bran, ask the manager to order it for you. It is readily available.

Almond Orange Wheels

Sandwich these cookies together with dabs of Buttercream Icing, or simply enjoy them on their own.

1 cup	shortening	250 mL
1 cup	granulated sugar	250 mL
1	egg	1
1/3 cup	orange juice	75 mL
2 tbsp	grated orange rind	25 mL
1/2 tsp	almond extract	2 mL
2-3/4 cups	all-purpose flour	675 mL
1-1/2 tsp	baking powder	7 mL
1/2 cup	ground almonds	125 mL
1/2 cup	Buttercream Icing (recipe follows)	125 mL

■ In bowl, cream together shortening and sugar; blend in egg, orange juice and rind and almond extract. Mix together flour and baking powder; gradually stir into creamed mixture.
■ Divide dough in half; shape each into roll about 10 inches (25 cm) long. Roll in ground almonds to coat completely. Wrap in plastic wrap or waxed paper; refrigerate until firm, about 3 hours.
■ Cut into 1/4-inch (5 mm) thick slices and place on ungreased baking sheets. Bake in 375°F (190°C) oven for about 10 minutes or until lightly golden. Let cool on racks. Sandwich pairs of cookies together with spoonful of Buttercream Icing. Makes about 40 cookies.

BUTTERCREAM ICING

1/4 cup	butter	50 mL
1 cup	(approx) icing sugar	250 mL
1 tbsp	grated orange rind	15 mL
1 tbsp	milk or orange liqueur	15 mL
1 tsp	vanilla	5 mL

■ In small bowl, cream butter; blend in icing sugar, orange rind, milk and vanilla, adding more sugar if necessary to achieve spreading consistency. Makes about 1 cup (250 mL).

(on baking sheet) Almond Orange Wheels ▶

Almond Chocolate Meringues

These delicate cookies with bits of chocolate will quickly become everyone's favorite. They're elegant enough to serve at a tea party.

3	egg whites	3
3/4 cup	instant dissolving (fruit/berry) sugar	175 mL
1 tbsp	cornstarch	15 mL
1/2 tsp	almond extract	2 mL
1 cup	chopped semisweet chocolate (about 5 oz/150 g)	250 mL
3/4 cup	finely ground almonds	175 mL

■ In bowl, beat egg whites until foamy; gradually beat in sugar, 2 tbsp (25 mL) at a time, until stiff glossy peaks form. Beat in cornstarch and almond extract; fold in chocolate and almonds.

■ Drop by heaping teaspoonfuls (5 mL) onto waxed paper-lined baking sheets. Bake in 300°F (150°C) oven for 20 to 30 minutes or until firm, dry and crisp. Let cool on baking sheets for 5 minutes; remove to racks to let cool completely. Makes about 40 cookies.

(left) Chocolate Nut Drops (p. 29);
(right) Almond Chocolate Meringues ▲

Chocolate Nut Drops

Everyone loves chocolate — especially in a moist, chewy cookie with nuts and a hint of orange.

2/3 cup	butter	150 mL
1 cup	granulated sugar	250 mL
2	eggs	2
1 cup	all-purpose flour	250 mL
1/2 cup	unsweetened cocoa powder	125 mL
1/4 tsp	salt	1 mL
1/2 cup	chopped walnuts, pecans or hazelnuts	125 mL
1/2 cup	chopped semisweet chocolate (about 2-1/2 oz/75 g)	125 mL
2 tsp	grated orange rind	10 mL

■ In bowl, cream together butter and sugar; beat in eggs 1 at a time. Stir together flour, cocoa and salt; stir into creamed mixture. Stir in walnuts, chocolate and orange rind.

■ Drop by heaping teaspoonfuls (5 mL) onto lightly greased baking sheets. Bake in 350°F (180°C) oven for 8 to 10 minutes or until firm to the touch. Let cool on baking sheets for 5 minutes; remove to racks to let cool completely. Makes about 55 cookies.

Gingersnaps

These old-fashioned favorites are a snap to make.

1/2 cup	butter, softened	125 mL
1-1/4 cups	lightly packed brown sugar	300 mL
2 tbsp	molasses	25 mL
1	egg	1
1-3/4 cups	all-purpose flour	425 mL
2 tsp	ginger	10 mL
1/2 tsp	baking soda	2 mL
1/2 tsp	salt	2 mL

■ In bowl, cream together butter, sugar, molasses and egg until light and fluffy. Combine flour, ginger, baking soda and salt; stir into creamed mixture and blend well.

■ Shape dough into roll 2 inches (5 cm) in diameter. Wrap in waxed paper and chill until firm, about 4 hours or overnight.

■ Cut dough into 1/8-inch (3 mm) thick slices and place on ungreased baking sheets about 1 inch (2.5 cm) apart. Bake in 400°F (200°C) oven for 6 to 8 minutes or until firm to the touch. Makes about 65 cookies.

Oldtime Icebox Cookies

Try a few variations on this recipe for a wonderful assortment of old-fashioned icebox cookies.

1/2 cup	butter	125 mL
1 cup	packed light brown sugar	250 mL
1	egg	1
1 tsp	vanilla	5 mL
1-1/2 cups	all-purpose flour	375 mL
1/2 tsp	baking soda	2 mL
1/2 tsp	salt	2 mL

■ In bowl, cream together butter and sugar until light and fluffy; beat in egg and vanilla. Combine flour, baking soda and salt; gradually blend into creamed mixture.

■ Shape dough into roll about 2 inches (5 cm) in diameter. Wrap in plastic wrap or waxed paper and refrigerate until firm, about 3 hours.

■ Cut dough into 1/8-inch (3 mm) thick slices and place on greased baking sheets. Bake in 375°F (190°C) oven for 7 to 9 minutes or until very lightly browned. Let cool for a few minutes on baking sheets; transfer to racks to cool completely. Makes about 4 dozen cookies.

VARIATIONS

Orange-Almond Cookies: Add 1 tbsp (15 mL) grated orange rind, 1/4 tsp (1 mL) almond extract and 1/2 cup (125 mL) finely chopped blanched almonds.

Ginger Thins: Add 2 tbsp (25 mL) molasses to the creamed mixture and 1 tbsp (15 mL) ginger to the flour mixture.

REFRIGERATOR COOKIE TIPS

Refrigerator cookie dough is firm and can be shaped into a cylinder by rolling it by hand on the counter. Wrap dough in waxed paper, plastic wrap or foil and refrigerate until firm enough to slice, about four hours or overnight.

• Refrigerator cookie dough can be stored in refrigerator for up to two weeks or frozen for up to two months. Thaw frozen dough overnight in refrigerator or let stand at room temperature until soft enough to slice.

• For perfectly round cookies, pack dough into small clean frozen juice cans opened at one end. Seal airtight with plastic wrap and refrigerate or freeze. When ready to bake, open the closed end and slowly push out

dough, cutting slices off as you push it out.

• For square cookies, line boxes from plastic wrap or waxed paper with plastic wrap, waxed paper or foil and pack dough into the box. Wrap airtight and refrigerate or freeze.

• Thin slices result in crisp cookies, thick slices make chewy cookies.

• Because of the high butter content in most refrigerator cookies, you don't even have to grease the baking sheets.

• To make cookies special, roll dough in finely chopped nuts, pressing a nut into each cookie before baking, or sandwich your favorite frosting, jam or jelly between baked cookies.

Chocolate Chip Cookies

Recipes for these perennial favorites abound, but a really good chocolate chip cookie can be a bit touchy to make. The following recipe calls for larger quantities of ingredients than most, which makes it a bit more tolerant to small variations in measuring. For a firmer cookie, add about 1/4 cup (50 mL) more flour.

1/2 cup	butter	125 mL
1/2 cup	shortening	125 mL
1 cup	granulated sugar	250 mL
1/2 cup	packed brown sugar	125 mL
2	eggs	2
2 tsp	vanilla	10 mL
2 cups	all-purpose flour	500 mL
1 tsp	baking soda	5 mL
1/2 tsp	salt	2 mL
2 cups	chocolate chips	500 mL
1 cup	chopped walnuts or pecans	250 mL

■ In large bowl, cream together butter and shortening; gradually beat in granulated and brown sugars, creaming thoroughly. Beat in eggs and vanilla.

■ Combine flour, baking soda and salt; blend into creamed mixture. Stir in chocolate chips and nuts. Chill for a few minutes or let stand at cool room temperature for about 30 minutes.

■ Drop by rounded tablespoonfuls (15 mL) onto lightly greased baking sheets. Flatten slightly and smooth edges to make 1/2-inch (1 cm) thick cookie.

■ Bake in 375°F (190°C) oven for 8 to 9 minutes or until golden brown around edges and still slightly underbaked in centre. Let stand on baking sheet for 5 minutes; remove to racks to let cool completely. Makes about 50 cookies.

VARIATION

Chocolate Chunk Cookies: For a super-deluxe version use 8 ounces (250 g) semisweet chocolate chopped into 1/2-inch (1 cm) pieces instead of packaged chips.

Coffee Hazelnut Crescents

A favorite for teas, these coffee-flavored nut crescents taste as great as they look.
Instead of dipping the ends in chocolate, you can roll the cookies in icing sugar.

2 tsp	instant coffee granules	10 mL
2 tsp	hot water	10 mL
1 cup	butter	250 mL
2/3 cup	sifted icing sugar	150 mL
2 cups	all-purpose flour	500 mL
1 cup	finely chopped hazelnuts or almonds	250 mL
6 oz	semisweet chocolate	175 g

■ Dissolve coffee in hot water; let cool. In bowl, cream together butter, icing sugar and coffee; stir in flour and nuts until well mixed. Chill for 30 minutes.

■ Roll small pieces of dough into logs 3 inches (8 cm) long and 1/2 inch (1 cm) in diameter. Shape into crescents on ungreased baking sheet.

■ Bake in 350°F (180°C) oven for 10 to 12 minutes or just until edges start to brown. Let cool.

■ In top of double boiler over simmering water, melt chocolate; dip ends of crescents into chocolate. Let dry on waxed paper. Makes about 8 dozen cookies.

(clockwise from top) Sugar 'n' Spice Cookies
(p. 33); Coffee Hazelnut Crescents;
Coffee Fingers (p. 33) ▼

Sugar 'n' Spice Cookies

Here's a wonderful recipe for children to help make because overworking and rerolling the dough doesn't harm it. Decorate with piped pink icing "flowers" if desired.

2-1/2 cups	all-purpose flour	625 mL
2 tsp	baking soda	10 mL
2 tsp	each cinnamon, cloves and ginger	10 mL
1 cup	butter	250 mL
1-1/2 cups	granulated sugar	375 mL
1	egg	1

■ Stir together flour, baking soda, cinnamon, cloves and ginger. In large bowl, cream together butter, sugar and egg; gradually add dry ingredients, mixing well. (If dough is very soft, chill slightly for easier rolling.)

■ On lightly floured surface, roll out dough to 1/8-inch (3 mm) thickness. With cookie cutters, cut into desired shapes; place on greased baking sheet. Bake in 375°F (190°C) oven for 5 to 8 minutes or until set. Makes about 50 cookies.

Coffee Fingers

Use your cookie press to make these. They're a little more time-consuming to make than some, but the delicate texture, flavor and appearance make them well worth the effort, especially for fancy teas. Freeze them filled or unfilled.

1 cup	butter	250 mL
1/2 cup	sifted icing sugar	125 mL
2 cups	all-purpose flour	500 mL
1/4 tsp	baking powder	1 mL
1/2 tsp	vanilla	2 mL
	FILLING	
3 tbsp	butter	50 mL
1 tsp	instant coffee powder	5 mL
1-1/2 tsp	hot water	7 mL
1 cup	(approx) sifted icing sugar	250 mL

■ In bowl, cream together butter and sugar; gradually stir in flour, baking powder and vanilla, mixing well.

■ Using cookie press fitted with star tube, press out in 1-inch (2.5 cm) lengths of dough onto ungreased baking sheets. (If dough does not press out smoothly, add about 2 tsp/10 mL more butter.)

■ Bake in 375°F (190°C) oven for 5 to 7 minutes or just until edges start to brown. Don't overbake. Let cool on racks.

■ **Filling:** In bowl, cream butter. Dissolve coffee in hot water and stir into butter; gradually stir in enough of the sugar for spreading consistency. Sandwich between 2 cookies. Makes about 6 dozen.

Honey Oatmeal Cookies

The ability of honey to retain water keeps these cookies moist. Freshly ground oat flour makes them especially good for anyone with a wheat allergy.

4 cups	rolled oats	1 L
1 tsp	baking powder	5 mL
1 tsp	cinnamon	5 mL
Pinch	salt	Pinch
3/4 cup	unsalted butter, softened	175 mL
1/2 cup	liquid honey	125 mL
1	egg	1
1 tsp	vanilla	5 mL
1/2 cup	raisins or chocolate chips (optional)	125 mL
36	pecan halves (optional)	36

■ In food processor or blender, process 2 cups (500 mL) of the rolled oats until in fine flour. Add baking powder, cinnamon and salt; process to combine. In bowl, blend together butter, honey, egg and vanilla; stir in oat flour mixture, remaining rolled oats, and raisins (if using).

■ Drop heaping teaspoonfuls (5 mL) at a time about 1-inch (2.5 cm) apart onto baking sheet. Flatten to 1/4-inch (5 mm) thickness; decorate with pecan halves (if using). Bake in 375°F (190°C) oven until lightly browned at edges, about 20 minutes. Let cool slightly on sheet; transfer to rack to let cool completely. Makes about 36 cookies.

HONEYED TREATS

Honey is available in several forms: comb honey is sealed in beeswax; liquid honey has been extracted from the comb and strained; creamed honey is liquid honey that has been seeded with finely granulated honey crystals, stored under controlled conditions until it's full of fine crystals, then beaten well.

• If kept cold, raw liquid honey will form coarse crystals. These are completely harmless; you can immerse the container in warm water until crystals are melted. Creamed honey may be turned into liquid honey in the same way.

• When you buy honey, think of how you'll be using it. Comb honey is suitable only for spreading. Liquid honey is easy to measure and to mix into a batter, while creamed honey makes the lightest cakes. Liquid and creamed honey are interchangeable in most recipes.

Saucepan Date Rolls

Like most refrigerator cookies, these ones are shaped into a roll and refrigerated or frozen. But there's no baking involved; to serve, simply thaw, slice and enjoy.

2 tbsp	butter	25 mL
1 cup	chopped dates	250 mL
3/4 cup	granulated sugar	175 mL
2	eggs, beaten	2
3 cups	crispy rice cereal	750 mL
1/2 cup	finely chopped nuts	125 mL
	Icing sugar	

■ In large saucepan, melt butter. Stir in dates, sugar and eggs; cook, stirring, over medium heat until thickened, 7 to 10 minutes. Stir in cereal and nuts, mixing well. Let cool to room temperature.

■ On waxed paper sprinkled with icing sugar, shape mixture into 2 rolls 1-1/2 inches (4 cm) in diameter. Roll in icing sugar to coat completely. Wrap in waxed paper and chill until firm, about 4 hours or overnight. Cut into 1/4-inch (5 mm) slices. Makes about 50 cookies.

COOKIE TIPS

Unless otherwise specified, have all ingredients at room temperature.

• *Cream butter, sugar, eggs and flavorings with an electric mixer. Use low speed or wooden spoon to stir in dry ingredients.*

• *Use bright shiny baking sheets for best results.*

• *Use baking sheets, not jelly roll pans, which have sides that deflect the heat.*

• *Bake in the middle of a preheated oven.*

• *When baking in batches, bake one sheet of cookies while you prepare the next.*

• *If you have only one baking sheet, line it with foil before baking the cookies. After baking, slide the foil off the pan and set the cookies aside to cool. Rinse the pan under cold water, pat dry and slide the next batch of cookies on foil onto the baking sheet.*

• *Let cookies cool for a few minutes on the baking sheet before transferring to a wire rack to cool completely.*

• *Store crisp cookies between sheets of waxed paper in a loosely covered container. Store soft cookies in an airtight one so they stay moist and chewy.*

• *If crisp cookies become soggy after storage, reheat them in a 300°F (150°C) oven for a few minutes.*

• *Crisp and soft cookies should not be stored together.*

Monster Oatmeal Chocolate Chip Cookies

Big cookies always go over in a big way at bake sales, especially if they're buttery-rich and crisp with lots of chocolate chips and nuts. Oats and wheat germ add extra flavor and nutrition.

1-3/4 cups	rolled oats	425 mL
1-1/2 cups	all-purpose flour	375 mL
1 cup	wheat germ	250 mL
2 tsp	baking soda	10 mL
1 tsp	salt	5 mL
1 cup	butter or margarine	250 mL
1 cup	lightly packed brown sugar	250 mL
2	eggs	2
1-1/2 cups	chocolate chips or raisins	375 mL
1/2 cup	chopped nuts	125 mL

■ Stir together oats, flour, wheat germ, baking soda and salt. In large bowl, cream together butter, sugar and eggs thoroughly; blend in dry ingredients. Stir in chocolate chips and nuts, mixing well.

■ Using 1/3 cup (75 mL) for each cookie, spoon dough about 6 inches (15 cm) apart onto greased baking sheets; flatten into 5-inch (12 cm) circles. Bake in 350° (180°C) oven for about 12 minutes or until golden. Let cool on pans for 5 minutes; transfer to racks to cool completely. Makes about 15.

VARIATION

For 3-inch (8 cm) cookies, drop dough 1 tbsp (15 mL) at a time, onto lightly greased baking sheet. Flatten slightly. Bake for 8 to 10 minutes. Makes about 6 dozen cookies.

Fortune Cookies

Here's a fun lunchbox idea: write special messages on 18 strips of 3- × 1/2-inch (8 × 1 cm) pieces of paper and put them inside fortune cookies.

3 tbsp	butter, softened	50 mL
3 tbsp	granulated sugar	50 mL
1	egg white	1
1/2 tsp	vanilla	2 mL
1/3 cup	all-purpose flour	75 mL

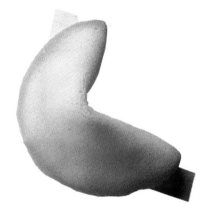

■ In small bowl, mix together butter, sugar, egg white and vanilla; stir in flour until well blended. Drop rounded teaspoonfuls (5 mL) at a time onto greased baking sheet; spread into 3-inch (8 cm) circle using back of spoon. Bake, one sheet at a time, in 400°F (200°C) oven for 3 to 4 minutes or until edges are lightly browned.

■ Place baking sheet on rack. Loosen cookies with spatula and turn over; place folded fortune in centre. Quickly and gently fold cookie in half; press edges together for several seconds. Grasp ends of cookie, place centre over rim of glass and gently press ends down to bend cookie in middle. Place each cookie in muffin cup to retain shape until cooled. Repeat with remaining cookies. (If cookies become too brittle to fold, return to oven briefly to soften.) Makes about 18 cookies.

Taco Cookies

Tease the mind and palate with this dessert that looks like a taco but is actually a cookie. Fill with lime sherbet and garnish with fruit.

2	egg whites	2
1/2 cup	granulated sugar	125 mL
1/3 cup	all-purpose flour	75 mL
1/4 cup	butter, melted	50 mL
2 tsp	water	10 mL
1/2 tsp	vanilla or almond extract	2 mL
1/4 cup	ground almonds	50 mL

■ In bowl, whisk together egg whites, sugar, flour, butter, water and vanilla just until blended; stir in almonds.

■ Drop 2 tbsp (25 mL) at a time onto parchment paper-lined or greased-and-floured baking sheets, leaving at least 8 inches (20 cm) between each. Using back of spoon, spread batter into 4-1/2-inch (11 cm) circle. Bake one sheet at a time in 400°F (200°C) oven for 6 to 8 minutes or until edges are just beginning to brown. Immediately remove with spatula and drape over empty paper towel roll to form curved shape. Let cool completely. *(Cookies can be stored in airtight tin for up to 1 week. If necessary, recrisp in 275°F/140°C oven for 1 minute.)* Makes about 8 cookies.

Christmas Cutouts

Leave these cookies plain or frost them with white Decorator Icing (sidebar, p. 44), adding colored sprinkles, silver shot or dragées.

1/2 cup	butter	125 mL
1 cup	granulated sugar	250 mL
1	egg, lightly beaten	1
3 tbsp	orange juice	50 mL
2 tbsp	grated orange rind	25 mL
2 cups	all-purpose flour	500 mL
2 tsp	baking powder	10 mL
1/4 tsp	salt	1 mL

■ In large bowl, cream together butter and sugar until light and fluffy; beat in egg, then orange juice and rind. Combine flour, baking powder and salt; gradually blend into creamed mixture. Cover and refrigerate until chilled.

■ On lightly floured surface, roll out dough to 1/8-inch (3 mm) thickness. Cut into Christmas shapes and place on ungreased baking sheets. Bake in 375°F (190°C) oven for 8 minutes or until lightly browned. Let cool on racks. Makes about 48 two-inch (5 cm) cookies.

(on tray) Thimble Cookies (p. 41); Sugar Cookie Jam-Jams (p. 42); Christmas Cutouts; Peanut Butter Logs (p. 43); Spritz Cookies (p. 44); (in square basket) Christmas Cutouts; (in round basket) Thimble Cookies (p. 41); Chocolate Madeleines (p. 43); Spritz Cookies (p. 44) ▲

Thimble Cookies

You can substitute jam for the red and green cherries but don't fill the centres until just before serving.

1/2 cup	butter	125 mL
1/4 cup	granulated sugar	50 mL
1	egg, separated	1
1 tsp	vanilla	5 mL
1 cup	all-purpose flour	250 mL
2 tbsp	sifted unsweetened cocoa powder	25 mL
1 cup	finely chopped walnuts	250 mL
	Red and green candied cherries, halved	

■ In large bowl, cream together butter and sugar until light and fluffy; beat in egg yolk and vanilla. Combine flour with cocoa; gradually blend into creamed mixture. Cover and chill for 30 minutes.

■ Shape dough into 1-inch (2.5 cm) balls. Dip in lightly beaten egg white; roll in walnuts. Place on ungreased baking sheets. Using finger or greased thimble, make indentation in centre of each ball. Bake in 325°F (160°C) oven for 7 minutes. Make indentations once more. Bake for 10 minutes longer or until set. Let cool on racks. Place cherry in indentation of each cookie. Makes about 2 dozen cookies.

MERRY COOKIES!

Bake a variety of cookie shapes to sprinkle with sugar, frost with icing or dip into chocolate for a festive array of Christmas treats. You'll find many recipes to choose from in this section, including Christmas Cutouts (p. 40), Thimble Cookies, Sugar Cookie Jam-Jams (p. 42), Chocolate Madeleines (p. 43), Peanut Butter Logs (p. 43), Spritz Cookies (p. 44) and Slice-and-Bake Shortbread (p. 48).

Sugar Cookie Jam-Jams

Vary these cookies for the occasion by using all sorts of cookie cutters. You can halve the recipe if desired, but before you begin, make sure all the ingredients are at room temperature.

2 cups	butter	500 mL
2 cups	(approx) sifted icing sugar	500 mL
2 tsp	vanilla	10 mL
2	eggs	2
5 cups	all-purpose flour	1.25 L
1 tsp	salt	5 mL
1/2 tsp	baking soda	2 mL
	Raspberry jam	

■ In bowl, cream butter with 2 cups (500 mL) icing sugar until light and fluffy; beat in vanilla and eggs. Combine flour, salt and baking soda; gradually blend into creamed mixture. Press into ball; chill if very soft.

■ On lightly floured surface, roll out about one-quarter of the dough at a time to 1/4-inch (5 mm) thickness. With 2-1/2-inch (6 cm) round cutter, cut out cookies. With small cutter, cut out holes in centre of half of the cookies. Arrange about 1-1/2 inches (4 cm) apart on ungreased baking sheets; bake in 375°F (190°C) oven for about 8 minutes or until lightly browned. Let cool on racks.

■ Sprinkle icing sugar over cookies with holes. Spread jam over whole cookies and top with sugared cookies. Makes about 60 cookies.

> *When trying a new cookie recipe, start by baking one or two cookies as samples to gauge the finished size, the amount of space to leave between cookies and the final yield.*

Chocolate Madeleines

The shell-shaped moulds used for these French delicacies are available at specialty cookware shops.

1 cup	butter	250 mL
1 cup	granulated sugar	250 mL
4	eggs, lightly beaten	4
1 tsp	grated orange rind	5 mL
1-1/2 cups	all-purpose flour	375 mL
1/4 cup	unsweetened cocoa powder	50 mL
1 tsp	baking powder	5 mL
Pinch	salt	Pinch
	Icing sugar	

■ In large bowl, cream butter thoroughly; gradually beat in sugar until light and fluffy. Gradually beat in eggs until smooth. Stir in orange rind. In separate bowl, stir together flour, cocoa, baking powder and salt; sift one-half over butter mixture and stir until combined. Repeat with remaining flour mixture.

■ Spoon tablespoonfuls (15 mL) of batter into greased and floured madeleine moulds. Bake in 400°F (200°C) oven for about 20 minutes or until tops spring back when lightly touched. Turn out onto racks and let cool. Dust with icing sugar. Makes about 2 dozen.

Peanut Butter Logs

The popular flavor of peanut butter makes these chewy treats delicious.

1/2 cup	butter	125 mL
1 cup	smooth peanut butter	250 mL
1/2 cup	packed brown sugar	125 mL
1/4 cup	granulated sugar	50 mL
1	egg	1
1 tsp	vanilla	5 mL
1 cup	all-purpose flour	250 mL
1 tsp	baking soda	5 mL
1/2 cup	semisweet chocolate, coarsely chopped	125 mL

■ In bowl, cream butter with peanut butter; beat in brown and granulated sugars until smooth and creamy. Beat in egg and vanilla.

■ Combine flour and baking soda; stir into peanut butter mixture just until blended.

■ Using large pastry bag fitted with #5 star tip or #2 plain tip, pipe batter into 3-inch (8 cm) jagged lengths onto lightly greased or parchment paper-lined baking sheets.

■ Bake in 375°F (190°C) oven for 10 minutes or until lightly browned. Let cool slightly on baking sheets; remove to racks to let cool completely.

■ Meanwhile, in top of double boiler over hot, not boiling, water, melt chocolate. Dip one end of cooled cookie into chocolate; let cool until set. Makes about 32 cookies.

Spritz Cookies

Use a cookie press and its different discs to make a variety of shapes. Sprinkle cookies with colored sugar before baking if desired.

1 cup	butter, softened	250 mL
1-1/4 cups	sifted icing sugar	300 mL
1	egg	1
1 tsp	vanilla	5 mL
2 cups	all-purpose flour	500 mL
1/4 tsp	salt	1 mL
	Decorator Icing (see sidebar below)	

■ In bowl, cream butter thoroughly; gradually beat in sugar until light and fluffy. Beat in egg and vanilla. Combine flour with salt; blend into creamed mixture.

■ Fill cookie press with batches of dough; press out shapes onto ungreased baking sheets. (If dough becomes too soft to hold shapes, chill.) Bake in 375°F (190°C) oven for 5 to 10 minutes or just until beginning to brown around edges. Let cool on racks. Spread with Decorator Icing (if using). Makes about 4 dozen cookies.

DECORATOR ICING

To 1 lightly beaten egg white, add a few drops of vanilla or almond flavoring. Stir in enough sifted icing sugar (about 2 cups/ 500 mL) to make firm icing that will pipe easily through pastry bag. If it's too stiff, add a few drops of milk. Divide among several small custard cups. Add enough food coloring to each cup to make bright colors. (Icing can be thinned slightly and painted onto cookies with small brushes.) Cover icing with damp cloth to prevent it from hardening.

Orange Coconut Crisps

Sheer delight is the only way to describe these tender-crisp orange coconut cookies.

3 cups	all-purpose flour	750 mL
1-1/2 cups	desiccated coconut	375 mL
1/2 tsp	baking soda	2 mL
1 cup	butter, softened	250 mL
1 cup	granulated sugar	250 mL
1	egg	1
1/4 cup	orange juice	50 mL
2 tbsp	grated orange rind	25 mL

■ Combine flour, coconut and baking soda. In bowl, cream together butter, sugar, egg, orange juice and rind; stir in flour mixture and blend well.

■ Shape dough into 2 rolls 1-1/2 inches (4 cm) in diameter. Wrap in waxed paper and chill until firm, about 4 hours or overnight.

■ Cut dough into 1/8-inch (3 mm) thick slices; place on ungreased baking sheets. Bake in 375°F (190°C) oven for 8 to 10 minutes or until golden. Makes about 96 cookies.

Rich Almond Wafers

These take about 15 minutes to make from start to finish.

18	(approx) graham wafers or biscuits	18
1 cup	sliced almonds	250 mL
1 cup	packed light brown sugar	250 mL
1 cup	butter	250 mL

■ Line ungreased 17- × 11-inch (45 × 29 cm) jelly roll pan with graham wafers; sprinkle with almonds. In small saucepan, combine sugar and butter; bring to boil over medium-high heat, stirring constantly until blended. Boil for 3 minutes.

■ Pour over almonds, spreading evenly. Bake in 350°F (180°C) oven for 7 minutes or until bubbling. Let cool slightly; cut into squares while still warm. Makes about 50 wafers.

Lemon Shorties

Cookies should be easy to make and delicious little mouthfuls — like these lemon shortbreads.

1 cup	butter	250 mL
1/2 cup	granulated sugar	125 mL
2 tbsp	grated lemon rind	25 mL
2 cups	all-purpose flour	500 mL

■ In large bowl, cream butter; beat in sugar until light and fluffy. Stir in lemon rind; gradually stir in flour until blended. Shape dough into 2 equal discs; wrap and refrigerate for 30 minutes or until chilled.

■ Between waxed paper, roll out dough to 1/4-inch (5 mm) thickness. With 2-inch (5 cm) floured cutter, cut out cookies and place on ungreased baking sheets; bake in 300°F (150°C) oven for 17 to 20 minutes or until lightly browned on bottom. Remove to racks and let cool. Makes about 3 dozen cookies.

VARIATION

Pecan Slices: Follow recipe for Lemon Shorties but omit lemon rind. Reduce flour to 1-3/4 cups (425 mL) and combine with 1/2 cup (125 mL) chopped pecans. Shape into two 9-inch (23 cm) long rolls. Wrap and refrigerate until firm, about 2 hours. Cut into 1/4-inch (5 mm) thick slices and bake as above. Makes about 6 dozen cookies.

MIX AND MATCH

- *Whole wheat or graham flour can be substituted for half the all-purpose flour called for in the recipe.*
- *An equal amount of packed brown sugar can be used instead of granulated sugar.*
- *When a recipe calls for raisins, you can substitute chopped dates, currants, chopped plumped dried apricots, chopped figs or dried fruit bits.*
- *When a recipe calls for coconut to be mixed into the cookie dough, you can use plain or toasted coconut. If the coconut is to coat the outside of the roll of dough before slicing, use plain coconut. Toasted coconut on the edges of cookies will burn during baking.*
- *You can substitute cocoa for chocolate in a refrigerator cookie dough. For each ounce (30 g) chocolate, substitute 3 tbsp (50 mL) unsweetened cocoa powder mixed with the dry ingredients, and add an extra 1 tbsp (15 mL) butter.*

Easy Sugar-Dusted Amaretti Biscuits

Amaretti, crisp almond cookies originally from Italy, are perfect with an after-dinner cup of coffee or with ice cream.

1 cup	blanched almonds	250 mL
1 cup	(approx) icing sugar	250 mL
1 tsp	all-purpose flour	5 mL
2	egg whites	2
1/3 cup	granulated sugar	75 mL
1 tsp	almond extract	5 mL

■ In food processor, process almonds and 1/4 cup (50 mL) of the icing sugar until finely ground; blend in remaining icing sugar and flour.

■ In bowl, beat egg whites until soft peaks form; gradually beat in granulated sugar until stiff glossy peaks form. Fold in nut mixture and almond extract.

■ On greased baking sheets and using pastry bag, pipe almond mixture into 1-1/2-inch (4 cm) wide mounds about 1-1/2 inches (4 cm) apart. Bake in 300°F (150°C) oven for 40 to 45 minutes or until light golden. Turn off oven; let dry in oven for 20 minutes. Remove biscuits to racks and let cool. Dust with icing sugar. Makes about 2-1/2 dozen cookies.

Pecan Slices (p. 46); Lemon Shorties (p. 46); Easy Sugar-Dusted Amaretti Biscuits ▲

Slice-and-Bake Shortbread

Enjoy the perennial favorite any time of year. Three fast-and-easy variations on the traditional theme make a nice change.

1 cup	butter	250 mL
1 cup	icing sugar	250 mL
1 tsp	vanilla	5 mL
2 cups	all-purpose flour	500 mL

■ In bowl, cream together butter, sugar and vanilla. Gradually blend in flour. Press into ball and knead lightly until smooth.

■ Divide dough in half; shape each half into roll about 2 inches (5 cm) in diameter. Wrap in plastic wrap or waxed paper and refrigerate until firm, about 3 hours.

■ Cut into 1/4-inch (5 mm) thick slices and place on ungreased baking sheets. Bake in 300°F (150°C) oven for about 20 minutes or until firm but not browned. Let cool slightly on baking sheets; transfer to rack to cool completely. Makes about 4 dozen cookies.

VARIATIONS

Chocolate Shortbread: To creamed butter mixture, add 1 tbsp (15 mL) water. Sift 1/2 cup (125 mL) unsweetened cocoa powder with the flour before adding.

Ginger Shortbread: Add 1 tsp (5 mL) ground ginger to the flour; stir in 1/3 cup (75 mL) chopped candied ginger at the end.

Hazelnut Shortbread: Replace 1/2 cup (125 mL) of the flour with finely ground hazelnuts or almonds.

Peanut Butter Cookies

Forever a kid's favorite cookie and a must-have with a glass of milk. This version is a little lighter than most recipes, but still packs in that old-fashioned satisfaction.

1/2 cup	butter, softened	125 mL
1/2 cup	granulated sugar	125 mL
1/2 cup	packed brown sugar	125 mL
1	egg	1
1 cup	smooth peanut butter	250 mL
1/2 tsp	vanilla	2 mL
1-1/2 cups	all-purpose flour	375 mL
1/2 tsp	salt	2 mL
1/2 tsp	baking soda	2 mL
1 cup	unsalted peanuts	250 mL

■ In bowl, cream butter with granulated and brown sugars until fluffy; beat in egg, peanut butter and vanilla. Combine flour, salt and baking soda; add peanuts. Stir into peanut butter mixture.

■ Roll dough, 1 tbsp (15 mL) at a time, into balls; place 1 inch (2.5 cm) apart on lightly greased baking sheets and gently flatten with fork. Bake in 375°F (190°C) oven for 10 minutes or until light golden brown. Let cool on rack. Makes about 3-1/2 dozen cookies.

Chocolate Chip Hermits

Pumpkin adds moistness and color to these soft spicy cookies.

3/4 cup	shortening	175 mL
1-1/4 cups	packed brown sugar	300 mL
2	eggs	2
1 cup	canned pumpkin purée	250 mL
1 tsp	vanilla	5 mL
2 cups	all-purpose flour	500 mL
1 tsp	baking powder	5 mL
1 tsp	cinnamon	5 mL
1/2 tsp	baking soda	2 mL
1/2 tsp	salt	2 mL
1/2 tsp	each nutmeg, allspice and cloves	2 mL
1 cup	raisins	250 mL
1 cup	chocolate chips	250 mL
1/2 cup	chopped dates	125 mL
1/2 cup	chopped nuts	125 mL

■ In large bowl, cream together shortening and sugar; beat in eggs, pumpkin and vanilla.

■ Combine flour, baking powder, cinnamon, baking soda, salt, nutmeg, allspice and cloves; stir into creamed mixture. Stir in raisins, chocolate chips, dates and nuts.

■ Drop rounded teaspoonfuls (5 mL) at a time onto greased baking sheets. Bake in 350°F (180°C) oven for 10 to 12 minutes or until golden brown. Makes about 60 cookies.

Chocolate Chip Hermits;
Halloween Bars (p. 52) ▲

Almond Cherry Bars

These moist bars are chock-full of cherries, nuts and chocolate chips.

1 cup	butter, softened	250 mL
1 cup	granulated sugar	250 mL
1	egg	1
1/2 tsp	almond extract	2 mL
2 cups	all-purpose flour	500 mL
1 tsp	baking powder	5 mL
1/4 tsp	salt	1 mL
2 cups	chocolate chips	500 mL
1 cup	maraschino cherries, coarsely chopped	250 mL
1/2 cup	slivered almonds	125 mL
1/2 cup	shredded coconut	125 mL

■ In large bowl, cream together butter and sugar until light and fluffy; beat in egg and almond extract. Combine flour, baking powder and salt; stir into creamed mixture just until blended. Stir in chocolate chips, cherries, almonds and coconut.

■ Spread evenly in 13- × 9-inch (3.5 L) ungreased cake pan. Bake in 350°F (180°C) oven for about 30 minutes or until golden brown. Let cool completely in pan on rack before cutting into bars. Makes about 40 bars.

Butterscotch Pecan Bars

These nutty bars take only minutes to make and are perfect for popping into lunchboxes.

1 cup	packed brown sugar	250 mL
1/4 cup	butter	50 mL
1	egg	1
1 tsp	vanilla	5 mL
1/2 cup	all-purpose flour	125 mL
1/4 tsp	baking soda	1 mL
1/4 tsp	salt	1 mL
1 cup	coarsely chopped pecans	250 mL

■ In saucepan, heat brown sugar and butter over medium heat, stirring, just until melted. Remove from heat; let cool slightly. Beat in egg and vanilla; stir in flour, baking soda and salt just until blended. Stir in pecans.

■ Spread evenly in greased 8-inch (2 L) square cake pan. Bake in 350°F (180°C) oven for 15 to 18 minutes or until golden brown and set. Let cool in pan on rack for 15 minutes before cutting. Makes 20 bars.

Almond Cherry Bars; Butterscotch Pecan Bars;
Lemon Meringue Slices (p. 60); Chocolate
Walnut Squares (p. 60) ▶

Halloween Bars

Moist orange bars with a yummy chocolate topping are perfect for Halloween parties or for trick-or-treaters.

3/4 cup	all-purpose flour	175 mL
1 tsp	baking powder	5 mL
1/2 tsp	salt	2 mL
1/4 tsp	cinnamon	1 mL
1/4 tsp	nutmeg	1 mL
2	eggs	2
1 cup	packed brown sugar	250 mL
1/2 cup	canned pumpkin purée	125 mL
1/4 cup	vegetable oil	50 mL
2 tsp	grated orange rind	10 mL
1/2 tsp	vanilla	2 mL
1/2 cup	raisins	125 mL
1/2 cup	chopped nuts	125 mL
2 cups	chocolate chips	500 mL

■ Combine flour, baking powder, salt, cinnamon and nutmeg. In large bowl, beat eggs; blend in sugar, pumpkin, oil, orange rind and vanilla. Stir in dry ingredients. Add raisins, nuts and half of the chocolate chips; stir until mixed.

■ Spread evenly in greased and floured 9-inch (2.5 L) square cake pan. Bake in 350°F (180°C) oven for 25 to 30 minutes or until top springs back when lightly touched. Remove from oven; sprinkle with remaining chocolate chips. When chips soften, spread evenly to make smooth frosting. Let cool; cut into bars. Makes about 30 bars.

Coconut Oat Thins

These golden, crispy oat squares taste terrific and are simple to prepare.

1-1/2 cups	rolled oats	375 mL
1 cup	packed brown sugar	250 mL
1/2 cup	flaked coconut	125 mL
1 tsp	baking powder	5 mL
1/2 tsp	salt	2 mL
1/2 cup	butter, melted	125 mL
1 tsp	vanilla	5 mL
1 tbsp	granulated sugar	15 mL

■ In large bowl, stir together rolled oats, brown sugar, coconut, baking powder and salt; stir in butter and vanilla just until blended.

■ Spread evenly in ungreased 13- × 9-inch (3.5 L) cake pan; press firmly with back of spoon. Sprinkle with granulated sugar.

■ Bake in 300°F (150°C) oven for about 25 minutes or until golden. Let cool on rack for 5 minutes before cutting with sharp buttered knife. Let cool completely before removing from pan. Makes about 40 squares.

Microwave Apricot Oat Squares

Your microwave oven makes these treats extra easy to prepare.

1 cup	rolled oats	250 mL
1 cup	all-purpose flour	250 mL
1 cup	packed dark brown sugar	250 mL
1/2 tsp	baking powder	2 mL
1/4 tsp	salt	1 mL
1/2 cup	butter	125 mL
	FILLING	
1-1/2 cups	chopped dried apricots	375 mL
3/4 cup	water	175 mL
1/2 cup	granulated sugar	125 mL

■ **Filling:** In 8-cup (2 L) microwaveable measure, combine apricots, water and sugar; cover and microwave at High for 6 to 8 minutes or until boiling and fruit is softened, stirring every 2 minutes. Uncover and let stand until lukewarm, stirring often.

■ Meanwhile, in bowl, mix together oats, flour, sugar, baking powder and salt; cut in butter until mixture is crumbly. Pat half of the mixture into 8-inch (2 L) square microwaveable dish; spread with filling. Pat remaining crumb mixture evenly over top. Microwave at Medium-High (70%) for 9 minutes or until set, rotating dish every 3 minutes. Cover with foil; let stand directly on counter for 10 minutes. Uncover and let stand on rack to cool completely. Cut into squares. Makes 20 squares.

FOR BETTER BARS AND SQUARES
Mixing and baking:
- *Mix dough just until blended; over-mixing will result in tough bars with hard tops.*
- *Use only the pan size indicated. If pan is larger, dough will bake faster and become tough. If pan is smaller, bars will be thicker with doughy centre.*
- *Spread batter evenly for uniform baking, thickness and texture.*
- *Check bars often as they cook. Over-baked bars will be hard and dry; under-baked ones doughy.*
Slicing:
- *Cut bars while slightly warm or completely cool unless recipe indicates otherwise (hot bars will crumble when cut).*
- *Use a ruler to mark off bars or squares evenly.*
- *Cut bars depending on the occasion. Small squares are appropriate for afternoon tea, large bars for after-school snacks.*
- *Cut a cross through the middle of pan first and work from the middle out to keep cuts straight.*

Pumpkin Bars

These spicy honey-moist bars are great for toting to bake sales or potlucks.

1 cup	packed brown sugar	250 mL
3/4 cup	butter, softened	175 mL
1/2 cup	liquid honey	125 mL
4	eggs	4
1	can (14 oz/398 mL) pumpkin purée	1
1 cup	all-purpose flour	250 mL
1 cup	whole wheat flour	250 mL
1 cup	chopped walnuts	250 mL
2 tsp	baking powder	10 mL
1/2 tsp	baking soda	2 mL
1/2 tsp	salt	2 mL
1/2 tsp	cinnamon	2 mL
1/4 tsp	nutmeg	1 mL
Pinch	cloves	Pinch

	ICING	
3/4 lb	light cream cheese	375 g
3 tbsp	liquid honey	50 mL
48	walnut halves	48

■ In bowl, cream together sugar, butter and honey until fluffy. Beat in eggs, one at a time; blend in pumpkin. Combine all-purpose and whole wheat flours, walnuts, baking powder, baking soda, salt, cinnamon, nutmeg and cloves; stir into pumpkin mixture just until blended.

■ Spread in greased 17-1/2- × 11-1/2-inch (45 × 29 cm) jelly roll pan; bake in 350°F (180°C) oven for 30 to 35 minutes or until top springs back when lightly touched. Let cool on rack.

■ **Icing:** In bowl, blend cream cheese with honey; spread over cooled cake. Cut into bars; top each with walnut half. Makes 48 bars.

LIGHTEN UP YOUR LUNCHBOX
Everyone loves a treat. For Pumpkin Bars, Peanutty Crispy Rice Squares (p. 55) and Peanut Butter Granola Bars (p. 57), we reduced the sugar, oil and butter and used unbleached flour. These nutritious snacks can be covered tightly and stored in the refrigerator for up to 3 days or frozen for up to 3 months.

Peanutty Crispy Rice Squares

Peanut butter adds a new kid-pleasing taste to crispy rice squares.

2/3 cup	corn syrup	150 mL
1/2 cup	smooth peanut butter	125 mL
4 cups	crispy rice cereal	1 L
1/2 cup	raisins	125 mL

■ In large saucepan over medium heat, melt corn syrup with peanut butter; stir in rice cereal and raisins until coated.

■ Spread mixture in lightly greased 8-inch (2 L) square baking dish. Refrigerate for about 1 hour or until firm. Cut into squares. Makes about 16 squares.

(centre) Peanutty Crispy Rice Squares;
(right) Pumpkin Bars (p. 54) ▲

Oatmeal Sesame Crisps

Crunchy oatmeal bars have been popular for generations. Here's a sesame seed version your youngsters will love. Pack a few extras in their lunchboxes so your children can treat their friends.

1/2 cup	butter	125 mL
1 cup	packed brown sugar	250 mL
1 tsp	vanilla	5 mL
1-1/2 cups	rolled oats	375 mL
1/2 cup	sesame seeds	125 mL
1/2 tsp	baking powder	2 mL

■ In saucepan, melt butter over medium heat; stir in sugar and vanilla and cook for about 2 minutes or until bubbly. Remove from heat. Stir in oats, sesame seeds and baking powder; mix well. Press firmly into greased 12- × 8-inch (3 L) baking dish. Bake in 375°F (190°C) oven for 7 to 10 minutes or until lightly browned. Let cool; cut into bars. Makes 48 bars.

Raspberry Cheese Squares

It takes only about 10 minutes to prepare these mouth-watering squares. A buttery cake is topped with creamy cheesecake swirled with tart raspberry jam. If you prefer, substitute your favorite jam or jelly for the raspberry jam. Store the squares in the refrigerator.

1-1/4 cups	granulated sugar	300 mL
1/2 cup	butter	125 mL
3	eggs	3
2 cups	all-purpose flour	500 mL
1/2 tsp	baking powder	2 mL
1/2 tsp	nutmeg	2 mL
1/2 lb	cream cheese	250 g
1/4 cup	raspberry jam or jelly	50 mL

■ In bowl, beat together 1 cup (250 mL) of the sugar, butter and 2 of the eggs until fluffy; stir in flour, baking powder and nutmeg until well mixed. Spread evenly in greased 9-inch square (2.5 L) cake pan.

■ In bowl, beat together cream cheese, remaining sugar and egg; spread carefully over batter in pan. Drop about 12 equally spaced small spoonfuls of jam onto cheese mixture. Using knife or spatula, swirl jam into cheese without disturbing batter on bottom. Bake in 350°F (180°C) oven for 35 minutes or until cheese is golden and tester inserted in centre comes out clean. Cut into squares; serve warm or cool. Makes 36 squares.

Chocolate Crunch Bars

These glazed no-bake bars sell well at a bazaar or bake sale and are easy for kids to make. Wrap bars individually and sell them one at a time or in groups of three for a special price.

1 cup	smooth peanut butter	250 mL
1 cup	packed brown sugar	250 mL
1/2 cup	corn syrup	125 mL
1/2 cup	liquid honey	125 mL
1 cup	chopped peanuts	250 mL
1 tsp	vanilla	5 mL
8 cups	corn flakes	2 L
2 cups	chocolate chips	500 mL
2 tbsp	shortening	25 mL

■ In large saucepan, combine peanut butter, brown sugar, corn syrup and honey; stir over medium heat until smooth. Remove from heat; stir in peanuts and vanilla. Gradually add cereal, stirring until well coated. Press evenly into a greased 15- × 10-inch (40 × 25 cm) jelly roll pan.

■ In top of double boiler over simmering water, melt chocolate with shortening. Spread evenly over mixture in pan; chill until set. Cut into 3- × 1-inch (8 × 2.5 cm) bars. Makes about 50 bars.

Peanut Butter Granola Bars

Here's a lunchbox treat.

1 cup	smooth peanut butter	250 mL
1/2 cup	packed brown sugar	125 mL
1/2 cup	corn syrup	125 mL
1/3 cup	butter, softened	75 mL
2 tsp	vanilla	10 mL
3 cups	rolled oats	750 mL
1/2 cup	flaked sweetened coconut	125 mL
1/2 cup	salted sunflower seeds	125 mL
1/2 cup	raisins	125 mL
1/3 cup	wheat germ	75 mL
3/4 cup	semisweet chocolate chips (optional)	175 mL

■ In bowl, beat together peanut butter, sugar, corn syrup, butter and vanilla until smooth. Stir in oats, coconut, sunflower seeds, raisins and wheat germ; mix well. Stir in chocolate chips (if using).

■ Pat into greased 13- × 9-inch (3 L) baking dish. Bake in 350°F (180°C) oven for 20 to 25 minutes or until light golden brown. Let cool on rack before cutting into bars. Makes 32 bars.

Raspberry Almond Squares

Bake two different kinds of squares in two different pans at the same time by doubling the crumb ingredients and using two different kinds of jam for the filling. Apricot, cherry, strawberry or pineapple would be a delicious alternative to raspberry.

1-1/2 cups	all-purpose flour	375 mL
1 cup	lightly packed brown sugar	250 mL
1 tsp	baking powder	5 mL
1/4 tsp	salt	1 mL
3/4 cup	butter or margarine	175 mL
1-1/2 cups	rolled oats	375 mL
1-1/4 cups	raspberry jam	300 mL
1/2 cup	sliced almonds	125 mL

■ In bowl, stir together flour, sugar, baking powder and salt; cut in butter until mixture is crumbly. Stir in oats.

■ Press two-thirds of the mixture firmly into greased 13- × 9-inch (3.5 L) cake pan; spread evenly with jam. Stir almonds into remaining crumb mixture; sprinkle evenly over jam, patting down lightly.

■ Bake in 375°F (190°C) oven for 30 to 35 minutes or until golden. Let cool in pan on rack. Cut into squares. Makes about 4 dozen.

EASIER THAN COOKIES

Easy-to-make bars and squares are just the thing for busy cooks who like to have treats on hand for teatime sweets, lunchbox snacks and totable bazaar items. They're quicker than cookies because there's no rolling, slicing, dropping or shaping. Bars and squares can be chewy, crunchy, fudgy, crispy, sugary or nutty — the same qualities that make cookies so popular.

Microwave Peanut Swirl Brownies

You can substitute white chocolate chips for the peanut butter chips in both the base and topping.

1 cup	chocolate chips	250 mL
1/2 cup	butter	125 mL
2/3 cup	granulated sugar	150 mL
2	eggs	2
1 tsp	vanilla	5 mL
3/4 cup	all-purpose flour	175 mL
1/2 tsp	baking powder	2 mL
1/4 tsp	salt	1 mL
1/2 cup	peanut butter chips	125 mL

TOPPING		
1 cup	chocolate chips	250 mL
4 tsp	vegetable oil	20 mL
1/4 cup	peanut butter chips	50 mL

■ In 2-cup (500 mL) microwaveable measure, microwave chocolate with butter at Medium (50%) for 3 to 4 minutes or until melted, stirring once. Let cool slightly.

■ In bowl, beat sugar with eggs; blend in chocolate mixture and vanilla. Combine flour, baking powder and salt; blend into chocolate mixture. Stir in peanut butter chips. Spread in ungreased 8-inch (2 L) square microwaveable baking dish. Microwave at High for 4-1/2 to 5 minutes or

until top is no longer sticky, rotating dish once. Let stand on countertop for 10 minutes. Set on rack and let cool completely.

■ **Topping:** Meanwhile, in small microwaveable bowl, combine chocolate and 1 tbsp (15 mL) of the oil; microwave at Medium (50%) for 2 to 2-1/2 minutes or until melted, stirring twice. In separate microwaveable bowl, mix peanut butter chips with remaining oil; microwave at Medium (50%) for 1 to 2 minutes or until melted, stirring once.

■ Spread chocolate mixture over brownies. At 1-inch (2.5 cm) intervals, drizzle with bands of peanut butter mixture. Pull tip of knife at right angles through bands. Pull knife through bands in opposite direction. Refrigerate for 1 hour or until topping is set. Cut into bars. Makes about 16 bars.

Lemon Meringue Slices

These slightly chewy squares have a melt-in-your-mouth shortbread base.

1/2 cup	butter, softened	125 mL
1/2 cup	icing sugar	125 mL
1 cup	all-purpose flour	250 mL
	FILLING	
2	egg whites	2
Pinch	salt	Pinch
1/2 cup	granulated sugar	125 mL
1 tsp	grated lemon rind	5 mL
2 tbsp	lemon juice	25 mL

■ In bowl, cream butter; gradually beat in icing sugar until light and fluffy. Stir in flour to make crumbly mixture. With floured fingers, pat evenly into ungreased 13- × 9-inch (3.5 L) cake pan; bake in 350°F (180°C) oven for about 10 minutes or until light golden around edges. Let cool.

■ **Filling:** In bowl, beat egg whites with salt until soft peaks form; gradually beat in sugar until stiff peaks form. Beat in lemon rind and juice. Spread over cooled base; bake in 350°F (180°C) oven for 20 to 25 minutes or until golden brown. Let cool completely in pan on rack before cutting. Makes about 40 squares.

Chocolate Walnut Squares

Full of crunchy walnuts, these thin cookielike squares are quick and easy to make.

1 cup	chopped walnuts	250 mL
1/2 cup	unsweetened cocoa powder	125 mL
1/2 cup	all-purpose flour	125 mL
1/4 tsp	salt	1 mL
3/4 cup	butter, softened	175 mL
1 cup	packed brown sugar	250 mL
1-1/2 tsp	vanilla	7 mL
2	eggs	2

■ Stir together 1/2 cup (125 mL) of the walnuts, cocoa, flour and salt; set aside. In large bowl, cream butter, sugar and vanilla until light and fluffy; beat in eggs, one at a time, beating well after each addition. Stir in walnut mixture just until blended.

■ Spread evenly in well-greased 15- × 11-inch (40 × 25 cm) jelly roll pan; sprinkle with remaining walnuts. Bake in 375°F (190°C) oven for about 15 minutes or until tester inserted into centre comes out clean. Let cool in pan on rack for 10 minutes before cutting. Makes about 50 squares.

Applesauce Bars

Rich with flavor and moist with applesauce, these bars are a great treat to make for a brown-bagging family.

1 cup	butter, softened	250 mL
1 cup	packed brown sugar	250 mL
1/2 cup	fancy molasses	125 mL
2	eggs	2
1/2 cup	unsweetened applesauce	125 mL
1/2 cup	light sour cream	125 mL
1-1/2 cups	all-purpose flour	375 mL
1-1/2 cups	whole wheat flour	375 mL
1 cup	chopped pecans	250 mL
2 tsp	baking powder	10 mL
1/2 tsp	baking soda	2 mL
1/2 tsp	salt	2 mL
1/2 tsp	cinnamon	2 mL
	DRIZZLE ICING	
3/4 cup	icing sugar	175 mL
2 tbsp	orange juice	25 mL

■ In bowl, cream butter, sugar and molasses until fluffy; beat in eggs, one at a time. Stir in applesauce and sour cream. Combine all-purpose and whole wheat flours, pecans, baking powder, baking soda, salt and cinnamon; stir into creamed mixture.

■ Spread in greased 15- × 10-inch (40 × 25 cm) jelly roll pan; bake in 350°F (180°C) oven for 25 to 30 minutes or until tester inserted in centre comes out clean. Let cool on rack before cutting into bars.

■ **Drizzle Icing:** Whisk together icing sugar and orange juice; drizzle over cooled bars. Makes 48 bars.

Credits

Recipes in THE CANADIAN LIVING COOKING COLLECTION have been created by the *Canadian Living* Test Kitchen and by the following food writers from across Canada: **Elizabeth Baird, Karen Brown, Joanna Burkhard, James Chatto, Diane Clement, David Cohlmeyer, Pam Collacott, Bonnie Baker Cowan, Pierre Dubrulle, Eileen Dwillies, Nancy Enright, Carol Ferguson, Margaret Fraser, Susan Furlan, Anita Goldberg, Barb Holland, Patricia Jamieson, Arlene Lappin, Anne Lindsay, Lispeth Lodge, Mary McGrath, Susan Mendelson, Bernard Meyer, Beth Moffatt, Rose Murray, Iris Raven, Gerry Shikatani, Jill Snider, Kay Spicer, Linda Stephen, Bonnie Stern, Lucy Waverman, Carol White, Ted Whittaker** and **Cynny Willet.**

The full-color photographs throughout are by Canada's leading food photographers, including **Fred Bird, Doug Bradshaw, Christopher Campbell, Nino D'Angelo, Frank Grant, Michael Kohn, Suzanne McCormick, Claude Noel, John Stephens** and **Mike Visser.**

Editorial and Production Staff: Hugh Brewster, Susan Barrable, Catherine Fraccaro, Wanda Nowakowska, Sandra L. Hall, Beverley Renahan and Bernice Eisenstein.

Index

THE CANADIAN LIVING
COOKING
COLLECTION

COLLECT ALL 8 BOOKS FOR A 500-RECIPE LIBRARY

EASY MAIN DISHES
Over 60 quick and delicious recipes for no-fuss meals

COOKING FOR COMPANY
More than 50 recipes for elegant-but-easy entertaining

SOUPS AND STARTERS
Over 60 fabulous first courses — plus snacks and appetizers

EASY CHICKEN DISHES
More than 50 best-ever ways to serve this family favorite

VEGETABLES AND SALADS
Over 60 recipes for garden-fresh goodness all year long

ONE-DISH MEALS
Over 50 marvelous casseroles, stews, pastas — and more!

MUFFINS AND COOKIES
The 65 tastiest recipes for muffins, cookies, bars and squares

GREAT DESSERTS
Over 60 luscious recipes to tempt any sweet tooth

W hether it's a fast and easy midweek supper for the family or a candlelight dinner with special friends, THE CANADIAN LIVING COOKING COLLECTION brings you more than 500 outstanding recipes for all occasions. Each of these 8 easy-to-use cookbooks features the very best recipes from the kitchens of *Canadian Living* magazine — the most trusted name in Canadian cooking. Sumptuous full-color photographs throughout highlight marvelous main dishes, satisfying soups, vegetables and salads, and mouthwatering desserts. Each recipe is complemented by helpful hints and serving suggestions and has been carefully tested by *Canadian Living* to ensure perfect results every time.

Collect all 8 titles for a complete, indispensable cooking library that makes it easy to put together delicious and satisfying meals that will draw raves from everyone at your table.

Canadian Living™ is a trademark of Telemedia Publishing Inc.   ISBN # 0-140-16569-X

EASY CHICKEN DISHES

More than 50 best-ever ways to serve this family favorite